THE INCREDIBLE
TRANSFORMATION
OF GREGORY TODD

Coming Soon from A J Sheppard:

Reflections from the Incredible Transformation

THE INCREDIBLE TRANSFORMATION OF GREGORY TODD

A Novel about Leadership and Managing Change

A J Sheppard

First published in 2015 by A J Sheppard
Copyright © 2015 A J Sheppard

A CIP catalogue record for this title is available from the British Library

Paperback ISBN: 978-0-9933424-0-0
Ebook ISBN: 978-0-9933424-1-7

www.ajsheppard.com

Book cover design by Samuel Nudds Design and Vision Tank

Typesetting and book design by Steve Passiouras at BOOKOW.COM

For my family

Foreword

*T*he *Incredible Transformation of Gregory Todd* has grown out of my quest to help others to transform their organisation and its culture. It is an educational novel which tells the story of a realistic transformation attempt. My hope is that it will prove enjoyable and insightful to those working in any kind of organisation, who are interested in leadership and change.

My view nowadays is that a transformation should only be heralded when an organisation has burst into life and excellent results are just the tip of its achievement. I love the limitless source of energy that such transformations liberate from within, and I have now dedicated fifteen years to pursuing them. I believe that each transformation needs to blend the right conditions in three fields: in leadership, in change-management and in the relevant subject-matter expertise.

My first encounter with proper transformation took me by surprise. It shouldn't have done. I had just become a management consultant with McKinsey & Company, and *transformation* was what we had been promising our client. But my expectations had already been shaped through my own experience. I had worked on the shop floors of a warehouse and an oil refinery before gaining bachelor's and master's degrees in manufacturing engineering from the University of Cambridge. I had then cut my teeth in industrial environments at Shell International and what was then Carnaud-Metalbox. I felt I had gained a realistic grounding in operations theory and practice, including Toyota's famed techniques for operations improvement (dubbed *lean manufacturing*). I thought this had qualified me with a reasonable grasp of what was possible. I was now being trained by an expert who had been bravely hired by McKinsey despite lacking the qualifications that the consulting company normally required. What he offered instead was experience in how Toyota had helped to transform its suppliers, through an approach that was as much about leadership and change-management as it was about Toyota's subject-matter expertise.

Through witnessing what this expert did and how he did it, my expectations were blown out of the water. Within four months, an organisation of around one hundred people had burst into life, and I had been humbled. The transformation had therefore precipitated another one in my own work life: I felt compelled to pursue similar achievements. I grew in this art of transformation by working them out in varied industries on different continents, before starting to train others to do the same.

If leading proper transformations can prove hard at times, training others to do so without the luxury of *showing* them has proved harder still. With hindsight, I can see that I should not have been surprised by this either. After all, my own expectations and learnt behaviours had only been overhauled by an expert *showing* me how to achieve more than I could have imagined. Therefore I started to envisage a *how-to guide* for such transformations: it would look like a business novel and *show* readers how to navigate a proper transformation through its characters. My goal was to offer a short cut to the type of experience that had transformed my own work life.

My mixed successes in training others made me realise that it would not be enough just to show readers a successful transformation. This is because however much I try to warn people to avoid common pitfalls, I find that they still gravitate towards them. My own theory here is twofold. Firstly, leaders tend to prefer to pioneer their own courses: many do not find it easy to follow a prescribed programme. Secondly, seasoned managers tend to tune out of the detail for anything that sounds obvious – such as the need to lead, structure and support any programme of change. I have found that leaders therefore tend to remain too optimistic of their organisation's capability to change, too determined to take short cuts and too constrained to make sufficiently radical step changes to their normal modes of operating.

The ultimate *how-to* guide therefore needed to help readers to *experience* such pitfalls so that they can go on to pioneer courses to avoid them in their own organisations. In essence, the value proposition of this book is therefore to equip you in the powerful art of transformation: blending the right conditions in leadership, change-management and subject-matter expertise. This is powered by the method of learning from mistakes – at the expense of the book's characters – to increase your chance of succeeding in your own organisation.

I believe that the right conditions in the first two fields – leadership and change-management – will be similar for successful transformations in any organisation. The third field of subject-matter expertise will of course depend on the nature of work that the organisation is undertaking. Its importance is paramount, to ensure a step change in results and to give credibility to the whole change process. Knowledge of world-class principles is not enough: expert capability is required to apply these principles to paint a picture of what excellent would *look like* for each organisation's specific processes and constraints. Equally, this vision is worth nothing alone, without capable leadership to make it happen and an effective change-management process to mobilise people in a way that will ensure that the vision is not just sustained but will continue to improve.

To bring *The Incredible Transformation of Gregory Todd* to life, I needed to set it in a lifelike organisation. It made sense to choose a backdrop to bring out my own core subject-matter expertise in manufacturing operations, while maintaining appeal for those working in other types of organisation. My solution was to set the book in a fictional business that makes sofas, which I trust keeps the content interesting and accessible enough to bring diverse readers beneath the surface of the same organisation. Those who have a particular interest in operations management may also notice that a good mix of capital-intensive and labour-intensive processes is involved, to bring out a range of principles and representative challenges.

There is, of course, already a plethora of books on leadership, as there is for change-management and operations management. As well as separating these fields for treatment, nearly all tend to dissect them further for analysis. My frustration is that in this dissection, the very lifeblood of leading, changing or operating an organisation seems to drain out. It is often hard to disagree with the content, but it is equally hard to reassemble the parts and integrate them within a moving canvas of organisational life which is full of particular pressures, personalities and politics.

Therefore, one thing that has kept me going in this undertaking has been my belief in the power of the educational novel. I love the potential for readers to experience lifelike situations because everything remains blended together, which is of course how we experience situations in real life. This brings the promise of effective and engaging *how-to* guides, but I can also see that it opens up potential for further benefits. For some there might be value in learning that they are not alone in challenges they are facing privately in their own workplaces. For others, an educational novel could serve as a rich case study, through sharing it with colleagues and discussing how to apply the group's learning. It should also be possible for experts to craft the calibre of role models which is sadly rare to experience in person.

Finally, my hope is that you might now be able to set all this analysis aside and simply immerse yourself in this story, set amid the typical complexity of organisational life. I hope that you will enjoy doing so – and that it might serve to release abundant life in your own organisation and beyond.

A J Sheppard, August 2015

1

UNRAVELLING

Gregory Todd dropped into his seat and shut himself in. The scent of showroom leather failed to calm his racing mind. He pressed the brake and turned on the ignition. The dashboard took an age to register his phone.

"Hello, Jane. Jane, I need to get the whole management team together tomorrow. No, everything's fine. Make sure you speak to each of them. They *need* to be there. Sorry Jane, I've got to go. Just leave me a voicemail with anything else. Thanks. Bye."

The wide tyres spat gravel back towards Doug Mountfield's country home. Gregory's estate was already unravelling.

The warehouse smelt of the smooth plastic sheeting that covered new sofas and chairs. Today this was blended with fresher notes from the occasional downpours. Buckets on the floor marked where the roof had been penetrated. At the edge of the warehouse the bulk of a man with short, silver hair and faded tattoos sat on his tatty throne and controlled the storytelling. His weathered face suggested he had a thousand similar stories to tell. His audience had gathered around on chairs and tables, according to seniority.

"So we ended up waiting in the car park," he continued. "Finally a battered Mercedes rolled up and five of them got out wielding baseball bats and crowbars." Big Dave paused to lure the youngsters.

"So what happened?" one asked.

"What do you mean, what happened?" he replied. Curiosity had been doused with condescension. "You would have hung around to find out?"

The far door was flung open. Big Dave pushed himself to his feet, triggering his band of workers to disperse deeper into the warehouse.

The storytelling had been interrupted by the suited Stephen Peasegood, the Operations Director. He was now swerving around the sofas that crowded the loading bays. "How's it going, Dave?" he called, raising his eyebrows expectantly while maintaining his speed.

"Not three bad, mate, not three bad," came Big Dave's uniform response. Stephen rewarded this with a raised thumb before he disappeared through the far door. He did not see Big Dave's return gesture.

Stephen made his way towards the stairs at front of the main building. He was irked not only by the sloth he had uncovered but also by the defiance he had read in the dispersion of the workers, like the brief skips of cocky pigeons who know they will be safe if they just avoid the feet of passers-by. Furthermore, they should have been working flat out to meet end-of-the-month targets.

Stephen calculated most things in life, including his appearance. Subtle labels and expensive accessories put him on a par with Gregory. Shaving his head had transformed his receding hairline into a trendy, aggressive edge. No other manager was as fearless as he in engaging with the more intimidating workers.

The operation he commanded was in a Victorian factory, a short way up Shrub Hill from the centre of Worcester. It was solidly built in red brick, with features crafted in distinctive yellow and black bricks. Originally part of the city's thriving glove-making industry, it ran alongside the Worcester and Birmingham Canal, just a few locks up from Diglis Basin, where this blended with the stately River Severn.

The boardroom on the first floor was their one pleasant facility for meetings. The large, uncluttered, oak-veneer table, black mesh executive chairs and huge flat screen would be good enough for most businesses. Around these, Fiona the design director had expressed Gregory Todd Ltd's design language through minimal artwork and textiles.

Despite being perfectly on time, he was the second-to-last person to arrive. He sat down quickly, exhaled sharply and made use of the time by tapping his phone. He always modelled a sense of urgency, but this time he had failed to draw a proper acknowledgement from his CEO.

Gregory squeezed his eyes with a finger and thumb. Nature's indiscriminate hand had given Gregory a generous head of hair. The greying sides added suave and suggested wisdom, when he was looking a little less haggard.

"Everything alright, Gregory?" Stephen asked. "You're looking a bit stressed."

"Thank you," Gregory replied. "Things haven't exactly been a bed of roses." Gregory replaced his titanium reading glasses and told everyone he would give Anna a couple more minutes. His laughter lines were not going to be exercised today.

Stephen still had enough time to get a proper coffee. He brushed past Eddie who was sharing a joke with Fiona. Eddie was a small, grey-haired sales director who revelled in his Scottish lilt. His forte for jovial small talk would never translate into top-line growth. Fiona was a bottled redhead and half-decent designer, although he only ever saw her work after it had been processed by Gregory. She was likeable, but she knew next to nothing about running a business.

He had already gained more experience in leading others than Anna, the finance director and the only other MBA in the company. Gregory was the only person worth following: a clear thinker who had demonstrated steel through his buyout. But Stephen was learning as much from what he would do differently. Gregory had allowed his edges to soften – to match his penchant for lilac shirts and classical music. His concern for people's feelings was now constraining growth. For example, Stephen would have fired Eddie months ago.

His cup rattled as he put the saucer down. It was a week early for their Quarter Three review, which meant that the results could be even worse than they feared. Their main performance measure was EBITDA, or Earnings Before Interest, Tax, Depreciation and Amortisation: an indication of the profit they were generating. It was still positive but they had been missing targets for a while. They had finally started to supply Aspiration but the online retailer was refusing to ramp up until their delivery performance improved. Some still pointed the finger at him but, as he always explained, it was mathematically impossible to meet the lead times Eddie had promised until Eddie improved his forecasts. In the meantime, he had continued to sweep his own backyard. Even Anna would not be able to find fault with his latest variance report, and he had postponed purchasing the new dye machines yet again.

Anna closed the door behind her and slid some warm pages in front of their boss. "Sorry I'm late, everyone," she announced. The platitude was riling. She was always at Gregory's right hand, never in the line of fire.

"Thanks, Anna." Gregory looked down at the document, keeping his back straight. "Right," he finally said. "Thank you for coming, especially when we're in the thick of it. You might already guess why we're meeting early. Despite all the good work, we're still looking short." The news punctured any remaining hope. Spirits deflated and groans escaped. Some looked to the ceiling; Stephen kept his eyes fixed on their boss.

"It's now about as serious as it can get. Mountfield hauled me in yesterday, and if he ever had any patience, it has finally run out. The way he sees it, we need to do two things. First, he's given us a date – Monday, 23rd October." There was enough of a wobble in Gregory's voice to suggest he had received a proper battering. "He's convened an emergency board meeting and we need to present him with a definitive turnaround plan. He needs to be convinced we can deliver at least two million EBITDA in the next financial year. The good news is that I managed to talk him down from something utterly unrealistic."

"23rd October is only four weeks away," Eddie said.

They could always rely on Eddie to add groundbreaking insight. "So what's the second thing?" he chose to ask.

"We need to deliver a run rate of £1.5m by the end of this year. So that's another £400k in the last quarter."

"We need to sell more!" Fiona exclaimed, turning to Eddie. "It always comes back to Aspiration."

Stephen knew what was coming.

"That's an operational problem!" Eddie protested. "We would be on plan if their customers hadn't continually complained about our late deliveries."

"And I keep explaining," Stephen said slowly, emphasising each word with a strike of his hand, "the *operation* is not the root cause." Eddie and Gregory had agreed a four-week lead time for Aspiration without consulting him. This was much shorter than the eight-week standard. Gregory had assumed that the forecasts would be reliable enough to make the frames in advance. Then cutting, sewing and dyeing a cover and fitting it to the frame should not take more than three weeks – in theory. "I've bent over backwards to find ways of delivering your promises. I've got the lead time data to *prove* we can meet Gregory's assumptions. But everything still depends on you getting the forecasts right. We never have the right frames in stock – because your forecasts aren't worth the paper they're written on."

"My information can only ever be as good as the customers'," Eddie replied. "If you can't work with our customers, then we're screwed. Maybe we should forget about Aspiration. Let's downsize and focus on the profitable lines. Get back to what we were doing before."

"No!" snapped Gregory. "Come on, Eddie. Downsizing has never been an option. Our whole mandate has been to grow the business. Look, I've tried to protect you but let me tell you Mountfield's actual words." He hesitated. " 'It's good for you that I'm rubbing your noses in your own s**t. Because if you don't clean it up by the New Year, I'll be swapping you all for a team that's already house trained.' "

"He really said those words?" Fiona asked.

"Yes."

Stephen liked straight talkers. *He* would have lost his patience by now too, if it was his money they were playing with.

"That's ridiculous. There must be something we could do about *Mountfield*," Eddie said.

"There isn't," Gregory said. "If there was, we would have done it already."

"We're still meeting our covenants," Anna said. "Can he really get rid of us?"

"Mountfield will always find a way to do whatever he wants," Gregory said. He waited for everyone to look at him. "If we can't convince him that we can meet our EBITDA targets, it's unlikely that any of us will still be here in the New Year."

"But it's an impossible situation," Eddie protested. "We're still profitable! I'd like to see him find anyone who could do better."

"No, you wouldn't," Gregory said. "I agree with you, but the argument is not valid with Mountfield."

"Look, there's no point sitting around feeling sorry for ourselves," Stephen ventured. He was not ready to see his own record tarnished.

"No one's suggesting we are," Gregory said immediately.

"Well, whether we are or not, surely our best form of defence is attack. We need to come out fighting." He had skim-read dozens of cases in which leaders turned around their organisations. This was his chance to write his own. "The secret is to mobilise our troops – don't forget there are a couple of hundred of us here. If others have turned themselves around, we can too. We just need to pull together and do the basics well. No company has a *right* to survive. But if anyone can, why can't Gregory Todd?" He thrust his seat backwards, rose to his feet and began rolling up the sleeves of his slim-fit shirt. Once at the white board, he ripped off the top of a marker pen. *+ £1m EBITDA* he scribbled, halfway down the left-hand side. "We need a plan to turn in another one million EBITDA, right? So let's start with revenue." He wrote *+ Revenue* just to the right and *– Costs* some way beneath it. "So what are the main factors influencing our revenue?" he asked, turning to the room.

"Sales," said Fiona. Excellent – she was not only willing to engage, she had also been listening.

"Right! But let's not fall into the trap of thinking only about Aspiration." He wrote *Aspiration* in the next column and *Non-Aspiration* underneath. "Also, let's not forget there are two ways of increasing revenue."

Gregory was on his feet but stood behind his chair, with his back against the window. He stared straight ahead, showing no inclination to intervene.

Stephen wrote *+ units sold* in a third column and, below that, *+ price per unit,* for both Aspiration and Non-Aspiration.

"Right – so we can increase sales volume or raise prices for each customer group."

"I can't see where you're going with this, Stephen," Anna said, glancing briefly at Gregory. "Don't you think we're already doing everything we can to increase sales? We know the problems. If you've got a new idea, then come out with it. Drawing a logic tree is not a new idea."

Gregory was now resting his elbows on the back of his chair. His lips parted as if he was preparing to intervene.

"You're right, Anna," Stephen said quickly. Like a judoka he had learnt to turn the force of an opponent's attack against them. "No one's saying it's easy to increase sales either way, but this process makes sure we investigate every option. First, let's lay them out in a *mee-cee* format."

Right on cue, Fiona appealed for a translation.

"Sorry, MECE stands for Mutually Exclusive and Collectively Exhaustive: what our list of EBITDA components needs to be. On the right-hand side we'll break each component down further, then analyse it. We'll need your help, Anna, with the figures for last year. Against each component we'll need a rough target for next year, together with which of us is responsible. This will help us to set direction. Then we need to do the same exercise for next quarter, prioritising the activities to give us the £400k we need."

He was on a roll. "We can use this format to prove to Doug Mountfield *how* we will deliver his goals. Every line item needs to be backed up by a sheet of actions and project plan. Make sense?"

An hour later, Gregory was returning from the window where he had taken a call. Stephen had only just moved over to support Eddie and Fiona in Gregory's absence. Gregory must have already challenged them to evaluate their own ideas, but their flip chart was still filled with wishful words and other people's responsibilities. By contrast, his own Cost Subgroup's whiteboard was already filled with a table of actions and estimates. His handwriting blended urgency with precision. Anna had remained behind her laptop throughout.

"OK everyone," Gregory said loudly. "It's getting on for one o'clock and we should have got far enough to continue on our own. Is everyone clear on the line items they're responsible for?"

Eddie said nothing, but then again he had hardly promised anything anyway.

"Good," Gregory continued. "Let's be more than ready on 23rd October. Let's blow Mountfield out of the water. OK?"

Stephen would do more than his fair share. Gregory would have to take responsibility for the rest.

"We need to take the initiative and show Mountfield a rough plan as early as next week. That probably means we need to meet this Friday to discuss the first draft. I'll confirm the time. Let's make Friday's numbers as accurate as possible. Don't discuss this with anyone outside these walls. Not yet. Any questions?" Gregory asked. "Good. Great work, everyone. Thanks for facilitating, Stephen."

Stephen was still buzzing as he strode out of the boardroom, in spite of feeling slightly peeved that Gregory had belittled his leadership as 'facilitation'. It was terrible if the business really was on its knees, but it had gifted him an opportunity that money could not buy. He pushed open the door at the end of the corridor. The subdued sound of radios blaring alone announced that it was lunchtime in the factory.

He stepped out onto the raised iron walkway which ran parallel to the front of the building, behind the offices. This platform offered a good view of the production area which stretched into the distance below, under the saw-tooth roof. A wrought iron, spiral staircase invited visitors to descend and see for themselves the quality of the hand-built furniture. The steps clanged under his leather soles as he jogged down and darted into one of the ground-floor offices beneath the showroom. He needed to leverage his own team, and there was never any time like the present.

2

THE MAGIC NUMBER

Peter's stiff black moustache revealed traces of the egg sandwich that he held in his left hand. His other hand held a mug of lukewarm instant coffee to his lips. The computer screen reflected his blotchy cheeks. His rounded stomach belied that this had been his lunch routine for years, since joining as production manager.

Something entered his peripheral vision.

"Oh, hiya." He straightened his back.

"Daydreaming, were you?"

"No." Peter gestured politely towards his empty chair and was shocked that his boss obliged. *What did he want now?*

"So much for the paperless office, then!" Stephen said. He wiped his finger along the pile of quality manuals on the round table beside him. "Look at the state of those," he said, inspecting his finger.

What would you rather me do? Tidy this poky office or run your petty errands? He breathed deeply and smothered the thought. "We tracked down those orders you asked about last night," he said. "One had been turned back at Pre-upholstery but Dave's given his word it'll make the 17.30." His fingertips performed a brief dance across piles of paper before selecting a printed sheet.

"Very good," Stephen said but did not even look at it. "We need to do more on costs."

Peter's throat turned dry. "Why?" he blurted. "We're still beating the budget." It was nearing the end of September and so the end of the third quarter too. He had diverted everyone to Upholstery to finish and ship as many large orders as possible. All non-critical deliveries of materials had been postponed. Every quarter he promised himself it would be different, but somehow it never was.

"We may well meet the *production* budget. But between you and me, we're still going to fall short on EBITDA. So next quarter we have to do more to bail out Sales. We need you to come up with some more cost-saving ideas – like the few I've already given you. Gregory needs a twenty per cent reduction and I need an initial list by the end of this week."

"Twenty per cent?" Peter exclaimed, driving his fingers through his wiry hair. "Where did that come from?"

"That's the big picture. The 30,000 feet requirement."

Stephen loved that phrase – no doubt because his head was always so far up in the clouds. "There's nothing more we can give, Stephen. Can't Sales do more? We've barely used any of the extra capacity."

"Trust me, Peter. I'm giving Sales the kicking they need. In the meantime we've got to bail them out with twenty per cent."

"That's impossible!"

"Nothing's impossible if you put your mind to it, Peter. Look what we've achieved this year already."

"That's just it. Where can we give any more? Labour? Materials? We're already as lean as we can get." The conversation was following a familiar pattern.

"You believe there's no room for improvement?"

The look from his boss jettisoned him straight back to his last appraisal. Some of the wounds were still open. "That's not what I'm saying." He was now being manoeuvred into yet another verbal minefield and had to learn from past mistakes. "I'm just saying that if another twenty per cent of savings were possible, the initiatives would be obvious. And if they were that obvious, *you* would be able to reel some off right now."

"You want me to do your job now as well as my own? You get paid to improve production, Peter."

"Stephen, I honestly don't think it can be done."

"So *think* differently, Peter. If you think how you've always thought you'll get what you've always got."

Peter's resolve crumpled. Overtime bans were the obvious answer, but morale and productivity would plummet. "We could try a *complete* overtime ban in Frame Assembly." It had never worked before as it was dependent on so much else. "It's not easy – we'll need Planning and Purchasing to change their habits of a lifetime." He sent his brain scanning for other ideas. "We could get rid of the last few lads we took on for Aspiration. They've never earned what they were promised anyway."

"Excellent – there you go."

"But we'll struggle when sales pick up."

"There's a solution for everything."

"I still don't understand why we're focusing on cost. Aspiration would place more orders tomorrow if we could deliver on time."

"Thanks, Peter," said Stephen quietly, with the quickest of smiles. "But I've finally got some good news – we're bailing out Sales there too. I think I've found a scheduling system that's perfect for our processes. Simon Tindale is leading that one – so once again all you need to worry about is production."

"Simon? He has never understood production." Simon's promises were never worth the paper they were printed on.

"He might say the same about your knowledge of planning. Let's all work together, but let him coordinate it. Think how much easier *your* life will be once planning problems are solved – you'll be able to focus on making sofas instead of chasing bits of paper." Stephen waved the sheet that he had been given.

Simon had always worked in planning. The only thing Peter had in common with Simon was that they were the only two people in the factory who still wore ties. Simon would never help production, with or without a new IT system. It was obvious – he just struggled to explain why.

"Be systematic with your ideas," Stephen said. "Take a variance report and against each line item list a few ideas and the percentage that could be saved."

He could already see what Stephen wanted. There would be a right-hand column for *amount saved* and a total figure at the bottom of the column.

"Can I leave you to draft it then? Gregory needs the finished version this Friday, so perhaps we can get together on Thursday?"

"*This* Thursday?"

"I'm not asking you to *implement* anything by then – just ideas. Brainstorm! And jot them down. Shouldn't take more than a few hours and we'll go through them together on Thursday. This is critical, Peter. This is now your number one priority."

He was trapped. Arguing would cost time and appraisal points. Filling in the numbers was much easier for now. Even a small change could lead to an epic battle if it survived through to implementation, but the current skirmish loomed the largest. He breathed deeply. "I'll see what I can do," he began, "so long as you realise the ideas could swamp us. I'm not committing to delivering any of them."

Stephen frowned. "Change is nothing to be afraid of, Peter. But yes, we're just talking about the first step for now. Twenty or thirty ideas. *Then* we can sit down together and talk about what and how we can implement."

Peter had been wrestled by logic into another submission. He reached for his vintage, electronic organiser that still served him well, despite the ridicule it attracted from his boss. He braced himself but mercifully there was a reprieve. "*Five pm* on Thursday?"

Stephen tapped his phone and steered them towards an earlier time.

Peter rose as his boss departed, out of bewilderment rather than respect. If only he had appreciated being much less burdened before Stephen had entered twenty minutes ago. Turning back to his computer screen, he tried to remember what had been weighing him down before. The sandwich was a bit crispy but he reasoned it was still the same inside.

3

HOME TRUTHS

RALEIGH Court graced a small village outside Worcester and symbolised the rapid elevation in Gregory's circumstances. He and Linda had bought the late Georgian manor just over a year ago. The first time they had approached he had felt that they had truly *arrived*. The drive swept past lawns and specimen cedars to an impressive red-brick façade, set off by a wide, signal-red door and white portico. It was nowhere near the value of Mountfield's London home, but it was in the upper echelons of Worcestershire's property market.

Gregory's Panamera turned into the driveway. The car had marked the buyout as much as the house. He had still only seen one or two around Worcestershire. Porsche's design language had come within his reach, but he had not been able to justify the sacrifice of practicality for the 911. All he wanted to do was to collapse on the sofa with a glass of wine, but this was their last evening before Emily went off to university. It had all happened so quickly. Thoughts swirled in his head like the damp leaves picked out by his headlights. *Emily wouldn't care if we lost this house – we've barely settled. The business was supposed to be underwriting her education. Linda's worry would be the upheaval all over again – and what others would think. As long as she is in the dark I can't expect any sympathy for working late. It was gallant to protect her from the uncertainty. And it gives me some space to fight the battle. I've still not prepared the lawns for winter. It would be a terrible time to sell.*

The idea for Gregory's management buyout had come from Doug Mountfield, his acquaintance at the golf club. He was the huge monocle-wearer who sat in the clubhouse reading the papers. A former weightlifter, he now exerted influence in private equity. Soon after Gregory had become managing director at Eden Furniture, Mountfield had introduced himself as a specialist in investing private wealth – including significant amounts of *his own children's inheritance* – in the leveraged buyout of small- to medium-sized companies. Mountfield had suggested that Gregory would never be able to prove himself as a *proper CEO* unless he could break free from Arthur's shadow. Gregory had laughed this off: Mountfield had no idea what motivated him. He had come to pity managers who put their families under excessive strain just to advance their careers. He recognised how fortunate he was to have ended up running a business of which he would never tire.

Gregory had been recruited by Arthur Eden when he had been in his late twenties. As an assistant editor in industrial publishing, he had concluded he did not want to languish in a small company that only ever created news and sold advertising. Eden was a respected name which designed, made and sold desirable, tangible products in which he could take pride. He landed a role as Eden's in-house copy editor with an understanding that he could develop his interest in sales and general management. He cringed when he recalled some of the answerless questions which he had boldly posed in those early years. Thankfully Arthur had been patient and had continued to mentor him. Ultimately, when he had been ready to step back from day-to-day management, Arthur had appointed Gregory as his managing director.

Mountfield had steadily infiltrated Gregory's playing circle and often joined them at the bar. He was an entertaining and knowledgeable character who made fun of his own lack of golfing physique. One afternoon the conversation had moved on to the topic of legacies. Mountfield had described his own legacy as having helped many other managers to have improved *their* legacies. Gregory's own motivation had matured into the notion of shaping an organisation to increase its reach and benefits to society. Gregory would never have gone into manufacturing if his principal motivation had been financial, but it was satisfying to hear that buyouts helped to reward industrialists for the personal risks they took to benefit society.

The main obstacle to buying out Eden Furniture had been the improbability that Arthur would ever part with the business he had built from scratch. Gregory could never have considered wrestling the business from the man who had done much more for him than his own father. Mountfield had then helped by explaining how ageing entrepreneurs normally lacked any exit plan of their own. Arthur would probably be grateful for the opportunity to entrust *his* legacy to Gregory's safe pair of hands. Most of the businesses Mountfield bought had never been put up for sale. He rarely trusted those that had.

The next time Mountfield had referred to his *dormant opportunity*, Gregory had been open to considering how the specifics might work. Linda had never been keen. She had been savvy enough to understand the essence of a deal, but she did not have sufficient experience to normalise the levels of risk that were involved. She had been particularly anxious about what they would have done if Arthur had taken offence. Linda doubted that he would have been able to find another position near enough and quickly enough to keep them on track even for a half-decent retirement. They had reached stalemate – there was no way he had been able to provide the guarantees she had been looking for. The tipping point had come when one of their friends had died suddenly, at the age of fifty-one. After that Linda had said that she would never stand in his way. Neither of them had wanted him to spend the last years of his life ruing a missed opportunity.

Mountfield had instructed him to prepare the initial approach without Arthur's knowledge, which had been the difficult part. Anna, Eddie and Fiona had all supported him in principle, but none had been prepared to invest a personal stake. Mountfield had still been willing to push everything through.

Gregory had leant heavily on Mountfield for their pivotal meeting with Arthur. It had taken place in a hotel that overlooked the River Severn. He remembered feeling as nervous as he had the day he picked up the first magazine he had ever edited. The moment Arthur entered the room, Gregory feared he had made the biggest mistake of his life. Arthur sat through five minutes of their presentation without saying a word. He then stood up and left, promising a formal response by the end of the week. After three tortuous days the call came: the Heads of Agreement was signed. Gregory felt like he had gained the whole world.

Their final valuation had been £6.2m, plus they had committed to invest a further £1.2m in new equipment to help them supply Aspiration, a new online furniture retailer. Mountfield's contacts there had helped them to secure an initial agreement to help satisfy the bankers. They had financed the deal through £5.1m of debt and £2.2m of equity. Gregory had contributed £100k, for which he had received fifteen per cent of the common shares. They had developed a strong plan to double EBITDA to £2.5m within three years. His personal stake would be worth £1.3m. He and Linda would be able to own their dream home outright and have plenty to secure Emily's future as well as their own.

He had become the CEO of Gregory Todd Ltd three months before turning fifty. The Mountfields had taken them out to celebrate in a hidden restaurant in the countryside.

It had taken only a few hours for the celebrations to sour. Just before they parted, Mountfield's demeanour had suddenly changed, as if he had packed away his charm with his monocle. It was the first time Gregory had ever seen the other side of Doug Mountfield. Nothing Gregory had done since had been good enough for him.

"Won't we, love?" Linda's words jolted him back into the present.

"Sorry?"

"We'll certainly miss having Emily around, won't we?"

"Of course." His smile was wasted on his daughter, who refused to lift her eyes. The lone sound of scraping cutlery underscored the mood. His private fears eclipsed any his daughter may have had.

"I'm sure you'll have a great time," he added, following the cue from his wife. "There's really nothing to worry about. You'll make loads of new friends. Soon we'll be pleading with you to come home for the holidays, you'll see."

He suddenly remembered there was a more specific issue. "Look, gorgeous, if you're still concerned about tomorrow I've said I'm sorry. I just can't afford a day off at the moment. You *can* understand, can't you?"

The cutlery ground to a halt. Chair legs scraped across the flagstone floor. "Sorry, Mum, I'm not hungry," Emily said, before hurrying out of the room and up the stairs.

"You could have made more of an effort, love. She's nervous, that's all."

He couldn't blame them: it had been his choice to keep them in the dark. Linda had no idea how Mountfield's eyes had flickered so quickly this time, from charm to dispassion to venom.

"So how was work?" Linda asked.

He looked up immediately. "Oh, you know. Results aren't great this quarter, to be honest."

"You'll be OK. You always are."

He *had* been. He had always held on to the belief that he was a good CEO. The question had now become whether he was good *enough*. "How was *your* day?" he asked.

"Infuriating!" she said. "You wouldn't believe how many window companies I've spoken to. The good news is that many do sash windows and double glazing isn't much of a premium these days. The bad news is that I can't seem to get them down to anywhere near the amount Marjory paid for theirs."

"Maybe we shouldn't rush into it."

"What?"

"It *is* the back of the house."

"I thought we'd agreed. They're ghastly. Totally out of keeping, and they're clouding over."

"I'm not saying we *shouldn't* replace them. Maybe it's just not the highest priority, that's all."

"We need to decorate before Christmas. And we need to replace the windows before we decorate. Anyway, we shouldn't be having this conversation now," Linda said. "Don't you think you should go after your daughter? Tell her how much you're looking forward to seeing her in a few weeks."

He froze. There was no way he could take tomorrow off to take Emily to university. When he had tried to explain, Emily had accused him of always prioritising work and golf over her. Therefore he had offered to forego his upcoming golf tournament so he and Linda could visit her for a full weekend, to check she was settling in OK. The presentation to Mountfield would now be the following Monday – which undoubtedly explained why Mountfield had scheduled it then, for his own convenience. Gregory wasn't bothered about missing the tournament, but any hour lost from preparation that weekend might now prove critical.

4

INCOME-STATEMENT GOGGLES

THE factory complex comprised three main buildings, imaginatively ti-
tled Building One, Building Two and Building Three. Just a few metres apart, Building One and Building Two were identical from the outside:
long brick-built factories with saw-tooth roofs stretching back from impressive Victorian façades. Building One comprised the reception area and two
levels of main offices, followed by Upholstery, Finishing and the warehouse.
Building Two comprised Sewing, Cutting and Pre-upholstery.

Peter rehearsed that evening's skittles match in his head as he hobbled
towards the end of Building One. His knee was one reason he tried not
make the walk too often: it had troubled him for years but apparently he
was still too young for a replacement. Wednesday-night skittles probably
didn't help, but that was non-negotiable. As he crossed the loading yard
he was forced to consider the woodshed. This occupied about a quarter of
Building Three – the smaller, concrete building at the back of the site.

If he were honest, the main reason he had not been to Building Three for
a while was to avoid getting dragged into yet another project. He had got
Josh off his back and allowed him to move machines on the condition that
he still met all his targets. The gamble may have backfired. The numbers
looked OK but he had allowed weeks to go by since someone had first
questioned whether he had really authorised the moves. Recent criticisms
had been more direct. The main hope was that Peter had received very few
complaints from the woodshed itself and none from Frame Assembly, its
internal customer.

As Peter approached the woodshed, the smell was just the same: fresh, sawn timber blended with machine lubricant. He surveyed the scene. *Oh dear*: little else had survived untouched. The machines were cramped together on the left-hand side. They had previously made good use of the space, through a logical layout with proper, straight aisles between the machines like bowling lanes. Now a large area had been vacated and taped off for no apparent reason. *What had Josh been thinking?* Only the area for planed timber and fibreboard at the far end looked relatively untouched.

Shafts of sunshine lit up the fine sawdust mist. If there was any good news, it was that everything looked a little cleaner. And it appeared Josh had not spent any unauthorised money: fresh lines had been painted over the crumbling, blackened trucking gangways. Still, with all the effort it must have taken to move the machines, he had not expected anything to look worse.

The prefabricated, sound-proofed office known as the *box* stood on one side of a faded, red roller door. This led through to the store of finished components, and to its immediate right there was now a large board with graphs and coloured objects which hung in patterns. The young man he was after was updating the board. He was in his early thirties, with broad shoulders and short, messy hair.

"Josh!" Peter called out, as the polo-shirted man began walking off into the factory. He resorted to a high-pitched whoop which cut through the cacophony of wood cutting and stopped him in his tracks.

He had recruited Josh as the woodshed team leader earlier that year. Peter had given him some stick in the interview because his surname Eden matched the company's old name. It had genuinely not crossed his mind then that Josh could have been related to the former owner. When he started with the firm, Josh had stirred things up by asking anyone who confronted him what *they* thought. He had enough of Arthur's free-spiritedness to make the rumours plausible, but people struggled to explain why he might have taken such an unglamorous position after his father – or grandfather, some suggested – had already sold it. In a factory culture rife with wit and wind-ups, Josh had hit the ground running.

"What the hell have you done here?" Peter asked.

"What do you mean?" Josh asked.

"It looks like all the machines slid to one side when you lifted the floor to sweep the dirt underneath." He made sure he did not look happy.

"Can I show you the rationale?"

"Not now. I need to see you about something else. Can we go next door?" He tilted his head towards Frame Assembly, where it was a little quieter.

Peter's three-quarter-length factory jacket billowed in a gust of thin, autumnal air. It was about time to switch back to long sleeves. Josh was still bearing sculpted forearms in his polo shirt, showing either the benefits or the foolishness of youth (or a bit of both, perhaps). The long summer had definitely come to an end. Soon everyone would be complaining about the lack of heating again.

The two walked side by side and stopped in front of the coffee machine. Peter reached through the flap of his jacket into an empty trouser pocket. Josh finally put a coin into the machine to bring his fumbling to an end.

"Oh, thanks very much," he said. "*Eight whipped* for me, please."

They manoeuvred into the fixed seating attached to a plastic table. Behind them mallets tapped, a radio blared and frames scraped across the floor, but it was quieter than the woodshed.

"So – feels a while since we last had a proper catch-up," Peter said. "I don't have time to give you proper feedback now, but I must say I was surprised to hear about the layout."

Josh did not flinch.

"Still, I suppose the main question for now is whether you're still running and keeping Frame Assembly happy?"

"We've solved their delivery problems, if that's what you mean." Josh's green eyes glinted. "But that doesn't necessarily mean they're happy."

Peter smiled. "Actually, that's what I want to talk to you about. The powers-that-be are after another round of improvements. Except this time they want twenty per cent."

"What about Aspiration?" Josh asked.

"If you had an easy answer for that then we would *all* be happy!" Peter joked.

"Not an easy answer but I'm sure you've heard of *five whys*. We can get to the heart of any problem by asking *why* in the right way five or so times."

"Go on, then," said Peter. He sensed a joke he might be able to trade elsewhere.

"Why aren't we selling to Aspiration? Because of delivery problems. Why? Because we're basing production on forecasts. Why? Because we can't make everything from scratch within current customer lead times. Why? Because our production lead times can be so long. Why? Because our *process* lead times are so variable. Why? Because no one's prioritised reducing and stabilising them. Why? Probably because we're preoccupied with costs. Why? Probably because that's how managers have chosen to view and dissect our organisation."

"That's more than five," Peter said with a grin. "Look, Josh. All I need to know for now is whether some of the things you've done in the woodshed could help elsewhere. Like the U-shaped cells – providing you don't screw up other layouts quite as much."

"Why U-shaped cells?"

"That's what I'm asking you – for goodness sake!" He had forgotten what Josh could be like. However bright he was supposed to be, he could struggle to answer the simplest of questions.

"U-shaped cells are a *solution*, Peter. Don't look for places to apply solutions; let's start with the problems we need to solve."

"Ok, cost. Cost is the problem. Where else can U-shaped cells reduce costs?"

Josh looked at him while he cupped his hands around his mouth. "Isn't there a bigger problem if operations are only ever associated with cost? What about customer service, capital, capacity or culture? Operations influence all these as well as cost every day! Why can't we be unshackled to improve *everything*?"

"Because cost is the current priority."

"For the business as a whole? Managers have probably assigned different priorities to different parts of the business. Why?" His team leader's pupils flared with passion. "Probably because they have dissected it along artificial lines – wearing *income-statement goggles*."

"I'm sure there's more to it than that, Josh." He was quite happy that he never got to see income statements. "Some things are beyond our concern, Joshua. Be careful what you suggest: if you keep offering, they'll keep taking."

Josh leant forward. "Then that's great. Just think what we could achieve if we redesigned all our processes systematically, end to end? Along the *real* lines from receiving an order to shipping it? We could take out loads of unnecessary cost – but we could also get the best out of the whole organisation. Including meeting Aspiration's lead times."

"So you want to sort out Planning now too?" Peter asked.

"Don't even think about departments at this stage. They're further examples of artificial lines – man-made barriers."

Peter shook his head. "Look, Josh, when I was your age I wanted to change the world too. When you get older and wiser you learn to be thankful for what you're *not* responsible for. And anyway, at the end of the day I can't see our factory looking much different to how it does today. If there are any other machines you want to move, let me know first. If it won't screw up the layout and actually delivers savings that justify the cost, I promise we'll look at it."

"It's not just about layout, Peter," Josh said, "although layouts *should* ideally end up looking very different. But we can also work around layout constraints. If we start with customer and business needs we can still design everything afresh: which machines we can dedicate for which products; when orders should be released; the sequence in which products will be processed; how they should be processed and how they should be passed on from one to the next. Then we can design how much manual help we need in the operation, from whom and how these people will be supported and managed. Then we can design the help we need to support them – for example, how the machines will be maintained."

"OK, OK, I get the point. We could tinker with everything, but at the end of the day I can't see us coming up with anything *that* different. Nothing that will reduce costs by *twenty per cent*!"

Alarmingly, this point did not seem to register with Josh.

Peter continued, "Look, if there really was that much potential, why wouldn't we have discovered it already?"

"Partly because the insight is new. And partly because of the way the business has been dissected, so that no one has been incentivised to develop the insight."

Peter tried to lean back but the stiff plastic chair would not comply. "So you don't think we've been trying? Look, Josh – I've served nearly twenty years as a production manager. If anyone can save even another ten per cent, I'll eat my hat."

"We've already achieved more than twenty per cent in the woodshed."

Peter's mouth opened but it took a moment to figure out what to say. "If you've got anything near that, then great. But as you said earlier, don't assume that anything you've done in the woodshed will apply anywhere else. Which brings me back to why I'm here!" He was beginning to get angry – it was like getting blood out of a stone. Sometimes he wished he could get away with being a bit more like Stephen. He looked around for inspiration. One of his more straightforward team leaders was in the far corner of Frame Assembly. "You'll have to excuse me," he said. "I've been needing to catch Milky for a while. Back in a minute." He swilled the cup and drank the bitter dregs. Then he tossed the cup into the bin and marched off for some brief respite.

5

OPPORTUNITY KNOCKS

JOSH moved round the table into Peter's chair so he could watch Frame Assembly. In the far corner Peter was now pulling at his hair, and Milky glanced over in his direction.

Milky's real name was Vijay: his nickname reflected his previous job as a milkman. He was a chirpy team leader who knew how to give and take a joke. Recently he had been the victim of one of Big Dave's legendary wind-ups. Milky was still in his forties but his hair had been silver and his face weather-beaten for years. When Dave noticed he had failed to sign out of his email account he composed a *send-to-everyone* email on Milky's behalf, inviting them to his retirement do. It had been perfectly gauged: Gregory had *replied all* to decline the invitation and to extend him best wishes for the future.

A gust of wind brought leaves skidding in from the yard. Josh's university tutors had considered him crazy to take this job. His friends knew different: he had never been shaped by the expectations of others. This company had always been in his blood. The irony was that now that the company had been wrestled away from his dad, his own influence was very much being shaped by the expectations of others: the expectations his managers had of him. He could see how the blend of his background, character, education and experience had prepared him to bridge the gap between management and the shop floor. But to others he was just a young man in a junior position, whose motivation they suspected. He had sensitively applied the freedom he had been afforded in the woodshed to transform it, and he had been biding his time for others to take note. This was the first time his boss had invited his broader ideas beyond his own area. The hurdle was now to avoid answering the wrong questions without alienating him.

One of the older frame builders plodded towards the coffee machine.

"Alright, Richard?" Josh called.

The quiet, rotund man turned slowly and shrugged his shoulders. He remained one of the most skilled and reliable frame builders.

"That good?"

The factory was running on empty: it had been leaking energy and good-will for years. Josh remained constantly alert to prevent the negativity permeating his own thoughts and feelings. Richard might well have yielded to it years ago. He now seemed to be weighing him up over the froth on his coffee.

"It's the end of the month," Richard said. "I've only had one proper work order today. But you can guarantee next week we'll be behind." He spied Josh's empty cup, "You don't want another one, do you?"

Josh smiled. "No thanks," he said. Management thinking had been driving ridiculous behaviour – to which they appeared oblivious. Efforts to *improve control* and meet monthly targets were driving variations in practices that introduced even more waste. Towards the end of the month when it became clear they were not on track to meet EBITDA targets, middle managers pulled forward as many high-value orders as possible. Then they starved the early processes to avoid bringing in new materials. For a while now this had meant that in the last week of the month, upstream processes had little to do and downstream processes were burning themselves out. A week later, at the start of the new month, this was reversed. Those doing the work despaired, but the more managers retreated to offices to assess progress against targets, the more they divorced themselves from reality and congratulated themselves on *pulling out all the stops*.

"I know how it is," Josh said. "Believe me, it will change."

Richard looked at him as if he was stupid.

"So are those the Montgomeries you're working on?" Josh asked.

"Uh-huh." Richard nodded towards Peter and Milky. "That's probably what they're talking about. Design should never have released them."

"I didn't think they had," Josh said.

"Eh?"

"I heard about the problem with the bottom rail. I spoke to the designer and he agreed to add two more dowels."

Richard looked stunned. Then he lapsed back into the gloom that seemed to fit him like his well-worn overalls.

"It's not just the Montgomeries. Our tools are knackered, the materials are flimsy, the kids untrained." He shook his head. "We're trying to keep it all together but no one else gives a fig."

"*I* do," Josh said. "And thank you – I know how much you're doing."

Richard looked at his boots. "They'll never change."

"We're all one company, Richard – there shouldn't be any *them or us*." He especially hated the disunity that had sunk in. They were supposed to be fighting the competition, not themselves.

"Try telling them that! We hardly *see* them any more." Josh waited: Richard had more to get off his chest. "Your old man was different. He would come and have a chat. And he listened." He looked away for a moment. "Until he sold us down the river."

"That's not how it was, Richard," he said. "He'll be glad that you're still here." It was true: his dad knew those who went beyond the call of duty. Despite his negativity, Richard still cared enough about the products to sacrifice his own earnings to help train the youngsters. The travesty was that instead of viewing Richard as an individual, some managers seemed to view him as just another person on the bottom rung who was indebted to them for a job. Such managers rewarded themselves more and Richard less, oblivious that they were in fact indebted to people like Richard for covering the cracks caused by their neglect. It exemplified the abuse of power that Josh despised.

Richard's cheeks grew a little ruddier and he turned to walk away.

"Keep doing the best you can, Richard. And keep your chin up."

Richard turned around. "Which one?" he said, pressing his chins against his chest.

Josh smiled. "See you later, Richard."

"See you."

Richard trudged back to his work area. He arranged three top rails in a long row on the floor and a bottom rail in front of each. He moved from one frame to the other and to and fro from the locker where he kept a makeshift container for the new glue. He then wandered off, presumably to get some parts. It was as easy to see potential here as anywhere, even when watching someone with Richard's experience. No wonder Richard was frustrated. He probably received work orders for three frames at a time because a planner or accountant had once decided this was the most efficient method of production. This was regardless of whether there were customer orders for all three. Furthermore, as long as the work orders came in threes, Richard would have limited scope to improve his station to reduce the time he wasted in walking or reaching.

None of this was yet worth pointing out to Peter: it could lead to an unnecessary argument or he might jump on improving Richard's productivity with disproportionate priority. Peter might also misinterpret such comments as lending support for the reintroduction of *time and motion*. This involved detailed time studies of an individual worker completing a task. It had been one of Peter's main improvement tools until earlier that year, when the industrial engineers who conducted them were themselves made redundant. The *stopwatch brigade* had never been popular: their main role had been to maintain the piecework system. This meant setting how much people got paid per product and prescribing how to work *smarter, not harder*. Operators knew that if they helped to find an improved method their piece rate would be reduced to reflect it. All this was now part of the cultural baggage that he needed to negotiate. If he had to fight just to be heard in his own organisation, the battles had to be chosen carefully.

Peter returned to the table, having stopped to get another coffee. "Sorry about that. Milky is up to his neck in it with the Montgomeries. Look, I've really got to be quick."

"No problem."

"You didn't want another one, did you?" Peter said.

"No, thank you," Josh replied. "Look, I know what you're after, Peter. I can put something together but please give me enough of your time so I can explain things properly. I'm sure we can give Stephen what he is after."

"If I give you more time, it won't be for a repeat of the discussion we've just had."

"Hopefully not. Let's get beyond the theory and apply the principles to our own processes. Let's imagine we have the chance to rebuild our factory from scratch."

"We don't."

"But let's ask ourselves, 'What if we could?' "

"There's no point dreaming if it's never going to happen. It's a waste of time."

"Please, trust me. Let me take you through a design process to give you an indication of just *how* different things could be."

Peter squirmed and flattened his moustache with finger and thumb. "One hour?"

"Two please, ideally. Then I can also give you confidence by *showing* you what we've already achieved in the woodshed. Consider that a scale model of what we can achieve end to end."

"Ah, the woodshed." Peter smoothed his moustache again. "The only possibility would be squeezing it in at seven am tomorrow. For one and a half hours max." He remembered his negotiation skills training. "*If* you can you then get me your list by midday."

"Tomorrow?" Josh asked. "Shouldn't we be involving the other team leaders first?"

"No. Why?"

"*I'd* want to know if someone else was discussing changes to my area."

"No, no. I wouldn't worry about that."

"Why not?"

"There's no time."

"Tell them that much then," Josh suggested.

"Eh?"

"If there's no time to involve team leaders properly, take five minutes in tomorrow's meeting to explain why. Better that than they find out you've submitted numbers behind their backs."

"That's up to me, Josh. Tomorrow at seven then?"

"See you then."

Peter rose to his feet and shook his head. He slapped him on the arm. "See you, kid."

"See you tomorrow."

Peter stretched his jacket and fastened a button.

Josh stood up and watched his boss hobble off. The odds were stacked against him, but his chance was still coming.

6

RETAIL THERAPY

GREGORY sat in the traffic and waited. The rainclouds had cleared but the winds remained. Branches of the sycamore trees opposite the factory remained mostly green and danced around in the sunlight.

He had wasted nearly two hours in a face-to-face meeting with his lawyer. Basically he had paid for him to confirm his worst-case scenario. The clock on his dashboard now read 16.04. His mouth was dry and his head ached. He had four missed calls and about fifty unanswered emails from earlier today. Fiona had been badgering him about new materials and he still had not looked at Anna's revised numbers. Part of him was not yet ready to do so.

Cars and bikes spurted out of the factory entrance. Familiar faces glanced at him. He wondered how many were working the dayshift purely for their own convenience. It also got to him how happy all his employees looked when leaving. And how they always left on the dot. He had always regarded it a privilege to manage one of the city's few remaining employers in manufacturing. He liked to think he was still following in the footsteps of yesteryear's benevolent entrepreneurs. He didn't like making anyone redundant, but times had changed and this had sadly become a fact of life. Workforces had changed too. A virus of entitlement had infected the country, and his company was not immune. Careers in manufacturing seemed particularly undervalued: employees wandered in like zombies and added insult to injury by springing to life as they left. How could he unlock this internal energy? He would make Churchillian speeches if it would make any difference. It might have done if there was an evident evil to rally his troops against, instead of the faceless and indefatigable market.

Gregory shook his head and cancelled the indicator. His getaway vehicle sped him away.

SofaZone was an unlikely retreat. Thankfully the store assistant did not appear to differentiate him from any other well-dressed customer with the potential to part with large amounts of money quickly.

Gregory paused inside the door to adjust to the latest layout. It was so irritating how they kept changing things around. The familiar sights and smells of new fabric and leather soothed his senses; this was still his domain. He counted two, three, four – just four of his suites on display. He made a beeline for the three-seater Foxglove: one of their most enduring sellers with washable, removable covers.

He tested the piping on the arm by lifting it between finger and thumb. He then lifted his woollen trouser legs and dropped onto the mixed-fibre cushions. He sank backwards and for a moment his body teetered on the brink of an involuntarily shut-down.

"Can I help you, sir?" asked the soft-spoken assistant.

The voice jolted Gregory. She had straight, blonde hair and was attractively dressed. There was some resemblance to a younger Linda.

"I hope so," he replied, with an engineered smile. "I'm in the market for a new sofa," he began. He tried to recall what it was like when a sofa was just something to sit on. "A good one, that's built to last."

"Well, you've picked a good one there, sir. That's an Eden."

He winced. It had made sense to keep the Eden brand name. He had considered repositioning it as *Eden: a brand of Gregory Todd Ltd*, but he was not that desperate for self-promotion.

"They've always been leaders in design and comfort. And it's made right here in Worcester, as you might know."

Full marks for assuming that he cared. These days more end-customers were seemingly treating sofas like consumables: not caring where or how well they were made, as long as they were cheap and looked OK. He leant forward to feel behind the valance and drummed his right leg on the floor. The staples that fixed the calico to the bottom rail did not feel even. Why was it so difficult to get this right? He had never felt sufficiently at home on the shop floor to prevent people trying to pull the wool over his eyes. Still, the calico seemed pretty well fitted – a far cry from the complaints he had personally followed up with SofaZone's Chief Purchasing Officer.

"The covers are removable and a hundred per cent washable. Many of our customers order replacement covers through us when changing their décor."

He reached under the skirting to scratch the top of the sofa leg with his fingernail and then withdrew it to inspect it for lifted lacquer.

"So how much are we talking?" he asked.

"This one, sir, is the large Foxglove sofa. It's £1495, or £1895 together with the armchair."

That seemed about right. SofaZone's mark-ups were already generous, but of course the prices did not reflect the discount he had been forced to grant last quarter.

"What are the options for upholstery?"

"Well, sir." She leant over to select a brochure from the coffee table. "This model has a fully removable cover. There are ten fabric choices but more than a hundred further choices in colour." She presented him with the brochure, which had colour cards for the highest sellers afforded through their dye shop. She was doing OK, but she had not shown him any samples or mentioned that the full range of choices could be viewed online. "The great advantages of the removable covers are that they're fully washable and you can change the covers to suit your decoration. Many customers choose to have different sets for summer and winter."

"I see. So how long would it take for mine to arrive if I ordered it today?"

"We say twelve weeks really, to be safe. Sometimes it's quicker but everything is custom built by hand, you see. You also get choices for the finish on the legs and for the fillings in the cushions."

"I understand: quality is worth the wait. Does anyone else offer anything similar?" he dared to ask, rising to his feet. He had already spotted a

Beauchamp in the neighbouring section. They were a similar, middle-end manufacturer who, he suspected, had also been talking with Aspiration. They offered similar designs in removable, fixed and leather covers. Like Eden, they had cut costs while stopping short of low-end features. For example, both companies had replaced unseen hardwood with fibreboard and used drop-in coil units on their mainstream models instead of fixed, tied coils. Yet to him a Beauchamp was simply not an Eden.

"Of course, sir. This one's a Beauchamp," she said, leading him over to it. He watched her run her hand over the top cushion. "Another gorgeous sofa. Also hand built. Retails at a very competitive £1295."

"Yes, but it's not necessarily better *value*," Gregory explained. "Which one do *you* prefer?"

"Well, they're both lovely sofas."

"Go on – if you had to make a choice."

The assistant crumpled under pressure. "I think they're on a par in terms of design and quality. Maybe the Beauchamp design is a little more edgy – and perhaps with the Eden you're paying a bit more for the name. My partner and I actually just bought a Beauchamp and we love it. But at the end of the day it really is a personal choice. They're both lovely sofas."

Any air of attractiveness evaporated.

"What do you think, sir? Do you need a few moments by yourself?"

"No, no," Gregory asserted, while raising his cheekbones. He had never considered himself anxious but wooziness had returned. Dryness spread to the back of his throat. "I definitely prefer the Eden. It has a classier look and feel." He swallowed. "Although I should of course consult my wife. I'm pretty sure she would prefer it too, though. It just seems a higher class." The assistant smiled and retrieved the promotional card that he had pushed to the back. "Anyway, I'd better get going. Thank you for your help."

"Not at all, sir. I look forward to seeing you and your wife soon."

He fixed his eyes on the door but his head felt light and his legs weak as he passed the sales desk. Fears assailed him. *Everything* he and Linda possessed, down to the clothes he was wearing, had come from money handed over for their products instead of competitors' products in moments like this.

He shook one of the doors several times before the other one allowed him to burst out into the fresh air.

This had always been the case for every business. Eden products remained highly desirable and the market was big enough for thousands of transactions every day. But the horizon had never seemed so distant.

He leant against the wall and bent over, to consider where he could throw up. *Every* bill *every* employee of theirs would *ever* face needed to be paid with monies from further purchases of their products. This realisation was not new, but it suddenly seemed impossible to sustain their existing level of business, let alone grow it.

His heart was racing. This was ridiculous: he had always been able to rely on a solid and healthy disposition. If it was just a virus, he would fight it off. He stepped tentatively towards his car. Safely seated, he closed his eyes. *Everything would be fine.* He recoiled when he saw his pale and clammy forehead in the rear-view mirror. It might be nothing more than a bit of stress, together with too much caffeine and too little sleep. The wine that had helped him to get off to sleep last night might also have played a part. He had cut back a lot prior to the weekend.

He turned on his ignition and searched for the *Serenade for Strings*. Good old Tchaikovsky. Now he just needed some time and space to get his head together.

Twenty minutes later, Gregory was safely seated in his office, which spread around the front, right-hand corner of the first floor, next to the boardroom. His head still ached and he was still having to concentrate on his breathing. He rummaged in his top drawer for painkillers and swallowed them dry. He found a muesli bar and tore it open. He had not eaten much all day – perhaps that was part of the problem.

Mountfield's voice still resounded in his head: "It's not a market problem is it, if Beauchamp is doing well?"

Running his own business was harder than it had looked. The more he learnt, the more there was to learn. He had to be leader, manager, motivator, strategist, peacemaker, coach and whip-cracker, all in one. Arthur had once assured him there was no need to be an expert in every functional area, as long as he could be secure enough to recruit, lead and develop experts. The problem was finding them. The truth was that if each of his senior managers had delivered their plans – which *they* had developed and had *promised* to deliver – there would be no problem. As a team player, he always cascaded the credit. But flak was something for which he was expected to bear full responsibility. At times it had been tempting to get rid of every one of them, but as his experiment with Stephen had confirmed, it took time for any replacement to learn the business, and there was no guarantee that other replacements would be any more capable. He still liked to believe that everyone should be given a chance, and one of his own strengths was getting the best out of others.

Since schooldays he had invented mnemonics to help him recall essay and thought structures. *SOFDS* was the one that had stuck to help him check whether every base was now being covered. He had been trying to get to *SOFAS,* but he now liked to think that the D in SOFDS reminded him that their designs had to stand out.

Strategy was OK: this was mainly his responsibility. He knew the market inside out and in their middle-market niche there was never going to be a great deal to revolutionise. There would always be the odd player that tried to experiment with wacky designs, but the main strategic needs remained: reducing costs and response times.

Operations were therefore a priority, hence he had recruited Stephen as a fresh operations director to replace the battle-weary one who had learnt to make too many concessions. Stephen was a bit green and a little prickly, but Gregory liked his confidence. He had already injected some top-level thinking and a sense of urgency. His initial cost plan would have been met if Aspiration's volumes had come through, and he had responded well by promising to do more on costs as well as getting their act together to meet Aspiration's lead times. Meanwhile, the middle managers were well qualified to look after the details. Peter, for example, was never going to be leadership material, but he provided the experience and stability that was controlling the bulk of the workforce in Production.

He had gained more confidence in *Finance* through the buyout, but their options were now limited because of the influence of Mountfield's team. Meanwhile, Anna had been learning to stretch the boundaries of what they were allowed to do within accounting guidelines.

Design remained one area in which they remained strong. All the feedback suggested their target customers never had any complaints about design – complaints nearly always concerned cost, quality or delivery. He had learnt to work well with Fiona: her artistic ability blended well with his knowledge of the market.

Sales was his own domain. Eddie had clearly not delivered in the past but he deserved some sympathy because his latest plan would have been met if Operations had got their act together on what were relatively simple products. Eddie would never be as good as he was at *hunting* new business or leading negotiations. For this reason he had recently taken the difficult decision to supervise both these areas personally. This was something that had to be done, although it had come at the cost of undermining their long-standing relationship. This had pushed Eddie to the brink of leaving the company, but thankfully Gregory had averted the crisis. When it came to *farming* existing customers, Eddie was second to none. Key players in all of their main customers loved him. If he had embraced the overtures he had received from Beauchamp he would have taken significant business with him.

His breathing had calmed. The current crisis could also be averted. He closed his mouth and tried to breathe normally. The pressure from Mountfield had been crushing him, but there was nowhere to go with it. He could not show any vulnerability to his team: they could never be his friends. He certainly could never admit any concerns or weakness to Mountfield. He closed his eyes and breathed in deeply. If he was honest, every interaction with his chairman was eroding his confidence and needlessly consuming hours of his thought life. Mountfield was diametrically opposed to Gregory's previous experience in so many ways. Arthur Eden had been a peaceful, larger-than-life gentleman whose presence had filled the factory. He had been a good man: too generous, perhaps, for the modern business world.

Gregory pinched the bridge of his nose and opened his eyes. This had been the very scene of so many of their candid chats, when Arthur had been on his side of the desk. But for years he had already been taking Arthur's advice with a pinch of salt, supplementing it with his own diet of management journals and biographies. It was these that had guided him to much of the low-hanging fruit which Arthur had left on the tree.

One of his deepest fears was that Mountfield was right. What if he *had* now reached the limit of his own capability? He had already done everything he had been eager to do. With so many variables in a business like this, he could not just carry on tweaking things without risking adverse effects. All significant levers had been optimised and everything was well controlled. Under Anna's keen eye, all managers had been incentivised to deliver improvements vs. budgets and they were reporting on all variances. Could he really take much more cost out of the operation? What more could he do apart from convincing a significant new customer like Aspiration to place orders?

He left his office and wandered down the corridor. Who could he turn to? Stephen was fresh out of his MBA and the textbooks he displayed behind his desk could well be full of green shoots of new ideas. He gave a cursory knock on Stephen's door before entering. He was at once relieved and angered by the clear desk: Stephen had already left for the day. Clearly Gregory needed to delegate more of his workload. For now he shut the door and scanned the intellectual capital on the bookshelves: *Corporate Value*; *Operations Management Theory and Cases*; *Lean Manufacturing: the Japanese way*; *Operations Performance Breakthrough*. He could do with some of that. He extracted the book and flicked through it backwards. A chapter on offshore manufacturing. People had been talking for years about sending at least part of their operation offshore, to developing countries where waves were cheaper. Automotive components… clothes… electronics… Of course, there was nothing on furniture. Yes, labour costs in China were a tenth of those in Worcester, but it was not easy to ship custom-built sofas halfway around the world. And this book was already out of date: Western firms were now starting to move manufacturing back home in the wake of China's wage inflation. He checked himself for defensiveness. Some of their standard covers were already sewn in Bangladesh, with mixed success. It would hardly help to reduce their lead times and it would suck even more management time.

He should probably challenge himself again. But at the end of the day, Arthur had taught him to take responsibility for his own decisions. He would not necessarily live a life mapped out by the road most travelled. Running a successful, Worcester-based furniture business was what he wanted to do. If he did not want to spend half his life on the other side of the world, he had to find a way of making this work.

He reached a chapter on lean manufacturing. 'Don't compromise cost or quality; improve both by reducing waste,' he read, shaking his head. In his first year as managing director he had been taken in by some consultants who had been recommended to him. They had crawled all over Upholstery, papering walls with flip-chart sheets and covering the floor with tape. The area had *looked* better for a while but the promised magic had never worked on the income statement except to conjure up a significant line of *exceptional expenditure*. The final straw was that the consultants then had the audacity to blame *him* that they had not achieved more. He should have known better: years earlier as general manager he had persuaded Arthur to let him bring in experts in Total Quality Management, or TQM. Back then it had all been about empowerment: they had shut down production and invested hours in talking to operators, all with zero payback.

The chapter on Six Sigma caught his attention. Someone at the golf club was constantly trying to sell him this approach. This was the name of another popular improvement programme, particularly in manufacturing businesses. He flicked through the pages looking for a proper definition. There was the notion of reducing variability, something about problem-solving, case studies, more case studies, something about programme management. There was little to dispel his suspicion that it was hardly rocket science. He looked back to see who had written it – the same author as for the previous chapters.

Maybe there *was* nothing new out there. Maybe he did just need people who could do the basics well. Was that all Stephen had learnt on his MBA?

Time would tell but it was running out. He needed to set a new course by the end of the week, and Wednesday had almost gone.

7

BETTER BY DESIGN

JOSH tapped on the open door. Thursday morning had not yet broken in the offices but in the factory the dawn chorus of pneumatic tools was already one hour old. He had thought long and hard about how best to use this gift of ninety minutes with his boss. First, he would try to bring insight to the root cause of many of their operational problems. Second, he would model how they could go about designing a better business from scratch. Third, he would show him what they had already achieved in the woodshed.

"Ah, hello mate," said Peter.

"Morning, Peter," he said. "How are you?"

"Oh, not three bad, mate. No new disasters yet, anyway," Peter said, with his eyes still fixed on his inbox straight ahead. He reached for his *Real men love skittles* mug, which was still steaming. "Won't be a minute. Kettle's just boiled – help yourself."

Josh ventured into the corner of the office and selected a mug that was less brown inside than most. It was emblazoned with a TQM logo. He dared to glance inside the fridge. Black tea would have to do.

Peter lifted a pile of papers and placed them on the floor. "Can you believe Stephen was giving me grief about this the other day?" he said. "He tried telling me to separate the important from the urgent! Yet he's the one who tells me how everything is more urgent *and* important than anything he dumped on me the night before."

It was time to listen, not to coach.

"It's time I need – not grief. Twenty emails since I went home last night," he continued. "Half of them from Stephen. It wouldn't matter so much if he actually *did* anything himself. He doesn't even ask – he just emails – without even a 'Hi Peter' these days, let alone a 'Well done' once in a while."

Peter sank into the dirty blue chair that had long been moulded to his contours. "Right, then. Sorry about that," Peter said. "It's just one of those things. Come on then, you'd better start taking me through your wonderful ideas."

Josh collected a few sheets from the printer tray before pulling up a chair alongside his boss. "Remember what I was saying about designing an end-to-end operation from scratch?"

Peter nodded.

"When you think about it, designing an operation is an obvious gap. No one would question that good *product design* is important, would they?"

"Maybe not, but it's not the only thing that matters."

"Exactly. So why do we not put the same focus into designing our *operation*? This is often just as significant as product design in determining overall customer service and costs. Yet we seem to be content with letting our operation evolve and then just trying to control it as best we can."

"That's a bit harsh," Peter said. "Don't forget what I said yesterday – the operation will never look that different as long as we're making sofas."

"Please try and reserve judgement for now, Peter. Let's start with a blank sheet of paper and imagine we're designing the operation from scratch. Consider it like a relay race, from receiving a customer's order to delivering it. What's the first thing we need to do?"

"Find the bloody fabric – if we've got it in stock."

"Before it reaches Production. We need to take the order, confirm the fabric is in stock, check credit-worthiness and so on. But if it was a relay race, this shouldn't take any longer than an hour, should it?"

Peter shook his head. "If that."

"So let's move to Cutting. How long would it take Shelley from the moment she starts laying out the fabric for one unit to handing on a complete bundle of pieces for sewing?"

Peter turned his palms upwards. "How long is a piece of string?"

"Let's say no more than one hour again," Josh suggested. Peter did not disagree. Josh accelerated through the same line of questioning for all processes through to despatch. He sketched boxes for each process on his sheet of paper from left to right, with times underneath.

"So if we add these up," he concluded, "we get… seven and a half hours. Now we're getting to the heart of our problem. What's the actual lead time we offer our customers?"

"About ten weeks, although I'm supposed to say eight," Peter said.

"OK. Let's imagine a sample of a thousand orders. What do you think a distribution plot of production lead time would look like?"

Peter fell silent, with his eyes fixed on the paper.

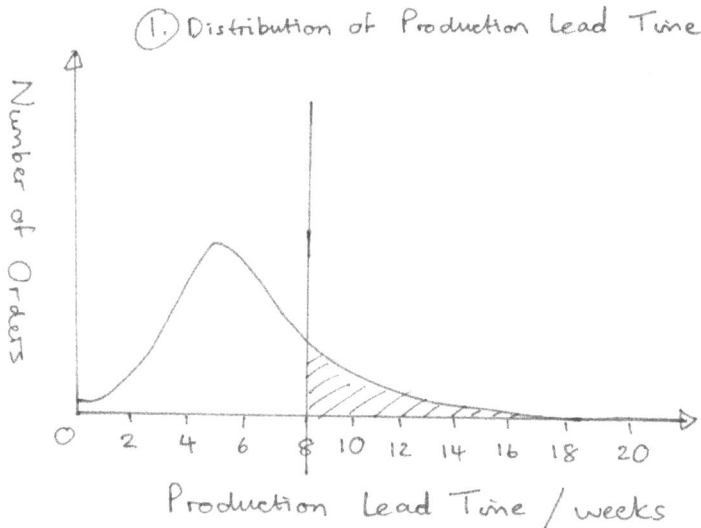

(1.) Distribution of Production Lead Time

"Let me explain what I mean," Josh said. He sketched two axes as the basis for a graph. Against the vertical axis he wrote 'Number of orders', and against the horizontal one he wrote 'Production Lead Time/weeks' and numbered it from zero to twenty.

"Within a thousand orders there is probably a handful that has been bullied through from start to finish in a day or two. For example, if it's a sample the customer is waiting for. The most typical value is probably four or five weeks." He drew a curve to peak above 4.5 weeks. "The problem is that the right-hand side will have a much longer tail." He continued the curve so it did not fully meet the axis until twenty weeks.

"As you say, we're supposed to quote eight weeks. So a lot of your expediting happens around here." He drew a vertical line at eight and shaded in the tail to the right. So we're going to be late on all these orders.

"Tell me about it," said Peter.

"But even if we say ten weeks, we'll still be late for all these orders at the end of the tail."

"In principle maybe," Peter said, "but we've become pretty good at expediting."

"I daresay, but prioritising some orders always means deprioritising others. We hide the extent of the problem because we still don't measure OTIF properly: the percentage of orders that are delivered On Time In Full (or OTIF) against even the ten-week standard. The real plot really does look like this – I did the analysis."

"Good for you. I'm glad you had the spare time."

"So the big question is what's causing this variability?"

Peter shrugged.

"It's built up from similar variability in lead times for individual processes: the total time before a product arrives at the next process, including waiting time. We said before that if it was a relay race we could get an order through cutting in less than one hour. But if we include typical waiting times, in a thousand orders the distribution plot would look like this."

Josh sketched out a similar graph with a similar curve, numbered on the horizontal axis from one to twenty days. "A typical lead time for the process might be four days but there's a long tail. Especially for orders with rarer lay characteristics. They can wait a long time in the hope that other units of the same pattern, design, model or shrinkage type will join them to make up a batch. So the killer solution is to design a system for each process to do this," he said, taking a thick marker and drawing a much taller and narrower peak.

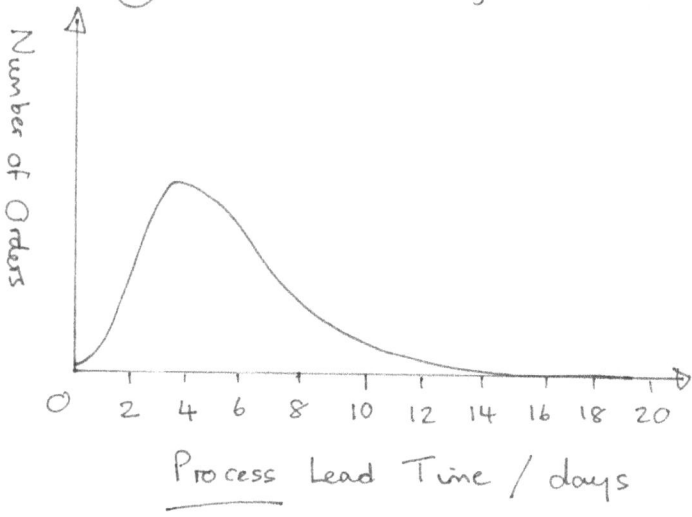

2.) Distribution of Cutting Lead Time

Number of Orders

Process Lead Time / days

FUTURE

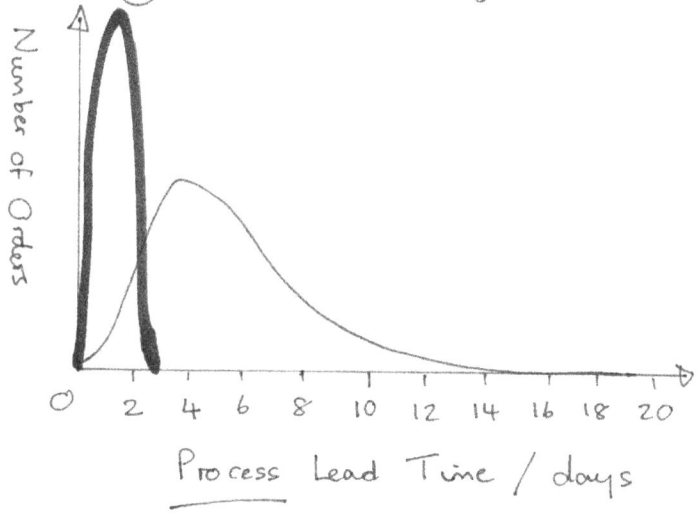

2.) Distribution of Cutting Lead Time

Number of Orders

Process Lead Time / days

Peter leant back. He grimaced and shook his head. His office phone started ringing. "Ignore it – it goes away eventually."

"So if we can design and sustain systems to do this for each of our processes, the overall picture would look like this," Josh continued, using the thick marker pen to draw a similar narrow and tall peak on the production lead time plot, "which would enable us to offer smaller customer lead times *and* guarantee to meet them."

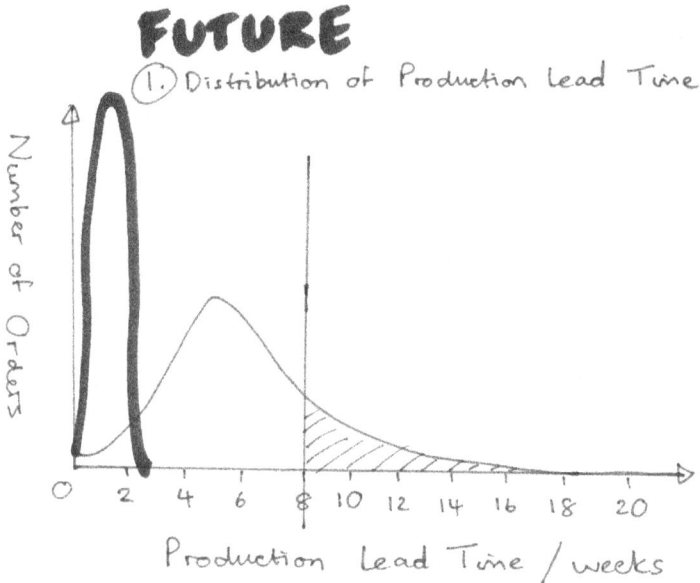

The phone finally stopped ringing.

"Thank goodness for that," Peter said. "Your argument is all theoretical. You know we can't cut *every order* within a two-day lead time."

"Why not?"

"Capacity! It's not unlimited, you know."

Ah, capacity. "OK, so what would you say our current capacity is, in units per week?"

"Overall?" Peter asked. "You should know that. It's eight hundred units. Or a thousand I should say now, with the new investments."

"That might be the most we have typically managed to *produce* in a week, Peter, but I don't believe it's our *capacity*. We can get loads more out of our current processes – I doubt we've come anywhere close to filling our capacity. Perhaps it's closer to *two* thousand units a week."

"Do me a favour!" said Peter. "If it's anywhere near that, why do you think we had to invest to get it to a thousand?"

Josh chose to say nothing.

"Whoa, Josh. You can't say things like that!"

"For labour-intensive processes we can always train more people. Capacity limits are determined by how much we can get out of equipment at individual processes. We may need to liberate capacity or improve reliability at targeted processes to support the overall flow improvements. If equipment is fully automated we should use Overall Equipment Effectiveness (or OEE). First, it can help to indicate how much potential there is to liberate. Second, it will help us to prioritise action to realise it."

"You don't need to tell me about OEE, Josh. I pioneered it here way before you arrived. The plant just isn't ready for it. OEE values would just be rubbing our faces in it."

"That depends on your perspective! Like any standard, is it there to condemn or can it help to reveal and prioritise improvements? Without it, we risk wasting even more money by throwing it at problems in the shape of new machines."

"You can't expect much from machines that are thirty years old."

"We've got more out of the woodshed's equipment, and we didn't buy any of the budgeted equipment."

"Be careful – we've not tried to hit the volumes yet. Anyway, you can't compare everything to the woodshed, Josh. It's completely different."

"You're right. Every process has different complexities. In the woodshed we have more components than anywhere else. In cutting, the complexity comes from batching, because the time per cut is independent of the number of layers cut together, right? If we had just one pattern and fabric we could cut *many* thousands of units per week. Practical cutting capacity is harder to define. But for our actual volume and mix we *could* calculate the minimum period where there is still enough capacity to cut all order types at least once. It needs to be just long enough to accumulate enough orders for the high runners to be layered and cut together, to compensate for the low runners that must be cut individually. My guess is that this minimum cycle time is only half a week."

"You would choose to cut products with only one lay? That's not going to do much for capacity, is it? Let alone machine utilisation!"

"That won't matter, will it, if we've already shown we can make all the orders that will ever be received in that time period?"

Peter hesitated, before shaking his head. "If utilisation goes down, costs go up. Anna would haul Stephen over the coals on his variance report."

Josh took a deep breath. It exasperated him when managers couldn't see the wood for the trees: some of the controls that managers prided themselves on most were the very things that were restricting their progress. "Reported *unit* costs might go up on some equipment," he said, "but real costs won't increase! Why should we let anything within our own power stop us from doing the right thing? Where measures or procedures unintentionally promote the wrong behaviour, let's help our leaders to strip them out, so they can properly take control of the business. Production targets are another example: they sound like a good idea but incentivise us to suck up cash irrespective of income."

Peter laughed. "You don't care about how much we make?"

"I care about how well we sell! And how well we are delivering these sales."

They were interrupted by a tinny melody. "*I work on the frontline,*" the lyrics proclaimed. "*I work to survive.*"

"Sorry about that." Peter's cheeks flushed. "I'd better get it." He finally found his phone. "Peter Nash."

Josh wandered to Peter's doorway to give him some privacy. It was tough – Peter's focus was rightly production, but there were so many other things that needed to change if the improvements were to be radical enough – and sustainable. It would be much simpler to talk to Gregory directly, but there was no precedent for any team leader to question the CEO's methods, let alone Josh with his personal background. He would have to wait for his time to come.

For now the right thing was to persevere with Peter. Not just to respect the chain of command, but also because he longed to help him understand how much better his factory could be. The difficulty was that explaining the theory would only ever get him so far: it would be a slow process for Peter to re-evaluate everything he had absorbed over so many years. It was time for him to encounter the changes in the woodshed.

Peter was still on the phone. Outside the office, the Upholstery jungle was rumbling. The processes had changed little since Josh had first discovered them as a schoolboy. Hoses snaked down from the metal canopy into a number of individual clearings below. Within one of them, a lone man paraded around a ragged carcass. One hand stretched fabric over the frame and the other forced a snake's head to spit staples in. Amid the chattering of tools across Upholstery, the carcasses were coming to life.

He had always loved the potential of factories to bond people together from all walks of life, to create things of value. It was now his second nature to sift this value in everything he observed: knacks from short cuts and characters from attitudes.

Upholstery still boasted some of the toughest characters, who went about their work with bristled chests and bared tattoos. They appeared as ready to spar with fists as they did with banter, jostling for position in the unspoken pecking order. If only he had free rein to turn this culture upside down.

As for now, even if he could convince Peter, it would take another seismic shift for them to influence Gregory and Stephen. It felt like trying to row the company to safety upstream, single-handedly. Managers seemed content to drift or even paddle against him towards the blind corner and the falls beyond. He clasped his hands behind his head and closed his eyes. He *had* what they needed: it was ridiculous that it was so difficult.

Helping Peter to encounter the woodshed transformation was the right next step, but even this would not be straightforward. The pressure Peter was under meant that he would be very reluctant to take the unnecessary risk of trying to transform the whole of Production. Instead, it would be much safer for Peter to try and keep Stephen quiet by cherry-picking one or two safer-looking solutions.

Peter would also have understood much more if he had got involved in the woodshed's journey, even though this might have compromised their solutions. Now the risk was that the solutions would be observed superficially, in oblivion to the engine that was driving them. Josh had carefully shaped this through insight in leadership and change-management and a cultural revolution had been forged through blood, sweat and tears. The woodshed had long been a dumping ground for difficult operators, and many of these were now going well beyond the call of duty. None had been motivated by the prospect of praise from the hierarchy, but it was high time they got some of the recognition they deserved.

"Sorry about that," Peter called out loudly.

Josh rejoined him in his office.

"Dave's on his way. So we've got another five minutes to put this discussion to bed. Our main difference seems to be your fixation with lead times, whereas our main priority is to reduce costs."

Josh sighed. What new angle could he use to make the most of this five minutes? "Can I ask what you understand by the term *waste*?" he asked.

Peter looked to the ceiling. "Anything that doesn't add value in the eyes of the customer."

"And you're familiar with the eight types of wastes? Those that Toyota defined to help them see the waste in their own plants?"

"We got that T-shirt years ago, Josh."

"Which one do you think is the worst of these eight wastes?"

"It's a trick question – they're all as bad as each other."

"The worst is *overproduction*: making too much or too soon. This is because of the amount of further waste it generates. For example, if you make a product too soon you immediately incur wastes of inventory and waiting – with the unnecessary costs associated with them. We can tackle overproduction through what we were talking about earlier, and in doing so you *will* reduce costs that you consider our priority. More than that, it will open up *new opportunities* to collapse costs. For example, once our production lead time is less than the customer lead time, we can start building every-thing to order. Just think how much that will help to collapse costs, as well as serving our customers."

Peter shook his head but was smiling. "We're already doing that, Josh."

"What?"

"We've been making everything to order for years."

It took a moment to work out what he meant. "We *finish* sofas to order, Peter, from inventory. What I mean is making everything from scratch within the time a customer is prepared to wait."

"So if you were in my shoes you would be willing to *guarantee* to Stephen that we could make everything *from scratch* within *eight weeks*?"

"No, we would need to convince Stephen first," Josh said. "Then Gre-gory. Not just for their go-ahead: we'll need the right conditions in change-management and leadership to drive the transformation, which will include reversing many of the management controls that we spoke about earlier."

"OK, OK. Fair enough. But you still believe that, theoretically, eight weeks are possible."

"No. Theoretically, I think that *two* weeks are possible."

Peter laughed out loud. "Two weeks?"

Big Dave hovered at the door, with a winged chair on his shoulder. No one should be allowed to risk injury like that, regardless of how much he could lift in a gym. Josh left it to Peter, as Big Dave's manager, to say something.

"Hey, Dave," said Peter, hobbling out to meet him. "Josh here reckons we could make *every* product from scratch – right? From cutting to packing – within two weeks! What do you think about that then?"

Big Dave hauled the half-wrapped chair to the ground and slowly straightened his back. "Well, if that's what the big man says, then bring it on." Josh had got to know Dave a bit recently through the informal factory football team. Dave's playing days were over but he was still the team's godfather.

"Alright, Dave?" said Josh.

"Hello, mush."

Josh gave Peter one last chance to say something, but it came and went.

"Dave, we can't let you risk your back like that," Josh said. "Please use a trolley."

Big Dave scowled. He stood up even straighter and his air of friendship disappeared.

"Yes," Peter said with a grin. "A back injury wouldn't look very good in the stats, would it?" He winked at Dave and turned to the offending product. "Come on then, where's the problem?"

On the back of the raspberry red chair, an area the size of a football was streaked with a slightly different shade. It was clearly a dye-shop problem, but an upholsterer on piece rate might have been incentivised to get it through unnoticed.

"No, that'll have to be redone," Peter said.

"Dangermouth said it had to leave on the eight o'clock. Apparently he spoke to you about it."

"Well, at least it's not on the front."

"Why don't we redo it and use a courier?" Josh suggested.

"No," Peter said. "No more couriers this month. You'll have to rewrap it and let it go."

He and Big Dave looked at each other. Then Big Dave wandered off towards the nearest trolley.

"So who's going to get to the bottom of the problem to make sure it doesn't happen again?" Josh asked.

"Are you volunteering?"

"Isn't Trevor the team leader of the dye shop?"

"He's got more than enough on his plate at the moment."

"If problems keep coming back, things will only get worse. Each fresh occurrence is a gift: a chance to capture the relevant data to solve the root cause."

"Then there's no need to worry if the gift will come round again." After a short-lived grin, Peter stepped towards the chair and tore off the label. "Look, I'll find out who let it through, if that will make you any happier."

"I shot the Sheriff," Dave sang loudly to the tune on the radio. The trolley had become his dance partner.

"Nice," Josh said. "No wonder they called you Twinkle Toes."

"And you the midfield enforcer," Dave quipped. He helped to lift the chair onto the trolley. "But I did not shoot the deputee!" Big Dave strutted off into the factory to leave him and Peter alone.

"Right – ready to see the woodshed?" Josh asked.

"Ready as I'll ever be."

Peter darted into his office to throw the ticket on top of a pile.

8

There's Something in the Woodshed

Peter led the way through Upholstery to the edge of the overflow frame store. Part of him welcomed the debates with Josh: it kept him on his toes. So long as he did not allow Josh to get too cocky.

"Look at this," he pointed out. "It's not just the woodshed that's been improving, you know." Over the last week the thicket of bare wooden frames had thinned to reveal the pedestrian aisle through to the loading yard. They passed a couple of operators who were still trying to marry up frames with some earmarked orders in an effort to make the month. "Now we just need to keep it here."

Josh made no acknowledgement.

"You can't run down inventory much more than this, Josh. Not if you want to run Upholstery smoothly."

"Don't consider inventory as something to keep topped up! If we can make everything to order, then each piece of inventory will have its own identity. The total inventory can then be determined from those distribution plots of lead time that we've just sketched. If we decide we have to release orders ten weeks in advance to stand a hope of completing most of them, what's the minimum inventory we lock in?"

"I've no idea."

"Ten weeks' worth."

That was cheating: Stephen always expected him to speak of inventory in monetary terms. "Hang on." They did know how many times their inventory was turned over every year. "Ten weeks' worth is about five turns a year. We're already there!" Even though Stephen wanted more.

"OK. So what if we can compress the variability trace enough to release orders five weeks in advance? How much inventory can we reach then?"

He was probably supposed to say five weeks, but it was all theoretical.

"Five weeks," Josh said anyway. "This would halve the total inventory, or double the turns! Think of what that would do for our return on capital employed. The point is that if everything is made to order, inventory should no longer be seen as something to top up: it then *results* from our design. If we reduce the variability of lead times, we can still reliably deliver orders while starting later, which enables us to collapse the inventory."

"So you still believe in *just-in-time*?" This inventory-reduction theory had emerged from Japan years ago but was now widely discredited. If Josh said no, he would be conceding that inventory-reduction theories did not work in practice. If Josh said yes, Peter had the proof to discredit him. Years ago Gregory had brought in consultants to help them upholster *just in time*. They had run down the finished goods inventory but they could only cope by increasing the frame stock upstream. The result had been an overall increase in inventory. And a lot of stress.

"That depends on what you mean," Josh replied. "Did they give you the analogy of the *river and the rocks*, where the water level in a river channel represents the waste?"

"I'm afraid so."

"By designing the systems we've been talking about, we'll put in safeguards to avoid failing customers while proving our ability to lower variability and waste. This will reveal more problems – rocks in the river channel – that have always been there, like inflexibility or poor reliability. By steadily removing these rocks we can further reduce the variability and waste."

They emerged into the relative brightness of the rear yard. One of the trucks was pulling away from the loading bay. Was it that time already? "That was hardly our experience," Peter said.

"No," continued Josh, "from what I heard you drained out the water without removing any rocks. No wonder the ship ran aground. It sounds like the consultants may have lobbed in a few extra rocks too – from the safety of the banks."

Peter laughed. "That sounds about right. How did you learn all this stuff, anyway?"

"Bit by bit, I suppose. This was the first factory floor I ever experienced. Whenever I've learnt some new theory I've always tried to think through how to apply it here."

"Well, you might well have read more than I have, but I've got a bit more experience under my belt. It's this that has taught me the value of flexibility, and your ideas to reduce variability don't sound very flexible at all."

"The only flexibility we need is to meet customer requirements. Is it better to sort out flexibility on the hoof, or to design how to provide the required flexibility in advance?"

They had reached the woodshed. "Alright. Time out, Josh. We'd better call a truce for now so you can show me what you've been up to. Just don't be disheartened if I find holes in things. It's better I do before Stephen does, trust me."

Josh led him into the *box*. He wasn't a bad kid but it was a relief to shut him up for now. That was fitting, just as Peter was putting Josh safely back in his *box*. *Oh, his wit was wasted in this profession.* He shut the noise out behind them.

"Right," Josh began. "Remember the first sketch we did in your office? Well, this flow diagram is conceptually similar but in more detail. It shows what used to go on in the woodshed." He pointed to two flip-chart sheets which had been taped together on the wall. They were covered with hand-writing, boxes and arrows and the title at the top read *Current State Material and Information Flow Analysis (MIFA)*. "Working from the left to the right, it shows all the processes and information, from knowing when we had to produce something to delivering it to Frame Assembly."

"All that just for the woodshed?"

"That's what we allow to happen when we don't design one simple and effective end-to-end system. Unofficial systems proliferate but the complexity remains hidden. Everybody has to work out for themselves when and how to do what."

"It should never have been that complicated."

"Exactly. But it was," Josh said.

Josh hadn't got his point: if people had been doing what they were supposed to be doing, it would never have looked like that.

"So we designed that system over there, instead," Josh continued. He looked at another diagram on the wall, which was entitled Target State Material and Information Flow Diagram. It also had hand-drawn lines and boxes, but that's where the similarity ended. For a start, it was on a single page of A3 paper.

"This showed we could achieve a two-hour response time. It took out so much waste that we could do the same amount with half the floor space."

"Anyone can reduce space by squashing machines together," Peter pointed out. "So what? It's not so easy to reduce something significant like headcount."

Josh screwed up his face: Peter must have finally found him out.

"I've been trying not to use that term here," Josh said.

"Eh?"

"I spent six months convincing the whole team here that they *count* more than that. But we *are* doing the same amount of work with two fewer people. Alan left because he did not like the new way of working. Ray was working full-time on the improvements until he retired."

"By two, then? Already?" Peter asked. This would put a smile on Stephen's face. A pulse of machine noise announced that someone else was joining them inside the *box*. He glanced back and groaned to himself. Graham stood behind him in his oversized black boots. Black plastic earrings stretched his lobes and matted dreadlocks were tied behind his back. Peter had endured enough skirmishes with Graham when he had been a regular upholsterer, but things had intensified when Graham had become a shop steward. Peter had finally got the upper hand by transferring Graham to the woodshed while he had been signed off work with stress.

"Sorry, Josh. Didn't mean to interrupt," said Graham, refusing to acknowledge Peter. "Just wanted to let you know, the cylinder arrived this morning. We'll fit it after our current orders. It'll be done by four."

"Great. Thanks, Graham. Hey, while you're here, why don't you explain to Peter how our new system works?"

Graham glared at Josh. After a long pause he adjusted his safety glasses, removed his gloves and pointed to the wall. "You explained this?" he said. Graham had still not had the decency to look in his direction.

"Not properly," said Josh. "Go on."

"We called this our current state diagram – it's how we used to work." He slid Josh's diary out of the way and knelt up on the desk. "Here are the weekly printouts we used to get from Planning to tell us what to make," he said, tracing his finger along an arrow running down the page. "Our last team leader used to spend a couple of hours batching them up before giving me a bundle of components to do together. I'd then set up the Balfour and cart them over to the machine, which was by the window. Then I set them down for John when I'd finished. Except sometimes he'd have a pile of other stuff to do, so he wouldn't get round to them for ages. For some models, John didn't need to do anything, so he'd go and have a smoke. Eventually everything would end up with Gerry in the store – if he could find a space."

Graham peered closer towards the right-hand side, lifting his safety glasses. "Here. Two months' worth!" he proclaimed, drilling his finger on the page for emphasis. "Two months' worth of components in and around his store, when we estimated it. Some models we hadn't made for years. We found enough Primula parts in the back to relaunch it. And an old two-stroke engine and a pair of wellies."

"OK, that's enough," Peter said. He was fed up with people tearing things down without offering anything constructive. "Just focus on what you're doing differently and how that is supposed to help."

"Well, Planning still sends us the printouts even though we told them we don't need them. We just respond to what our customer – Frame Assembly – needs, when they need it, and everything's pulled through. Gerry gutted his stores and reorganised them so he knows where everything is. He tours Frame Assembly every hour and brings them what they're supposed to need.

Whenever he withdraws a set of parts, he takes off the kanban that's attached to the back rail and hangs it on our production board."

"Can you explain what a kanban is?" Josh asked.

"We made some small wooden shapes. Each one says, 'Produce another set of these.' We just cycle through each of the products on the board, producing one set for each kanban. It takes us two hours to cycle through the lot. Nothing to it, really."

"So if that's true, Gerry should only need two hours of stock?" Peter asked.

"Well, we're not quite there yet," Josh said.

Peter grinned. That was his point: in practice nothing was as simple as people like Josh liked to make out.

"Mainly because we haven't improved Frame Assembly yet. This morning, for example, they wanted a week's worth of Montgomery components in two hours. That kind of variability always introduces waste, but it's nearly always of our own making. Someone probably made a knee-jerk decision this morning to make Montgomeries without considering the consequences."

Josh did not understand the bigger picture: it had been a strategic decision to keep Frame Assembly productive. Neither of them had a clue what it was like as the production manager, having to keep everything in balance.

"But once we've implemented the kind of end-to-end system we've been talking about we'll have smoothed out this unnecessary variability and we can remove the associated waste," Josh said.

Another lecture had started. Peter looked around to drop the hint that he was ready to *see* something.

"Thanks then, Graham," said Josh. "We won't take up any more of your time. See you later." Graham nodded towards Josh and ignored Peter before another spurt of machine noise emphasised his departure.

"He's changed his tune a bit," Peter said.

"He's a good man," Josh said.

He was bound to be hiding some war stories.

"Come on, let's go and look at some U-shaped cells," Josh said, inserting his ear plugs.

Peter leant in towards Josh as they walked to the machines. "So is this really your final layout?" Peter asked.

"Well, nothing's ever final, but yes, it's good for now."

"I guess you've picked up already that it looks a bit of a disaster." *There was no point beating about the bush.*

"How do you mean?"

"The old layout was clear and logical. Now it's a mess."

Josh tilted his head. "We didn't start the design by considering what looked good from an onlooker's perspective. Watch how Graham is working."

Graham was unloading a part from a machine. He turned to a neighbouring machine, unloaded another part and set it in a third machine. It was like a moving jigsaw.

"The machines are in U-shaped cells to minimise the time parts spend waiting for the next process and the time wasted in transporting parts. The U shape has also given us maximum flexibility to define different ways of working."

"What happens when a machine breaks down? You've created no end of problems."

"If a machine breaks down, Peter, that *is* the problem. The new way of operating won't *cause* this problem. But yes, it might expose it, so that we can begin to address it."

"Oh, great. Just what we need, then. Something to highlight our problems."

"Of course it's not *all* we need, Peter. We need to *solve* problems instead of burying them with waste, like excess inventory, equipment or lead times. We need to build a culture that is able to respond urgently with countermeasures and solve root causes where we can. *That's* what will make us stronger."

Peter pulled his jacket around him. "So you admit you've no magic answers to prevent breakdowns?"

"No magic answer, Peter. But TPM is beginning to come through for us."

"Pardon?"

"Total Productive Maintenance. It's an approach to maintenance that engages all stakeholders to maximise equipment performance."

"I know what it is! I was the one who introduced it years ago! I just didn't realise anyone was still doing it."

"We resurrected it just for the Balfour, since it's fully automated and our capacity constraint. We're not just tackling breakdowns, though. OEE showed that changeovers were a much bigger problem."

He pulled them over to the Balfour to get a proper look. It did look incredible, but he knew what to look for. Sure enough, there was an absorbent pad on the floor. He traced the trail of grime with his finger and turned to Josh with a smile. "What was I saying? You can put lipstick on a thirty-year-old machine, but it's still a thirty-year-old machine."

"That's the faulty cylinder Graham mentioned," Josh said. "Because the machine's cleaner we've noticed it long before it fails."

"Spring cleaning is easy. The hardest part is convincing people to keep it that way. It will never last."

"No," Josh said. "The *hardest* part was convincing people to reduce batch sizes. Everyone thought I was crazy."

"Maybe you are."

"Thanks. I would have been if I had tried to do so without reducing changeover times. Come on, you said you're short of time. We've talked a lot about *flow* and you've seen a little about how *process effectiveness* supports it. You've also seen the fruit of developing *people* to sustain it. I need to show you the fourth component of our improvements: how we manage *performance* to realise the benefits."

Josh led Peter back to the big board next to the *box*. There were four hand-drawn graphs at the top of the board. "For quality, we measure complaints we get back from Frame Assembly," Josh explained. "For cost, we measure man-hours versus plan, and for delivery we measure percentage of kanban completed against plan and the number of stock-outs. Anything that prevents us from meeting our targets is recorded in this table below, together with the short-term fix and who is doing what by when to fix the root cause."

It looked OK, but there was nothing new: they already had performance measures coming out of their ears. "Look, Josh," he said, "you're right, I had better be getting back."

"Can I quickly show you the cockpit chart I use for weekly reviews?"

"Some other time, perhaps. Look, I can see you've been busy and it's great that you've reduced headcount. Can you get me the figures to show that you're still meeting your targets – just in case Stephen tries to pull it apart? And can you get me that list of ideas for other areas by lunchtime? I'm meeting Stephen at three."

"No problem."

"Thanks. See you later," Peter said. He found himself shaking Josh's hand. He walked into the yard in a slight daze. There was one certainty he could celebrate: a headcount reduction of two would look great in the spreadsheet next to the term *U-shaped cells*.

9

NOT GOOD ENOUGH

SOUTH Parade ran along the river from Worcester's old limestone bridge. Flanked by brick hop warehouses, it led to a pedestrianised area. The old quay was now a great vantage point from which to throw bread to the scrummaging swans beneath. The railings should have been the only hazard for Stephen to negotiate with his two-year-old daughter, but some bright spark had placed fountains in the paving nearby. He had finally managed to distract her away for a bit of leaf shuffling.

Stephen looked at his bag of bread and smiled. Little in his personal life had turned out as he had planned, but things were not all bad. He had survived the time with his daughter and was still smiling, but he would now be late returning to work. He emptied the bread over the railings and took pleasure in marching away quickly enough to force some of the pigeons to take to their wings. The majestic cathedral towered over the river ahead of him, until it was obscured by the giant wall of red sandstone blocks. He slowed down. The wall was a fascinating patchwork: no two blocks looked the same but they still held together, forming what was probably the greatest wall in the city. There was surely a metaphor here for building success through processes of different shapes and sizes. He cut through the wall at the Watergate, past plaques up the weathered wall that commemorated record water levels since 1670. The haven of the monks' precincts slowed him down another gear: there was no real need to hurry.

Peter was sitting on the sofa, beside a young man in factory blues. "Sorry to keep you waiting, Peter," said Stephen, consulting the calendar on his phone. "It's another one of those back-to-back days."

Peter rose as he walked past.

"Right then, let's talk numbers," Stephen said. To his surprise, they had been joined by the factory worker.

"Do you remember Josh?" Peter said. "I brought him along to explain some of the improvements we've already made in the woodshed."

Stephen slipped his jacket round the back of his chair. "Ah yes – Joshua Eden!" he said, reapproaching the doorway. "How could I forget, given the amount of trouble it caused when we recruited you?" Stephen grinned and shook his head. "But don't worry, my position will never change: I don't care who you are, if you're the best person to run the woodshed."

Stephen turned to Peter. "Well," he continued, "if you need the moral support I don't see why he shouldn't join us – if you can keep things confidential, Josh. We're just blue-skying possible improvements in Production, that's all. We don't want anyone to think the company is in trouble."

The two men stood over his shoulder as he opened up Peter's spreadsheet. He immediately scrolled to the bottom. "Seven per cent?!" he said. "We need a lot more than seven per cent!"

He quickly scrolled upwards. "Why is Upholstery next to nothing? And Pre-up only two? When the woodshed's thirty-eight?"

"That's what I've brought Josh here to explain."

"No, what I mean is that you're implying that the woodshed is in a much bigger mess than the rest of the factory." While Peter searched for an explanation, he looked over his other shoulder. "What do you reckon to that, then, Josh?"

He did not look particularly offended. "When did you last see the woodshed?"

"I go to gemba all the time, Josh. Genchi genbutsu and all that."

"The reason he's asking is because we've started making changes there already," Peter said. "The thirty-eight per cent has already been delivered. Right, Josh?"

"Yes."

Stephen shook his head. His grandfather had instilled in him that managing rank and file was a privilege, which allowed society to benefit from his education. But it was painful to work with people who were innumerate.

"The thirty-eight per cent is against budget," Josh added. "We've delivered thirteen per cent against last year."

"Eh?"

"Our budget included three extra people to deliver the planned increase with Aspiration."

"You budgeted for three people you didn't need?" He swung to face Peter, who took a step back.

"We *would* have needed them if we hadn't made the improvements."

Stephen rubbed his eyes. "Why don't you both pull up a chair?" He gestured to a small round table. "Go on, take a seat. Both of you." Josh and Peter each dragged out a heavy blue chair with a chrome-plated tubular frame.

"Let's leave aside budgeting crimes for now," Stephen said to Josh. "Tell me, what exactly did you do?"

"We redesigned everything."

"People are working *smarter*, not *harder*," Peter chipped in. "For example, machines are closer together, so operators can now work on two machines at once."

"That would be a fifty per cent labour reduction."

Peter looked ruffled. "No, not every operator. But we've done whatever's been possible, right, Josh?"

"We've made a good start."

Stephen was amazed that any good news had come out of Production by itself. He had not been aware of any problems with the union. "If you've already made substantial changes, how did you manage to do this so easily?"

Josh's lips parted and then closed. "No one said it has been *easy*," he said. "We've been working flat out for six months."

People always complained about working hard, but unless they had pulled all-nighters on an MBA they wouldn't know the meaning of hard work.

"It did help that I could promise no one would lose their jobs because of the improvements," Josh said.

"You promised what?" It was getting worse. "Never make any promises regarding headcount."

Josh leant back in his chair.

"For three reasons," Stephen continued, counting them out on his fingers. "First, we're not a charity. Second, we can't afford people to take their foot off the gas. Third, you have no right to make promises anyway."

He had succeeded in silencing him.

"Anyway – it seems you may have got away with it this time. If it wasn't easy, what was the biggest challenge?"

Josh took a long breath. "Coaching people to change bad habits."

"Yes, yes. I understand all that," Stephen said. "I mean, what was your biggest innovation?"

Josh stroked his lips with his forefinger.

"Did you modify any equipment, for example?" As an economist he did not have a typical background for an operations director. So he was always on the lookout for one or two technical nuggets that he could pass on when required.

"Nothing major," Josh said. "*Some* modifications to reduce set-up times, so we could reduce batch sizes."

"Great – give me a concrete example of how you reduced a set-up." He was finally getting somewhere, although he feared it would be nothing new. In the Operations Module of his MBA he had learnt how Toyota had used Set-up Reduction decades ago to reach the efficiency of American carmakers, without the same economies of scale.

"The Balfour used to take thirteen minutes. Now it's down to about fifteen seconds."

Stephen's eyes shot upwards. "Wow. That's – less than two per cent of the baseline. How did you do that?"

"We used an approach called SMED: single minute exchange of dies."

"Go on."

"It's a standard six-step approach," Josh said. "First a couple of operators videoed everything from the normal production rate of the last piece to reaching the normal production rate of the new piece. Second, we differentiated between components that had to be *internal* to the changeover and those that could be done *external* to it. Third, we rearranged tasks so that the external tasks – like preparing tools – were done while the machine was still running." Josh sat more upright in his chair. "Fourth, we worked on honing the remaining internal tasks – like keeping colour-coded inserts at the machine to ensure we don't have to adjust for length. Fifth, we reduced the time of the external tasks – like organising tools on shadow boards next to the machine. Sixth, we agreed on the fifteen-second standard."

"Excellent," Stephen said. "Sounds like progress." It had been a hope too far to avoid getting tangled in the weeds. "So what would it take to get thirty-eight per cent in Upholstery?" he asked, dragging them back to the big picture.

"Upholstery is a different kettle of fish, Stephen," Peter protested. "It's always been in the spotlight, undergoing improvements. And upholsterers are already paid per piece, which keeps productivity high."

Peter was a typical middle manager: stuck in his ways and valuing comfort over ambition. Stephen's role was to push him to achieve more than he thought was possible.

"Come on, Peter," Stephen began, "we only need to achieve an *average* of twenty per cent improvement and you've already demonstrated that thirty-eight per can be achieved." Twenty per cent was the perfect number: low enough to be credible and high enough to stretch people so that if they only delivered half the goal, it would still be worthwhile. "What do you reckon?" he asked, turning to Josh. "Can you get me twenty per cent in Upholstery?"

"You'll only achieve a fraction of the potential by trying to reduce costs by department. If you're asking me, we shouldn't even have a separate Upholstery department."

Wow! I've unearthed a fellow maverick! Peter failed to share his enthusiasm. "Go on."

"I would redesign our operations end to end. Upholstery would be integrated within a value stream for each product family – one for Aspiration, for example."

"We tried value streams," Peter said. "They didn't work."

"We have only ever had them in name," Josh said. "So far they've never been any more than names for product categories. All products can still go through all areas."

"But you think they can help?" Stephen asked.

"They could be instrumental in transforming this company. If you consider each as a narrow slice through the company, I would take one at a time and work deeply with everyone through phases to diagnose, design, implement and refine new ways of working. A narrow and deep approach is the proven path to sustainable transformation."

"How long would you need?"

"Sixteen weeks for each value stream."

"Four months? How many are you talking about?"

"That depends on your vision and capability. Maybe two, maybe three or four."

"A whole *year* for the entire operation? We can't wait that long. Why sixteen weeks? Why not fifteen? Or five?"

"Sixteen is about right. I know the woodshed is only part of a value stream but we used the same time, albeit with a smaller team. We took two weeks to diagnose the opportunity, two to design the new system, ten to implement and coach and two to refine. If it was any longer we'd have lost the pressure created by the expectation to change," Josh claimed. "Any shorter and we could not have designed detailed enough solutions with the right people."

"Did you have a lot of help from Peter?"

Josh looked at his line manager. "He gave me the freedom to get on and do it."

"Just as I thought. Once Peter and I get fully behind this, we can make things happen more quickly than you could imagine."

"You can make changes happen as quickly as you want, but it doesn't necessarily mean you will transform anything," Josh said. "Time is needed to design credible details and to take people with you."

"Four months should be long enough for the whole plant," Stephen declared. "Two months for each building."

"For surgery, maybe. You might stop the bleeding, but you won't cure anything."

"Don't feel bad because we can speed things up. That's our job. Right, Peter?"

Peter squirmed. "We can certainly make things happen," he said. "But I can see Josh's point about taking time. If we want to make big changes to how people are working I would agree that four months is not long at all. But I also don't think we *need* to change a great deal. So maybe we can prioritise a few changes for those four months. I'm a firm believer that if ain't broke, don't fix it."

"Right," said Stephen. "Anyway, time for action. However we decide to implement," he said to Josh, "do you think you could deliver twenty per cent?"

"No," said Josh, "not *however* we decide to implement."

"OK, OK. Forget about how you implement. In theory, how much improvement potential do you think there is?"

Josh looked at Peter who was shaking his head. He remained silent.

"How much potential?"

Josh looked at him for a moment. "That depends on how much you and the rest of the organisation are able to change."

Peter coughed.

Stephen smiled. "I like your style, Josh. But for now, twenty per cent would be fine. So the action for the two of you, then, is to revise this spreadsheet, showing a total of at least twenty per cent."

Peter closed his eyes and hung his head.

"I'd also need some proper examples, Josh, to show that the twenty per cent is achievable. How long would you need to generate enough of a blueprint for the main processes?"

"I wouldn't."

"What?"

"That's the reason for the diagnose and design phases – we need to work with process owners to develop and test solutions if they are to have any hope of being sustained."

Stephen drummed his finger on his lips. Josh was now verging on the obstinate. "Ok – four weeks you said to diagnose and design solutions in one value stream, right?"

"Yes – with a full-time team of five people."

"A full-time team? What planet are you on? The whole point of this programme is to reduce headcount, not increase it."

"If you want to see a transformation, resource it," Josh said. "Transformation rarely happens accidentally."

Factory people were always asking for extra money or extra people. "Everyone is working flat out. If I could have freed anyone else from their current roles, they would already have been laid off. We don't have any fat left in this operation."

"I'm not suggesting you look for idle people. I'm asking you to prioritise what you are asking people to do."

He nearly had a point. "You don't need to talk to *me* about prioritisation, Josh. Look, I'll do what I can and if you're lucky, I'll free you up an operator or two."

"Good, but we need to represent other functions too."

"Not if you're just looking at production ideas, Josh."

Josh kept quiet.

"So what do you think, Peter? I'll give you and Josh and a little team three weeks to diagnose and design changes in all the main processes. Let's call it a feasibility study. Then if the ideas are any good, we can have another conversation with Josh about implementing value streams."

"Three weeks to confirm whether twenty per cent is possible, without implementing anything?" Peter asked.

"Pretty much."

"We can give that a go," Peter said, looking at Josh. "Although I can't guarantee we'll confirm twenty per cent."

"Good," Stephen said. Josh had lost his tongue. "What do you think, Josh?"

"I've told you what I think."

"I don't think you and I are that far off, Josh," said Stephen.

Peter's resistance had withered away as normal.

"Good," Stephen said and retreated to his desk. "OK then, Josh. Can you excuse Peter and me for a while?"

Josh stared at him. Then he pushed himself up from his chair. "I'll see you later, then."

"Yes, thanks Josh. Close the door if you would."

"See you, buddy," said Peter.

When the door had closed, Stephen rocked back in his chair.

"What a character!" he remarked. "Is he always like that?"

"Like what?"

"Arrogant," Stephen said. "And a bit vague."

"Well, he *can* be a bit stubborn," said Peter. "He has some good ideas but I wouldn't trust his judgement on the twenty per cent. He's still young."

"Oh, I like that," Stephen said. "I call it optimism. He hasn't been around long enough to absorb what can't be done." He sustained his look for emphasis, as a pianist would achieve with his damper pedal. "Where did he learn what he's done in the woodshed?"

"Oh, it's fairly standard stuff."

"So why hasn't it been done before?"

Peter's eyes widened. "I haven't had the time to get involved in details like that!"

"Whoa! Calm down, Peter. There's no need to take it personally. Look, has Josh got what it takes?"

"For what?"

"To lead this feasibility study," Stephen said, leaning on the table. "You're right – you and I are far too busy to do it. I need to know if he can lead a team to deliver results in three weeks, or whether he'll just wind everyone up. It needs to be done properly, with strong analysis. We can't afford to waste twelve man-weeks."

"Wouldn't Gregory have some concerns about giving Josh extra responsibility?"

This was something he might not have properly factored in: sometimes he was too objective for his own good. "Peter, no CEO worth his salt would let a bit of politics get in the way of doing the right thing." He trusted that

Gregory would meet this standard. "Anyway, is there anyone else who could have done what Josh did in the woodshed?"

"Not really, no."

"There you are, then. Let's assume that Gregory will back anything that makes sense. So get him started: let him choose two operators to work with – as long as they are ones we can live without."

10

KICKING OFF

WORCESTER was shrouded in fog, which enhanced the mystery that had descended on the factory on this Monday morning. Gregory kept a watchful eye from the front as managers carried out his orders to round people up into the canteen. Many hesitated on walking in: the familiar tables had been replaced by rows of seats facing an impromptu stage.

He looked at his watch: starting promptly at eight o'clock had been wishful thinking. His fingers stretched within the soft, lined pocket of his worsted trousers and he bounced on his toes. Bodies slowly flushed forward. Joshua Eden was already sitting in the very front row, as if to suggest he still held some kind of special authority. It was an untimely reminder of one of the tiresome people issues that made his job much more complicated than it needed to be.

His workforce resembled a patchy blue carpet. After the buyout they had saved on transitional costs by sewing the *Gregory Todd* logo over the *Eden Furniture* shirts. It was now evident how shabby some of the old shirts had become. Now would not be the right time to replace them, even if they could capitalise the expense to keep it outside their EBITDA numbers…

They had only made the decision on Friday to launch the change programme today. It had just turned October, and their sense of urgency would disarm Mountfield by demonstrating bold, decisive action before the 23rd. The main risk was rocking a boat that was already unstable. This was the first time he had addressed the whole company in the cold light of day. It was essential to deliver the right message.

Stragglers were being shepherded from the vending machine. As an English graduate he had always felt comfortable addressing an audience, but he had never done so with such little energy to feed his nerves. He strode out quickly.

"Good mor—" He recoiled from the screeching microphone. Barry, the maintenance team leader, had the guile to grin as he sauntered to the stage.

"Go on Bazza, give us a song!" a voice that sounded like Big Dave's shouted from the back. It released a wave of laughter and a chant of "Bazza! Bazza! Bazza!" Barry's surname was White, and Dave had set him up at one of the Christmas parties they used to hold, with a karaoke performance of 'You're the First, the Last, My Everything' by Barry White. Barry turned to acknowledge the crowd, but it was hard to look cool with such a red face.

Gregory seized the interruption as a gift. "Hello?" he tried again. "That's better. OK, you'll be pleased to know that I'm just the support act. Barry will be on later," he said. The laughter was not emphatic, but it was a healthy recovery.

"So good morning everyone! For anyone who's new here, I'm Gregory Todd. If you *are* new here, for that matter, welcome. Take a look around. Collectively, we are Gregory Todd Ltd. You might be wondering why we have this strange set-up here this morning. The answer is twofold. First, in the interest of improved communication, we wanted to bring you up to date with the business situation. Second, it's an opportunity to launch a programme which needs your help to succeed."

Blue light from the projector was shining in his eyes. He stepped aside and glanced back at the screen. "So here's the agenda. I'll set the context. Then Stephen Peasegood will explain the Operations part before Eddie explains the Sales part of the initiative we are launching today. And we'll end with some time for questions. But if you do have any burning questions as we go please shout them out. OK? Good."

The sewing machinists were easy to spot, midway down the left side. Many were young and glamorous: he had to keep his eyes moving.

"During this time we have gone from strength to strength. A chief measure of success is EBITDA, a form of the profit we make. Another is ROCE, the return we get on the money we have put into this business, which is invested in things like our machines and raw materials. Although we've normalised the graphs, you can see from the trends that despite good work we have recently struggled to maintain the same rate of progress. This results from a number of factors."

The sales team were sitting in a row near the front. He looked at them for long enough to make them uncomfortable without humiliating them.

"Firstly, we are facing stiffer competition than ever before. Some of this is coming from the Far East, where people are paid a fraction of our own wages. Secondly, the market is becoming more demanding. For example, Aspiration, our new online customer, has demanded short response times that have previously been unheard of for our market. Thirdly, the cost of our materials keeps increasing. For all these reasons, to maintain our success we need to become even better than we are today. We need to find better ways of doing more, with less. If we stay still, we'll effectively slide backwards. So we *need* to increase sales and reduce costs. In essence, we need to *break through* to a whole new way of doing business – even better than we've done before. So this is exactly what we are calling the initiative to get us there: *Breakthrough*."

Remembering that his phone now put him in control, he advanced the next slide and turned to see their new *Breakthrough* logo swirl around on the screen.

He waited for some murmurs and sniggers to die out. Had he not made it clear that their situation was now serious?

"The initiative will focus on two parts: Operations and Sales. That doesn't mean that other areas aren't important – like Design of course – but these two are our immediate priorities. We know how easy it is to keep doing the same things the same way. But if we keep on thinking the way we've always thought, we'll never get better than we are today. Some of you will already have things you are itching to improve. Some of you may feel that we haven't listened to you well enough in the past. If that's the case then I want to say sorry, and I promise it will be different this time. This is why I am here this morning, together with the rest of the management team. We need your help. We can only *break through* if we all pull together. And show respect for what we are trying to achieve together."

A hand was already raised. His heart stiffened: it was Barry. In trusting others with recruitment they had ended up with team leaders like Barry – and Joshua – who were more like *ring* leaders.

"Yes, Barry. Do you want to sing already?"

Barry swallowed hard and fidgeted. "It's you lot that's singing!" he shouted. "To the same old tune! If you really wanted to save money, you wouldn't keep cancelling purchase of the new dye machines. I must have replaced six circuit boards in machine twelve over the last six months. Each one must have cost a few hundred quid. It's a false economy."

"Thank you," Gregory said. "And sorry if I offended you with the banter. It's a good question, although things aren't always as straightforward as they might appear. Peter, do you want to answer that? I know you're deeply involved."

Peter stood up and rubbed his forehead. He had not taken in any of the coaching he had been given about his unspoken communication. "We're aware of the situation, Barry. As Gregory said, the economics aren't as simple as you point out, I'm afraid. I'll keep monitoring it. As Gregory said though, it's a good question. Please keep them coming."

Peter had recovered well but the audience was getting restless.

"Thank you, Peter," Gregory said. "I'm keen to crack on to make sure we cover the specifics of how *Breakthrough* will work. So let me invite Stephen up here. For anyone who doesn't know, Stephen Peasegood is our operations director."

Stephen strode towards him and beamed towards the audience. He gave him a final cautionary glare before releasing the microphone. The last thing they needed was a Stephen Peasegood show.

"Thank you," Stephen said. "And now this is the part where Barry takes requests. No – I'm only joking."

The flogging of the dead horse was met with predictable groans. Gregory stood at the side where he could survey the audience. He folded his arms and lifted a clenched fist to his teeth. It could be a long few minutes.

"This really is an exciting time for the company and for Operations in particular," Stephen continued. "I've only been with the company for a year or so – why don't we have a show of hands to see how many of you have also joined in that timeframe?"

A few hands were raised half-heartedly.

"Well, I *know* there are a few more than that, but perhaps it's still a bit early on a Monday morning! Anyway, the first thing to say is that there are two main components to the Operations part of *Breakthrough*: *Planning Breakthrough* and *Production Breakthrough*."

Gregory dropped his fist and looked around: Stephen was back on track. The talk moved on to the Enterprise Resources Planning – ERP – system that they had committed to investigate. Stephen was confident that the right system could finally organise them to achieve Aspiration's lead times. He was wary about expensive overruns, but most of the spend (including the training) could be capitalised, and much of it could even be delayed until the system had already started to slash operating costs.

Stephen moved on to talk about production improvements. On Friday he had boldly suggested that these could contribute as much as £50k towards next quarter's target.

Stephen started repeating Gregory's apology about mistakes from previous change programmes. "But that was all before I joined," he said. "Since then we've been doing a lot of good work, stabilising the operation and controlling materials spend. That's why the stage is now set for a *kaikaku*."

Gregory closed his eyes. What was Stephen playing at? The last thing Production needed was more jargon.

"*Kaikaku* is the Japanese word for a major step change. That's what is needed to refresh a business, where everyone has the chance to think about what they are doing and to find a better way of working. You might have heard of the Japanese word *kaizen*, which means one of many smaller, continuous improvements. After this *kaikaku* I trust that continuous improvement via *kaizens* will be second nature to us."

More murmurs spread through the audience.

"The most important thing is to echo Gregory's promise that this time, things will be different. If you feel you're not being listened to, my door and

Peter's door are always open. We have a policy of absolute openness, which we know is important for success. The future of Gregory Todd depends on us.

"So what exactly are we doing, going forward?" Stephen continued. "Well, as I mentioned, we need to find out exactly how much potential there is in each area, but as a guideline we're aiming for an average of twenty per cent in every area."

Despite inevitable scoffs and gasps, most people still seemed to be listening.

"I know that sounds a lot, but you'll be encouraged to hear we've already shown in the woodshed that *more* than that can be delivered. Josh Eden was involved there, so we've asked him to help with *Breakthrough* in the rest of Production."

Gregory's mouth dropped open. *What was Stephen doing?*

"And given that the majority of you are involved in Production, I've asked him to come up and say a few words about how that part will work."

Gregory stood bolt upright and withdrew his hands from his pockets.

"Thanks, Josh – over to you."

There was a ripple of applause as Joshua took to the stage. There was even a wolf whistle from the back. He stood still on the stage and smiled as if he owned it. "Good morning, everyone," he said.

Gregory cupped palms around his mouth. *Keep it quick; don't promise anything.* Then he would sort this out.

"I'm very pleased to have been asked to lead these changes – many of you know how much this place means to me. We have huge potential and I genuinely believe that with the right support, this business will be transformed. We need to redesign everything we do from receiving an order to delivering it. Let's work together in the right way so that everyone is respected and involved. This way we can transform our culture as much as our processes."

Gregory tried to get Stephen's attention: some might receive this as seeds of revolution.

"We've agreed to spend the first three weeks on a feasibility study, working with many of you to generate initial ideas and to confirm the overall potential. My hope is that we can then embark on a series of transformations, to help you to diagnose and design detailed solutions in your own areas that serve the end-to-end operation. To avoid this sounding abstract, let me give you a flavour of what our transformed business might look like. You can expect to see changes in four areas. First, in *flow*: how all people in all processes have been connected as one to serve our customers. Second, in *process excellence*: capacity might well be doubled *and* quality guaranteed by improving the effectiveness and efficiency of existing processes. Third, in *performance management*: everyone will be clear on their part to play, and they will feel supported in surfacing and solving problems in order to succeed. Fourth, in *people*: we will all be thriving, because we feel valued, we're having fun and we're fulfilling more of our potential."

Joshua looked around and smiled broadly. "Who wouldn't want to be part of a workplace like that?"

Gregory started moving along the wall towards the front: Joshua's platform had to be removed as soon as possible. It was clever and subtle subterfuge: in planting grand illusions he could reap enough disillusionment to rock the boat, in conditions that were already stormy.

"We have a mountain to climb," Josh continued, "but we need to keep together and challenge ourselves to keep our minds open. To model the importance of working across existing boundaries I'm going to be working with three people from different areas. Nigel Travis from Pre-upholstery, Sue Johnson from Sewing and Chris Thomas, who has recently joined the Sales team. Please can the three of you stand up?"

Chris the fresh-faced sales recruit stood up and saluted the crowd. Nigel slowly dragged his spindly frame to its feet. The veteran operator with a mane of grey hair and thick-rimmed spectacles bowed slightly before sitting down again. After a small commotion a petite young lady with blonde ringlets was made to stand by those seated around her.

"Thank you," Josh said. "And thanks too to Graham Cairns who has taken over from me as team leader in the woodshed."

Gregory was on the brink of retaking control himself when Stephen finally got the hint. Joshua caught sight of Stephen tapping his watch.

"Finally, to practise what we preach, we don't want to make any presumptions about your current challenges. Therefore, before we do anything, we would like to spend two days working alongside you in every area. Please consider this as your first opportunity to share your concerns and ideas. Please be honest with us and keep an open mind: the sign of this will always be your willingness to participate and to consider anything that has a rational basis."

Stephen now stood up and reached for the microphone.

"Thank you, Josh. So that gives you an idea of how we *might* run *Production Breakthrough*," he said. His glance to Gregory seemed to confirm that Joshua had veered a little off-piste.

"That's all we really need to say at the moment about the Operations part of *Breakthrough*. Obviously there's much more we could say, but we also need to find out what Sales will be doing to pull their weight." He looked at Eddie and smiled. "So Eddie, over to you. And while you come up, let me reiterate how excited I am about this opportunity and to say thank you in advance for all your hard work."

As soon as Eddie took the microphone, Gregory beckoned Stephen over. He led him out quietly through the double doors at the front of the canteen. "What were you thinking?" he demanded.

"What do you mean?" Stephen replied.

"I had no idea that Joshua was involved."

"You've got a lot going on, Gregory. I couldn't involve you in every detail."

"Don't you know who he is?"

"Of course. But why is that relevant?"

He opened up his palms. "Can't you see?"

"What?"

"He's trying to stir things up."

"How?"

"By creating unrealistic expectations," he spelled out more slowly. "That will only lead to disappointment and unrest."

"There's nothing wrong with a strong vision."

It was not entirely clear whether Stephen was trying to wind him up. "You honestly think he's reliable?"

"From what I've seen and heard, yes. One hundred per cent reliable – just not always predictable. But that's not a bad thing. He's already delivered more than I would have predicted in the woodshed."

"The woodshed – exactly! When did anything good come out of there?" He tried to smile. "Did you sanction him wasting two whole days just chatting to people on the shop floor?"

"No, that was a bit of a surprise."

"Exactly – that's what I'm worried about. You'll have to put a stop to it."

"Look, Gregory, if I didn't think he was the right man for the job I wouldn't have asked him. I guess I just assumed that you would trust your operations director to find the right people to improve operations."

"Don't make it personal, Stephen. You just need to understand the politics here, that's all."

"And I wasn't born yesterday. I get your concern, but I honestly think he's the best person for the job. And we can't pull the plug on his involvement now."

"And whose fault is that?"

"Look, if it's the unpredictability you're concerned about, I'll stay on top of it. If he speaks again, we can get him to use slides that we can check in advance."

Gregory weighed up his options. "Don't let him promise anything without my approval. I'll have to have a chat with him too."

"Relax, Gregory. It's not as bad as you fear. But yes, I'll keep you informed of everything if you'd like."

"Good. I'm not overreacting, Stephen. We're entering the most critical of times. I can't afford to have anyone rocking the boat – no matter who it is."

He put a hand on Stephen's shoulder to direct him back towards the double doors. "Other than that, I think it's going OK. What do you reckon?"

11

ACTION STATIONS

Sue had been so shocked when Josh had first approached her that she could not remember saying yes. She had never been first pick for anything. Now she was being led into the alien next-door territory of Pre-upholstery. The concentration of men had never bothered her – she had grown up surrounded by brothers. Her only fear was how much people would expect her to know. Sewing was the only thing she had ever been good at.

The pre-upholsterer they were approaching had already pretended not to notice her twice. Even so, he seemed to have a kind face – he was not one of the lairy ones.

"Oi, Clarky," said the team leader who had been chaperoning her. "Do you know Sue?"

Clarky turned his head sideways. "Um, hi," he said, straightening up. "Hello."

"Sue's part of the *Breakdown* initiative you heard about earlier morning."

"Excellent!" Clarky said, smiling. "Big Dave called it another BOHICA." "What?"

"*Bend Over, Here It Comes Again.*"

The team leader laughed but Clarky stopped when he caught Sue's eye. "Sorry," he said. "No reflection on you. You know how it is though, when you've heard it all before."

"Remember *RIGHT FRIST TIME*?" Clarky's team leader continued. Sue's stony face was misinterpreted as a request for enlightenment. "For some reason management decided to hang these massive golden letters on the wall that spelt *RIGHT FIRST TIME*. Only Big Dave swapped two of the letters so that it read RIGHT FRIST TIME. It was well over a week before anyone noticed! Classic!"

Clarky's weak smile refocused his team leader.

"Anyway," he said, "Sue needs to spend some time with us this morning learning the ropes in Pre-up. Sue, Clarky is probably the best you can get."

Barry suddenly popped up behind Clarky's shoulder. He delivered a foul innuendo and disappeared.

"Sorry about that," Clarky said. "He's always like that but never around when you want something fixed."

"Don't worry, I know what he's like. We see a lot of him in Sewing, but rarely paying much attention to the machines."

"I'll leave you to it, then," said the team leader. "Clarky, I'll put you on day-rate for the rest of the morning. How long are you with us Sue?"

"Just 'til lunch – then I have to go to Upholstery."

Nigel was spending his first period after lunch in Frame Assembly. Milky had given him inevitable stick before leaving him with his old friend Richard. The two of them made an odd pair: Richard plump and ponderous; Nigel scraggy and tense. Both were in the same boat: neither was prepared to compromise on quality, yet both were still here, mainly because it was difficult to transfer their skills anywhere else in the area. Even if their skills were no longer appreciated here, at least they were still making a difference. Occasionally Richard had flirted with contract joinery. It had promised to double his wages, but at his stage of life he placed greater value on stability.

"Cheers," Richard said, as Nigel passed him two lengths of wood. "So how come you're doing this thing with Josh, then?"

Nigel patted down his wild mane. "Don't know, really. He just asked me."

Richard placed the first of the left arms in position and then looked up.

"Why *do* you always build in–" Nigel's friend waited patiently for him to overcome his stammer "– batches of three?" he asked. Josh had told them to question everything, and the thought had just occurred to him.

Richard straightened his back. "More efficient, I guess. I don't know – we've always done it that way."

Nigel smiled. That was one of the clues Josh had told them to expect.

"So you just said yes?" Richard said, after laying out the last of the left arms.

"Eh?"

"You just said yes? To Josh?"

"Pretty much." Nigel stuck out his bottom lip and nodded. It did sound strange – he had always been happier in the background. He could always see what people were doing wrong but had learnt to bottle it: he had always been hampered by his inability to get his words out.

"He was in here the other day. He thanked me," Richard said.

"Yeah?"

"Simple, isn't it? Shouldn't have made a difference, but it did. I can't remember the last time anyone said thank you and meant it." Richard stared straight ahead for a few moments, screwing up his face. "Yes I can," he said, looking back at Nigel. "It was probably his old man."

"Who – Arthur?"

Richard smiled.

"Oh, so that's finally official is it?" queried Nigel.

"Of course. Weren't you here years ago, when he came in for work experience? As a teenager?"

Something vaguely resonated with him, but Nigel struggled to picture the teenage Josh.

"He spent a week in Frame Assembly. They said to treat him like an apprentice. So we did, with all the usual tricks. Some he saw coming, but if we caught him out he just laughed. Other apprentices were always on edge, trying to prove themselves – but Josh was unshakeable. Even then."

"So why do you think he came to work here, then?"

"Don't ask me. I can't understand *anyone* coming here if they had a choice. You're the one working with him."

"Maybe he feels he can turn this place around."

"As a team leader? You've got to be joking."

"Why not? He speaks his mind. And he knows his stuff."

"Exactly. You wait till he starts talking about the problems."

Surely some of Richard's gloom was misplaced – otherwise Nigel would have to return to Pre-upholstery. If it *was* to be short-lived, at least he would have more chance of reclaiming his sought-after position by the window.

"Have a look at that, behind you," Richard said. "That was one of their latest ideas."

Richard was exceptionally tidy. The only item on his cabinet was a sawn-off washing-up liquid bottle.

"Remember our old adhesive? Six months ago they got rid of it in favour of this stuff, because it's supposedly cheaper per kilo. It dries so quickly we can't use our guns. So we've gone back to the ark and are using brushes. Even then the tubs keep drying out so we have to chuck away half of it every half hour. But they still call it progress."

He held the toxic tub at arm's length.

"Get a load of this." Richard pulled out the bottom drawer of his cabinet. It was full of yogurt pots and washing-up liquid bottles. "The whole family is collecting them – it's ridiculous."

"Do they know about the problem?"

"Of course they do. Hell broke loose when they brought it in."

"So what did they say?"

"They made it clear the decision had been made. This is the only glue now sanctioned to make frames."

"What about Milky?"

"He's given up. He says Peter's *looking into it* but we hardly ever see him. Apparently he took it to Michelle in Purchasing but there's nothing she can do either. The place we used to buy the old glue is no longer an *approved supplier.*"

"That's crazy! *Something's* got to be done!" Nigel was becoming jittery. "They told us this morning to challenge anything that doesn't make sense."

Richard glanced at him once, then again. "You're not serious?"

Chris had been working for Gregory Todd for two long months. This was supposed to be his first proper job, nearly a year after graduating in international business. The starting salary was not great, but he was able to save money by living with his grandparents in the Worcester suburb of St Peters. He had got on well in the interview with Eddie McGivern the sales director, who had promised him an *integral role in marketing a new brand*. The problem was that since he had joined, Eddie had spent hardly any time with him at all. There was no sign of the new brand. His biggest contribution had been helping clueless sales people with their spreadsheets. Then late last week Eddie had personally commended him for a temporary assignment with the *Production Breakthrough* team. It was hardly glamorous but it offered a welcome respite from reading trade magazines.

Today was the first day he had set foot in the underworld of Building Two, which housed Sewing, Cutting and Pre-upholstery. From the outside it was a red-brick building, finished in yellow and black bricks just like Building One. Salaried staff and visitors always came and went through the reception in Building One, straight into its swanky offices, boardroom and design studio. Behind them the hand-built upholstery area looked fairly primitive but bright and relatively straightforward. Any entrance at the front of Building Two had been bricked up long ago: workers seemed to disappear in and out of crevices round the back. The official access to Building Two was through a sheltered trucking corridor from Upholstery. Although only a few metres away from the main building, it seemed closer to a science fiction film set. Operators glided on platforms up and down each of four long cutting tables that dominated the building. Each time they went, another layer of cloth was unfurled. When the table was laid a mechanical beast at its head pulled in and digested its fabric meal. A servant frantically tried to keep up, collecting and sorting scraps of cut cloth from the beast's rear end.

Chris longed to ride on one of the platforms but instead he had been assigned that morning to the compact sewing area at the front – effectively the far end – of Building Two, next to their *Production Breakthrough* team room. The machines were relatively tame and uninteresting, but the female machinists were anything but. He would have been happy enough to have been paired with someone like Sue. The trouble was that the team leader had somehow overlooked all the babes and put him with a woman as old as his gran.

"Now *that's* a posh tie. What do you reckon, Maureen?"

"Ooh, very suave. Let me see, is it real or is it on elastic?"

"Get off!"

"I'll gladly slip it off if you like."

He knew his face and neck were overheating. "You're supposed to be showing me the process."

"Well, take the hot seat then." Maureen drew her heavy frame to her feet and ushered him into her chair.

Her bejewelled hand passed him a cover. "Here you are, Bab. This one is scrap, *just in case* you mess up. Now mind the pedal. It controls the needle: you control the fabric. We need a stitch all the way up here. Let me start you off."

Maureen flicked a few switches. He squirmed as she extended her leg to his left and reached over his shoulder. He leant as far away as he could. Jewellery jangled in his ear but he still tried to keep an eye on the needle. After a smooth whirr she lifted the fabric and showed him a seam. "That's all there is to it. Now your turn then, Bab."

Within seconds he had produced a similar whirr, but the needle was buried in clumps of fabric and thread.

Stephen was buried deep in a nested *IF* function within his spreadsheet. He had finally resorted to counting the brackets on the screen when a knock at the door interrupted him. He cursed under his breath and was surprised to see two older operators in his doorway. They looked more like comedy partners than hard-working, direct labour. One was heavyset like Oliver Hardy, the other thin with a mane of wild hair like Stan Laurel.

"Yes?"

Laurel stepped forward and adjusted his glasses. His ears were crimson. "I'm Nigel. With," he took a deep breath, "Josh. You said in the canteen to tell you if things don't make sense."

"Yes. Absolutely." He now felt bad that one of them had a stammer.

"I've been with Richard on the shop floor. In Frame Assembly. He's told me—"

"You're still on the shop floor? Didn't you get the message?"

"What message?"

He shook his head. "Gregory's knocked it on the head. We can't afford to waste the time."

Laurel and Hardy looked at each other.

"Please tell Josh, you should all focus straight away on getting ideas down on paper. Sorry – the message should have got through."

The double act turned towards the door.

"Was there anything else?" he asked.

Laurel pointed to a container that Hardy was holding. He seemed just about to whimper and scratch the top of his head!

"This glue is supposed to be cheaper. But it's rubbish. They prefer what they had."

Stephen swung round on his chair and checked another spreadsheet. "Well, whether we like it or not," he said, spinning back on his chair, "it's saving us £10k a year."

"Bulls**t!" Hardy had found his tongue. "We use at least double 'cos it keeps drying. We keep throwing it out. And it slows us down."

"Is that a washing-up liquid bottle?" Stephen asked.

"That's part of the problem – it dries and blocks up the nozzles."

The operator was getting worked up but clearly no one had challenged him to solve the right problem. They always channelled energy into arguing against improvements instead of thinking creatively how they could *make them work.* "Have you looked at alternative guns?" he said, to give them a helping hand.

Hardy looked shocked – but had clearly taken over from his friend. "Why? It's the glue that's the problem."

"Not if there's a suitable gun. Have you checked?"

"There's nothing wrong with the guns!"

"You should raise this with your team leader. That's Vijay, isn't it?"

"Yes – Milky," said Hardy. "It's not his fault. He's had a go at Peter and Peter's mentioned it to Purchasing but no one's doing anything about it. That's why we've come to see you."

"Absolutely. But we need to make sure we're solving the right problem. We shouldn't avoid saving costs just because no one wants to change. Remember, if you think the way you've always thought, you'll get what you've always got."

"What if we *want* what we used to have?!"

"Then there'll be no progress."

"You call this progress?" Hardy said. "We can barely make anything with this stuff!"

Finally. If you kept on pressing the right buttons you always got to the real issue. And it was nearly always about pay. Yet if pay was really that bad they would have already taken their labour elsewhere.

"Look, let's be rational about this," Stephen said. "If the total cost per unit really is greater than the last one, then absolutely we should investigate further. If you've looked at the market and there are no guns that can apply this particular less-expensive glue, then we need to search for other less-expensive glues that *can* be properly applied. Only in the last resort, when we have the full fact base, could we authorise a step backwards."

Hardy turned and walked off surprisingly quickly. Laurel remained.

Stephen shrugged his shoulders. He could not have been more reasonable.

"So who's going to do all that?" Laurel asked.

"Your team leader. Once you've got the data, Peter can also help make the case and I'm always here for extra support. So, thanks again for letting me know," he said, rising to his feet. "As I said, you are absolutely right to challenge anything that doesn't *appear* to make sense. Keep on questioning and good ideas will follow."

"So that's that?" Laurel said.

"That's the way forward, yes."

"Right then. Thanks for your time," he murmured. Then he left.

"Thanks. Have a good afternoon," he said. He got up to close the door. Then he returned to his spreadsheet.

12

TREASURE HUNT

Production Breakthrough had only just got out of the blocks and they were already limping. Josh had never expected transformation to be straightforward but he *had* hoped that the launch of *Breakthrough* might result in some early momentum. Instead, Peter had refused his request to use the training room next to his office as a base. It could have sent a powerful message: that *Breakthrough* was at the heart of the business, and they would have been equally accessible to both managers and operators. Peter wanted to reserve the room for *proper* training, even though this would be integral to everything they would be doing. It was hard not to read between the lines, but Peter had restated his case after meeting with Stephen. His *Production Breakthrough* team was now tucked away in the old apprentices' room, located behind Sewing in Building Two.

While his team were in the throes of building trust on the shop floor on the first afternoon, the plug had been pulled. Neither Peter nor Stephen had the decency to discuss this with him: they had communicated through Nigel that it was deemed a *waste of resources*.

Management support would be critical to achieving and sustaining any benefits. Unless this could be evidenced through managers removing obstacles or following up new methods on the shop floor once they had been implemented, the support of managers would prove to be no more than lip service. With these early warning signs, Josh had already been fending off doubts as to why he was even bothering. The woodshed had been hard enough. What bothered him as much was the prospect that he was being personally misunderstood. He could *see* the factory coming to life and how to get there. He could see it delivering more than the managers could dream of – if only he could open their eyes to see it too.

He had used the rest of Monday to bring forward the training on how to map the flow of material and information through the operation. This morning they would return to the shop floor to start the mapping, as soon as Chris arrived. The Material and Information Flow Analysis (or MIFA) was the full version of what he had sketched out for Peter in his office. It would reveal opportunities across the organisation but, perhaps more importantly, it would also model engaging it as a whole.

Through the grimy glass in the team room's door, he could see Chris approaching.

"Sorry I'm late," Chris mumbled as he shut out the whirr of the sewing machines. Avoiding eye contact, he lumbered across the suspended flooring towards the coffee maker that Sue had brought in from home.

"Good afternoon, Chris," Nigel teased.

"Is it?" Chris quipped back. He filled a plastic cup with coffee.

"Please be on time, Chris," Josh said. "It's essential we model the behaviour we want to see in others." He chose to ignore Chris' scowl. "Nigel, why don't you quickly share with Chris what you were just talking about?"

"What, about Dangermouth?"

"No – about team leaders," Josh said. "And let's respect people please, by using the names they would choose."

"Oh. Just that I'd hate to be a team leader. All you get are problems. Most of them you can't solve but you still get all the flak."

"So what were you suggesting?" Josh prompted.

"I don't know really. Just that there's got to be a better way. It would be good for everyone to know who is meant to solve which problem. Like the new adhesive. Is that what you meant?"

"Yes, that will do for now. Thanks, Nigel. We will develop this further when we start covering performance management. In essence that's all about supporting and equipping the right people to solve the right problems. But today we're continuing with flow, by doing the current state mapping we prepared for yesterday. Some call it Material and Information Flow Analysis (MIFA). The end goal is like the diagram you saw in the woodshed, but it will cover the entire customer order fulfilment process. This means everything we do from receiving an order to delivering it to the customer."

Nigel filled his cheeks and slowly exhaled. "How long have we got?"

Sue was partially hiding behind her wavy locks.

"Let me recap. The customers are top right, the suppliers are top left. The material flow is from left to right along the middle of the diagram. The information flow is typically from the customers through to production and back to the suppliers. We use standard symbols to ensure we capture the right level of detail. Each process is represented by one box, with data below it. Sue, can you remember how we define a process, to capture the right level of detail?"

There was no answer.

"Are you OK?"

Sue swept her hair away and sat up. "I've never done anything like this before."

"Most people haven't. It's like tracking a relay race, following how the baton is passed on from whoever takes the instruction from the customer to whoever cuts the first piece of wood and so on. At each stage we need to understand *how* someone knows what to do, *when* they start and *what* they do with any instruction or material they receive. It's better to be curious than knowledgeable. The best mappers are those who can listen and empathise. I think you'll excel at both."

"Won't it save time if we write down what we already know?" Chris asked. "I already know the orders are entered straight into the Manworks database, for a start."

"Good, but that's not specific enough. The point of walking the flow is to make sure we *see* what goes on for ourselves. You'll find all kinds of things going on, such as data being scribbled in notebooks and informal spreadsheets. The golden rule is to always ask, *Please can you show me?* And ask if you can take photos of what you see to document the current process."

"What if people feel we're checking up on them?" Sue asked. "And getting them into trouble."

"We need to reassure them. If people are doing something different it's often because there's a problem with official assumptions. We need to commend them for their initiative – but we also need to surface the problems. At every stage make sure you can answer the question, *If I were in that role, how would I know what to do next and when?*"

He had everyone's attention. "Good. So, who can remember how we define a process?"

"I do remember that bit," Sue said. "Wherever material can stagnate either side."

"Excellent. And every location of material should be marked separately. If it's uncontrolled, mark it with a bell curve and the estimated quantity above it. Inventory can only be considered controlled if its location, quantity *and* method of replenishment are all controlled – but we'll talk more about that when we go on to design the future state.

"Right – here's a list of information we should gather for each process. This will help us to get a feel for quality, cost and delivery, where problems occur and much of the information we will need to design the future. Try and get a feel for the range and variation of process cycle times, but let's also use the R-05-02 as a typical product and common reference."

"The what?" Chris asked.

"Jasmine two-seater. R-05 is the Jasmine range, 02 means two-seater." Nigel explained.

Josh smiled and nodded. "Any other questions?"

"OK – we've got until the end of tomorrow. I'll lead for the rest of the morning. Then I'll come and go, while each of you takes a turn in leading. Tomorrow morning I'll have to leave you too as Gregory has asked to see me."

"Oooh – what have you done now?" Nigel asked.

He struggled to smile. Jane's email had come out of the blue, with no explanation. He had not spoken to Gregory for years. For twenty-four hours his mind had been a battle scene, filtering what he *should* say to Gregory from everything he *could* say. In the meantime there was other work to do.

He stood up and loosened his shoulders. "Come on," he said. This attempt at smiling was more successful. "Let's get going."

Sue opened the door and hunched her shoulders. "Nice day," she said iron-ically. They could have had better weather for their second morning of mapping the current state.

"Beautiful," Nigel replied.

It was hardly rain; just dreary drizzle with no end in sight. The dye machines used to occupy a separate section in Building Two, which would have been much more convenient on a day like today. The dyeing process now took place in a building that used to belong to the exhaust centre next door.

Sue raised the clipboard she had been given above her head before trot-ting across the car park. She had never worn heels to work but that morning she wanted to feel a little taller. Chris and Nigel strode beside her. They ap-peared to be getting on a bit better than yesterday, when Chris had showed Nigel scant respect for how much he knew about the processes. He seemed to have no idea how stupid some of his questions were. At one stage even she was embarrassed when he had to be told that MDF stood for medium density fibreboard. Still, Josh must have seen something in Chris worth choosing – it was probably just with her that he had made a mistake.

Josh had asked her to lead the mapping through the new dye shop yester-day afternoon. Thankfully the dye shop had postponed and now that Josh was with Gregory, Nigel had agreed to take over. He was concerned about his stammer, but at least he knew what he was talking about. The thought of leading anything made her clammy, let alone the prospect of going up against Trish, the notorious dye shop operator.

"So why did they put the dye shop out here anyway?" Chris said.

"Progress," Nigel said. "That's their word for a change they want. If *you* want something, it's called aggravation."

She could never do what Josh had done yesterday. He had persistently and kindly drilled deeper to unearth all kinds of challenges, problems and complications. Surely these weren't ordinary skills, even for a team leader.

Her head had been too saturated to take in much beyond Cutting. The small consolation was that the rest of the factory had seemed a bit less unfriendly as she had walked through it that morning. That would never be the case in the dye shop where Trish ruled the roost. Trish embodied everything about the estate in Worcester that was much tougher than her own.

They reached the small opening in the dye shop's roller door. Nigel refused her invitation to step through first. Thankfully Chris had no such qualms.

The humid air was thick and sweet. Juddering machine noise joined the assault on their senses. They lined up on the inside of the door, pinned back by a herd of plastic trolleys. Each was laden with sewn covers. The far door swung open as a balding man backed through it. "HAS NUMBER THREE FINISHED YET?" he shouted. It was Trevor, the dye-shop team leader. Matted strands hung from his sweaty scalp, and he had battled his way past several trolleys before he noticed his guests. He slowly straightened his spine and lifted heavy eyes to the clock above them. "Sorry guys. It's even worse today. Neither of the machines is back up and Trish is off sick. I haven't even had a coffee yet. Can we do it later this week?"

Chris was holding his phone up in an effort to photograph the chaos. Nigel was squeezing between trolleys and inspecting the printed work orders within them. Given their inattentiveness, Trevor was looking to *her* for a response. Compared to Trish he was a teddy bear: if they accomplished nothing today they might face Trish tomorrow. *What would Josh have said?*

"Why don't we give you a hand to get things straightened out," she suggested. "Then maybe we could chat over a coffee."

Trevor winced but Nigel had already started, separating the bins with dyed covers from those that had yet to be dyed. Once he had found the units for machine seven, Trevor seemed to soften. "So you guys are coming up with some clever new ideas, are you?" he said with a smirk.

"I don't know about that," said Sue.

"Well, as you could probably tell, we could do with some help."

"We've just come here to do the mapping for the time being."

"Well, while these guys are busy, why don't we have a chat in my office?"

Trevor seemed open and was taking her seriously. "The only thing, though, is that Josh insisted we walk every process on the shop floor."

"No need," he said. "I can tell you anything you need to know in the office. Everything's on the computer."

It was a fair point, one that Josh may not have appreciated. She signalled to Nigel that she was going with Trevor. Chris intercepted the signal and scampered over to join her.

"You want to tag along, do you?" Trevor said. He used his sleeve to wipe his brow as he led them to his air-conditioned office.

"When everyone's here and the machines are running we can cope with whatever is thrown at us. But if you have any suggestions we'll gladly consider them."

Sue smiled. It was a kind way of suggesting he did not expect too much from them.

"You could organise the trolleys a lot better," Chris said.

She glared at Chris as Trevor stopped. "This morning is not typical," Trevor said. "We're short staffed and they didn't pick up our second delivery. The underlying problems are our machines. They're on their last legs, but the new machines have been cancelled yet again."

"Why?" Sue asked.

Trevor grinned and rubbed his thumb and fingers together. "At the end of the day, this business is Gregory's money-making machine. For every spare pound he finds, do you think he's putting it into production or into his pocket?"

"Do you really think he's like that?" Sue asked.

"Of course. All his senior managers are in it together. They're as thick as thieves, that lot – literally! Ask Peter: he's a great manager but he's stuck between a rock and a hard place."

Sue's short-lived optimism had been engulfed in low cloud. The company was already fixated with penny pinching and reducing headcount. Josh had tried to convince her there was hope: that they could still genuinely help people to find better ways of working. But how was that possible if people's main needs required more money and more people?

13

POINT BLANK

"COME in," said Gregory, in response to the knock at the door. It was more of a reflex than an invitation. He placed his finger on the current row of numbers and raised his head. A young man in factory blues stood before him.

"Joshua!" Gregory straightened his back.

"Jane said you wanted to see me?"

"Yes." This felt a bit awkward. He glanced at his screen. "Sorry – I didn't realise she had managed to book you in. I suppose you had better come in anyway. Do you want some coffee?" Gregory asked. He was in need of another one himself.

"Thanks – if you're having one."

He phoned through the drinks order. Arthur's son lingered in front of the glass doors, looking at the view beyond.

"Beautiful, isn't it?" he said.

Joshua smiled. "One of the best views of Worcester."

It wasn't bad. Stone spires and towers shared the skyline with concrete blocks. Brick chimneys silently rued the metal flues that had sprung up around them. The entire settlement served as a living storybook, much to the bemusement of the grand Malvern Hills in the background, which were still coming to terms with their relatively new urban neighbour.

"Please, take a seat." He guided Joshua to the A-1-11 armchairs beside the other window. Joshua had the decency to check his trousers for grease before sitting on the leather. Gregory lifted his own trouser legs to prevent them from creasing, before sitting in the opposite chair.

"Well, I should start by telling you how much of a surprise it was to discover you were running part of the change programme." His smile was strong. "Just like it was when I first discovered that you had somehow managed to join the company under my radar."

Joshua leant back in his chair. His deference may have waned, but it was not exactly disrespectful.

"So I thought it was time to clear the air," Gregory continued. "Whatever is motivating you, Joshua, I trust we can leave any personal differences aside. I'm trusting you to get on with your job the same as anyone else."

Joshua nodded. "Thank you."

"So you have my full support."

"Really?"

"Of course."

"Does that mean you're willing to change?" Joshua asked.

His arrogance was staggering. "You're expecting *me* to change?" He was prepared to accept criticism – from anyone who was entitled to give it.

"Would you say you have shaped this business yet as your own?"

It was clear whose influence Joshua was trying to herald.

"Of course I have, Joshua. Your father was trusting me to make major decisions as general manager way before I even became managing director. I've pretty much shaped this business into what it is today."

"So if the business still needs to change, isn't it likely that your thinking needs to change first?"

"Oh, very clever. Has someone put you up to this?"

"You need to model openness to change. Otherwise, if you view *change* as a programme to be managed, are you effectively assuming that change is required from everyone *except* you?"

He leant forward and spoke straight at Joshua. "This is my business *to* change, Joshua. I can understand it if you find it hard. Most people *do* find change hard, in itself."

Joshua had the audacity to smile. "Change isn't some homogenous commodity, Gregory. Changes can be good or bad. Some of those who are resisting change most strongly are only doing so because they care. They're the ones you need to be listening to."

"Of course changes can be good or bad! But the numbers don't lie, Joshua. They'll tell you I'm running a tighter ship now than ever."

"Too tight a grip can suffocate."

He had overstepped the mark. "Look, if you've got something to say, speak plainly. Otherwise I haven't got the time to listen to this."

"You're pressurising people to report what you want to hear, Gregory. Problems are suppressed, mistakes are hidden and risks are discouraged. We're stagnating. Encourage healthy disagreement! Listen to us and get the most out of us."

"No one who knows me would ever accuse me of not getting the best out of people."

"Maybe that's the point. What if you've surrounded yourself with individuals *because* they don't disagree with you? And what if they're as blind to the potential as you are?"

"You're way out of line, Joshua. Of course I'm open to change. Who do you think initiated the whole ruddy programme of change that you're involved in?"

"I've been tasked to reduce production costs."

"So do you want the job or not?"

"If you really want to transform this place, arrest its decay. With one bold, calculated risk you can set off a chain reaction of bold, calculated risks to transform this company forever."

"Joshua, let me make myself clear. I didn't invite you here to lecture me. Especially on taking risks."

"Then take the risk of overhauling the organisation properly. Redesign it to meet its challenges. Change contracts to get people working together. Dismantle the individualism fuelled by overtime and piecework. Get rid of those who are unwilling to help us succeed as one team."

"Maybe I should start with you."

Joshua did not baulk. Gregory's eyes fell first, wandering to his logo on Joshua's shirt which concealed the Eden one beneath.

"Don't assume you know anything about me, Joshua. I took a bold risk to take control of this company and I did it with a clear vision for improving sales – and operations."

"A *top-to-bottom* vision won't be enough. We also need an *end-to-end* vision."

He had been about to pull the plug on the conversation but something about this grabbed him. He quickly evaluated the costs versus the benefits of letting him continue. He folded his arms. "You think we're not managing end to end?" he said with a smirk.

"You want the truth?"

"*Your version* of it: go on then."

"Many organisations never properly commit to improvement. But for those that do, improving an operation can be compared to packing for a journey," said Joshua, holding a large, imaginary suitcase in his hands. "There are two opposite ways to improve results. The top-down approach is to squeeze the case. Managers jump up and down on it until everything fits within their targets. The workforce is kept in the dark and ends up bruised and battered. Management becomes exhausted and despised.

"The second approach requires courage: it involves more risk and more reward. Open the suitcase and involve everyone in taking out what is not needed. Work out together how best to pack what we really need. It is hard work, but it will also energise people. With the smaller, agile case you'll wonder why you ever put up with hauling the original one around for so long."

"Very nice," he said. "Did your dad come up with that little analogy?"

"Pretty much – it just developed from a chat we were having."

It was no surprise that he had been discussing their situation with his dad. "Look, Joshua," he said, leaning forward, "I still have the utmost respect for your father. But I need to know that your loyalties are correctly aligned within what is now my organisation. What I need from you right now – as one of our team leaders – are practical ideas instead of philosophies. Without rocking the boat, if you know—"

Knuckles tapped on the door and it opened immediately.

"—if you know what I mean."

Jane recoiled. "Sorry, I didn't mean to disturb you."

"No, no, please come in. We were just having a chat. Thanks, Jane." He removed a glossy trade magazine from the table. The chinaware chatted awkwardly as Jane transferred it. The two men were soon alone again. The mood had mellowed slightly as Jane's perfume lingered.

"Sugar?" he asked.

"No thanks."

He poured the coffee in silence. "How is your father, then?"

"He's well," said Joshua. "The same as ever."

He looked up and reciprocated Joshua's smile. "He's still living up Rainbow Hill?"

"Yes."

He had lived in the same house for ages. It might have been one of the city's pre-eminent homes in Georgian times, but it was now surrounded by one of the more run-down parts of the city. Situated on the next in the series of hills that skirted the city, it had a good view of Worcester's historic centre. The building was no doubt still immaculate, but today it might be worth no more than Raleigh Court.

"He still has the same phone number too."

Gregory looked up and this time could afford to reciprocate Joshua's smile. Arthur might well have mellowed a little by now, too.

They both drank some coffee before Joshua leant forward.

"Gregory, you should know that whatever happened is in the past, Dad and I still want nothing more than to see this company prosper." His eyes were wide.

"If that's the case, you had better come clean. Tell me, why *did* you apply to work here after I took charge? As a front-line leader, of all positions?"

"To help save it," Joshua replied. The truce had been brief.

"Well, that's very noble of you. The company needs saving, does it?"

"Yes."

"So you didn't think of saving it while your dad was in charge?"

Joshua had no answer.

Gregory swiftly finished his coffee and replaced the cup on the saucer. "Look, I'm afraid I don't have time for any more of this. If you *do* genuinely want to help, then you can start by getting us your *production* ideas by Monday."

"Monday?" said Joshua. His shoulders drew upwards and his arms fell into his lap. "Stephen gave us three weeks."

What?

"He gave us three weeks for the feasibility study."

"For the whole study, maybe. We can't wait that long for initial ideas. I need to develop the vision – as you yourself implied."

"Did Stephen mention anything about implementing one value stream at a time, after the study?"

"No."

"We're working on end-to-end blueprints for all the flows. With your support we can start delivering the Aspiration transformation straight after the feasibility study. After sixteen weeks you'll see huge benefits, including the lead times."

"Again, that's very noble, but Stephen and Simon are already taking care of the Aspiration issue."

"With an IT system?"

"Yes."

"I can't see how that will solve problems on the shop floor. How can it make sense to *spend* money trying to manage complexity when we can *save* money by simplifying it?"

"All leading companies have these systems, Joshua. The business case is long established."

The upstart had been silenced. "Look, Joshua. I just need to know whether you are with us or not. Will I have your initial production ideas by Monday? Yes or no."

"Yes."

"Good. Well if you'll excuse me I have a lot more to be getting on with. As you now have too." He rose to his feet and so did Josh. "Look, Joshua," he added. "I don't have a problem with you being here if you keep your head down and do a good job. I want us to get on. And I welcome everyone's ideas, including yours. OK?"

Joshua looked at him but did not say a word.

"Goodbye, then," Gregory said. "All the best."

"See you later."

Gregory closed the door and he rested against it. Joshua was young but he was every bit as self-assured as his father. It might prove safer keeping him inside the company where they could keep an eye on him.

Josh rubbed his stubble as he stepped onto the iron walkway: hours had flown since he had come in to brief the night shift that morning. His conscience had been clear when speaking to Gregory, but everything he *could* have said now started to flood into his mind. He could not be sure how much had reached Gregory: his eyes had seemed clouded throughout. How could he open people's minds enough for them to glimpse how closed they were?

At times he could have wept for the business. Couldn't anyone see what was going on? Managers were congratulating themselves on progress while everyone else privately despaired. Gregory's need for control was constraining them all.

He leant on the handrail. If he was being misunderstood, his father had endured this first. He loved spending time with his dad, who would never have let his business go without a fight or a plan. Josh would continue to play whatever part he could. He trotted down the spiral stairs, past the empty training room.

"Josh!" came a yell from Peter's office. "Just the man! You got five minutes?"

He checked his watch. He grimaced before walking over. "No more than five, Peter."

"Great – come on in."

Peter cleared a chair. "I need to talk to you about performance-management boards. Stephen cited yours in the woodshed and claimed they could be worth up to five per cent in every area!" He smirked. "Have you got any evidence I can use to the contrary?"

"The board's just a tool, Peter. It won't improve anything by itself."

"Exactly! That's what I told him."

"But in the hands of a good manager it's invaluable. Someone who is seeking out the right problems to solve. That's the core of good performance management."

"You want people to *go looking* for problems?"

"The problems are there whether we find them out or not. Is it better to surface them or to bury them?"

"That depends on how many you already have."

"Maybe, but I would rather bury none and prioritise which problems I solve first. Then we can model the right culture of embracing, prioritising and solving problems collaboratively. Every problem is an opportunity to improve. If we really *need* to improve by twenty per cent it's only bad news if we *can't* surface twenty per cent's worth of problems."

"Come on," Peter said. "*Every problem is an opportunity*, eh? I probably got that particular T-shirt before you were born. I can assure you I still have more than enough of those opportunities, all day, every day."

"So you feel responsible for solving them yourself?"

"Who else is there? Team leaders raise them to me and Stephen dumps them on me."

"What if you created tools and expectations to help team leaders prioritise and solve their own problems?"

Peter pulled a face.

Josh leant back in his chair. "Hey, I've got to call Graham. Excuse me." He rearranged his appointment and then unfolded a sheet of paper from his back pocket. "Look at this," he said. "This is what I wanted to show you before. It's Graham's weekly cockpit chart for the woodshed. It has all of the most important information he needs to drive decisions in what is now his area. On the left is a graph for each of his main Key Performance Indictors (or KPIs) versus target, which includes last week's data."

"You don't think we have enough KPIs?"

"Yes!" he said. "Far too many! If an indicator really is *key*, we need someone to be thinking about how they're influencing it all the time. The more indicators anyone has, the less *key* they become. That's why we only put four on here. They need to be specific, too – something each leader is responsible for and can influence. You could have four or five KPIs for Production and cascade each to the relevant area for each team leader."

Peter took the sheet and spread it out on the lowest of his piles.

Josh continued, "On the right is a table to log main problems – gaps to target – and what is being done about them this week. If every team leader had one of these, it could focus them on your expectation that they address the main gaps themselves. You could just follow up with them once a week to challenge and support them, using the chart as a focus."

"When would I do that?"

"In a dedicated one-to-one meeting."

"What, with each of them? Individually?"

"Yes."

"Every week?"

"Yes."

"Are you crazy? We already have *more* meetings in this place than KPIs!"

"Too many *ineffective* meetings, yes," Josh said. "Not enough efficient, effective ones. A well-prepared cockpit chart like this could facilitate an effective review in half an hour."

"I have seven team leaders. That's – half a day every week!"

"Then look at it like this: if you're responsible for production performance, why *wouldn't* you invest ten per cent of your time in high-quality interactions with your direct reports to review and manage it? If you do this well, you'll also be modelling to everyone how to manage their own areas. They'll walk about with your questions in their head and they'll bother you less during the week if they know they'll have this protected time with you."

"They already have that. Every week we meet to review the KPIs as a team. That's always going to be more efficient than meeting individually."

"And how effective are those meetings?"

"Everyone hears what's going on. And anyone can raise any problem they like."

"So have you noticed what kind of problems gets raised?"

"Their priority ones."

"It's always other people's problems. Most people wouldn't feel comfortable to air their own problems in a group, if they were aware of them. Not in our current culture."

"Well, that's their problem then," said Peter. "If you'll excuse the pun."

"It's everyone's problem if we're not improving. You could use your own one-to-one with Stephen to elevate those problems which need his help to be solved."

"Are you serious?" Peter said, shaking his head and laughing. "He's already told me he *pays me to come up with solutions, not problems*."

"Maybe we could discuss it with him together?"

"Nice idea, Josh, but if he doesn't listen to me he's hardly going to listen to you. No offence. Anyway – getting back on track, Stephen is suggesting *virtual boards* – lists of problems that we keep on a central spreadsheet on the Z drive. What do you think?"

"Well, one advantage of a real board is that it's big enough for the whole team to see and use."

"Come on," said Peter, smiling. "Surely any big board is just there to impress visitors. Do you really think the operators care what format the information is in?"

"Yes. They're the ones filling it in. And the format means the information is never hidden."

Peter raised his eyebrows. "Let's see how long it takes for them to lose interest. Anyway – I've got enough to go on. I'll have a think about what to put in Stephen's spreadsheet."

"Keep that if you like." Josh left his copy of the cockpit chart on the table. "Share it with Stephen."

"I'll think about it. Thanks for stopping."

"You're welcome. Will we see you at our short daily update tomorrow?"

Peter furrowed his brow. "What time?"

"Eight am," Josh replied. "The same time every day. People have started to ask why you're not there. And it's essential for you to hear what we're discovering."

"I'm sure you won't find much that will surprise me, Josh. Anyway, you know what it's like." Peter peered in his hand-held organiser. "No, sorry. There's no way I can do tomorrow."

"What about Friday? You're already coming to the future state design training at 8.30 – so come early."

"OK – go on then."

"Thank you. Please can you double check that Stephen will come and introduce Friday's training? It's about redesigning our operations so it's critical that our operations director takes the lead."

"Of course."

"Thank you. And can you make sure Simon and Barry are there too? It's essential that Planning and Maintenance take part."

"Stephen's told them already. We'll all be there. Just remember to think twice before you suggest anything in front of Stephen."

14

Special Ops

THE workplace was filled with the Friday feeling. Sue could almost smell the fish and chips that used to herald the weekend, even though the canteen service had been replaced by vending machines ages ago. Today would be particularly special: Josh would start giving them answers.

"Morning!" said Sue, closing the door.

"Morning, Sue," said Josh. He looked up from a sheet of scribbled notes and diagrams.

"It's a bit quiet in here."

Chris was bent over their informal masterpiece that covered the cluster of desks. Failing to acknowledge her, he drummed eraser shavings away with the back of his hand. Then the number displayed on the calculator was transferred to the bottom of the diagram. A large *Planning Board* now hung on the team room wall. Her name was written on one of the rows, and there was a column for each day of the week.

"Are you OK?" Sue asked Josh.

"I'm not too bad, thanks."

"Not great?"

He sighed. "Life would be a lot simpler if people said what they thought and did what they said."

"That depends on what they were really thinking," she said.

"Maybe!"

"Coffee?"

"I'd love a tea, please."

Nigel joined them at his standard 7:52. By five past eight it was looking unlikely that any managers or members of their support team would be joining them for their eight o'clock update.

"I've just had an email from Peter," Josh announced, "to say that he and Stephen can't come."

"I thought *Breakthrough* was supposed to be everyone's priority?" Nigel said.

"They're at another *Breakthrough* meeting – about Planning."

"That's not very good planning, then," said Chris. Josh indulged him with a smile.

"Boycott *their* meetings," Sue said. "Drop them last-minute emails and see how they feel."

"That wouldn't exactly model the culture we want to see, would it?" said Josh. He was smiling but it felt like a telling-off. "Let's do our own update now and hope that others will still join us at 8.30 for the Target State Design training. We won't need long for an update as we're still working together on the Current State MIFA. Any lead time figures for us yet, Chris?"

"Total value-added time per product is 413 minutes. Divided by the total inventory, which is eighty-four days' worth."

"That's lower than normal," Nigel commented. "It's the end of the month."

"Which gives less than one per cent value added."

That didn't sound very good. Nigel shook his head, possibly because he still had misgivings about the analysis.

"Thanks, Chris," Josh said. "Don't read too much into the value, but it gives a flavour of the potential. It's safe to say that this number will be a lot higher with our designed Target State."

"What sort of value would be considered world class?" Chris asked. "In your opinion."

Nigel covered his face.

"Well, another reason for not reading too much into the value is that it depends on the specific processes. For us, the long wash cycle has already inflated our value-added time. An excellent design for our processes might reach ten per cent, just to give you an idea."

They were really supposed to get ten times better?

"Let's move on," Josh said. "I need to introduce you to the board you'll have seen on the wall. In the training session we'll be outlining the process of designing a target state MIFA for the operation. Then we will dismantle this into loops that will be assigned to each of you to develop and implement, with the relevant line managers and stakeholders."

Sue froze. Was she supposed to have any idea what he was talking about? She was a good sewing machinist and she could organise people to do things that she herself knew how to do. But she only had a handful of qualifications and she was way out of her depth.

"Don't worry," he said, as if he was reading her mind. "I chose each of you for a reason and I'll give you all the support you need."

He was kind, but he barely knew her.

"We'll develop an overall plan for major milestones in each phase for flow, process excellence, performance management and people. Then every Friday each of us should plan our next week by taking our objectives from the plan and breaking it down into daily end products. Once again, if you are new to structuring your work like this I'll give you all the support you need. I hope you'll find it's a good discipline."

Her concerns were now eclipsed by the immediate one of wiping her clammy upper lip without leaving a white moustache.

"You really expect us to write something different for every single day?" said Chris. "What if we're working on something bigger?"

"Then it's just as important to break it down into daily end products. This is the way of maintaining pace. It will focus you on bite-sized pieces of work and ensure we practise what we will be preaching to the rest of the factory. If we don't hold ourselves accountable to daily targets, why should anyone else?"

Nigel shuffled in his seat. "If there's a good reason we can't get something done, we shouldn't punish ourselves."

"No one said anything about punishment," Josh replied. "If we can't meet daily targets, on what basis can we be confident of meeting monthly targets, or indeed goals for the whole change programme? Is it better to surface a problem sooner or later?"

If Nigel still seemed confused, Sue did not stand a chance.

"In terms of the fourth component of people, each of you will also need to work with people in the right way to release potential and to ensure changes can be sustained."

Nigel leant in towards her just as she was blotting her lip. "God help boy wonder, then," he whispered.

It was 8:40 and no one else had joined them. Josh put his phone away after leaving a couple of messages. "I think we'll start the training."

The refilled coffee pot would be wasted.

"No one's coming?" Nigel asked.

"The planning meeting has been extended. Stephen, Simon and Peter are all involved. I can't get hold of anyone from Maintenance."

"Nothing unusual there, then," Nigel said.

Sue shook her head. *Why would anyone not want to learn how to improve?*

"Shouldn't we postpone it?" Nigel asked.

"Normally I would, but you need to start using this information as soon as possible. So I think it's best that we press ahead now ourselves. We can run another session with the others as soon as they can manage."

"It doesn't bode well if managers can't even turn up to their stated priorities," Nigel said.

"Especially if they'll still be expecting others to commit to any changes," Sue added.

"Exactly."

Josh sat on the front of his desk. "Come on, everyone. I never suggested it would be plain sailing. A large part of this role is influencing others – we'll have a separate training session on that soon."

"It shouldn't be this difficult. Aren't we all supposed to be on the same side?" said Nigel.

"Don't lose heart. We will transform this place, I promise."

His face was like flint, but people always made promises they couldn't deliver. She would be happy if they could just make life easier for a couple of people. If they could make a few changes that would make people's lives easier, Sue knew that would be enough for her.

"Let's start the Target State Design training. I will present you with a general process you could use to design any operation from scratch. We'll bring it to life by seeing how it applies here. The end product will be an initial end-to-end vision for our operation."

"Are you following a proven framework? From any particular text book?" Chris asked.

"Nothing was available off the shelf so I devised this design process myself. Some books cover some of the principles but most are based on automotive components, so their applicability tends to be limited to operations with a few variants which can be made to stock. Making sofas to order involves a more typical level of complexity, so the process I give you now should also be applicable to most other make-to-order operations. We can call it SPECIAL OPS – a mnemonic for ten steps that we need to go through."

Ten? Sue sank a little deeper.

"We need to start, though, by assuming the right posture. To develop good designs for many different solutions you need to practise what I call being *hypothesis driven*. This means starting with an overall hypothesis – an idea of what something could look like – and then testing it with data to confirm or adjust it. We need this skill to apply each step of the SPECIAL OPS process to our own operation. Being hypothesis driven is the key to overcome inertia and drive towards a better solution quickly. Otherwise in the face of so much data and so many opinions you may be trapped with analysis paralysis. Or you might just settle for incremental change."

Chris's face was contorted. "Hold on," he said. "Are you telling us to start with the solution?"

"An idea of it, yes."

"Not the problem?"

Josh smiled. "The answer is both. With enough experience we can already understand some of the root problems. For example, we've already seen that in a manufacturing operation the cause behind much waste is in the variability of process lead times. A good hypothesis is an educated guess of a solution, which you can test with data to see if you're right."

Nigel squirmed. "Isn't that a bit irrational?"

"No, it's completely rational. But it is *also* intuitive. We shape the educated guess from experience, but if we find data to show that any part of it won't work, or won't deliver significant benefits, we will change it."

Nigel did not lift his gaze. Sue was ready for Step One.

"You do need to be careful, though, not to reveal too much of your hypotheses too quickly with those you're trying to influence. It helps to have enough of a private hypothesis – or vision of the solution – at the beginning, but then to lead the critical stakeholders through the process of developing their own solution. Again, we'll cover this in our training session on influencing skills."

Nigel gave the slightest of nods.

"So do you already have a hypothesis of what this whole factory could look like?" Chris asked.

Josh looked at each of them. Part of her hoped that he would not be arrogant enough to say yes. But then he would be hypocritical if he said no.

"Yes," he said matter-of-factly, "I do."

"Cool," said Chris. "So can't you just show us?"

"No."

"Why not?"

"Partly because you will learn more by discovering it for yourselves. And partly because if I were to give you the solution now, you might then be tempted to get it done in your own way. Now, we need to move on. We're setting out to design a new way of doing everything from receiving a customer order to delivering it, with minimal waste." He was speaking quickly and his enthusiasm was infectious. "Reducing waste is central to everything. Remember: waste is anything that costs time or money but does not add value in the eyes of the customer." He pointed to a flip-chart sheet that they had posted on the wall earlier that week:

EIGHT WASTES:

WAITING of parts or people;

INVENTORY of raw material, Work In Process (WIP) or finished products;

MOTION within a process;

OVERPROCESSING to an unnecessarily high standard;

TRANSPORTATION between processes;

OVERPRODUCTION of more products than required, or sooner than needed;

REWORK of a product to achieve the right quality, or scrap that is produced;

POTENTIAL within people that is neither liberated nor put to good use.

"Please learn these. To become a world-class company, everyone should learn to see and to eliminate these types of waste."

The wastes themselves made sense, but no one had explained *how* they were supposed to reduce them. Did Josh still think he could do so where people were already short of money and people? Why couldn't Nigel think to ask him that?

"Right, we're ready to start the ten-step Target State Design process. I'd like you to imagine we're designing the operation from scratch. You have a blank sheet of paper. Where would you start?"

Nigel shrugged.

Sue was not going to embarrass herself.

"What about our customers?" Chris suggested.

"Good idea," Josh said. "Shouldn't every good design start with a specification?"

Four hours later even Nigel was looking punch drunk after the onslaught of new material. They had got out into the plant several times to see practical examples but Sue had failed to take in much beyond the first half hour.

Only Josh's summary of the morning session was now keeping them from lunch.

"So how is everyone feeling?" Josh asked.

He must have known – although Sue could answer in a number of different directions: shattered, saturated, sinking… Yet she still felt that if anyone could help her, Josh could.

Nigel's arms remained folded.

"Great!" Chris replied, glancing at the others. "Let's do it." Nigel cast him the look on her behalf.

"Have any of you heard of the concept of a training cycle? It might help to normalise how you may be feeling at this point – unless you're Chris. Remember, the purpose of this morning's training was only to give you an initial awareness. The best way of learning is by doing: you will get to grips with this as you try and put it into practice."

On a fresh flip-chart sheet he drew a cross that separated four quarters. Moving clockwise from the bottom left quarter he wrote: *Unconscious Incompetence, Conscious Incompetence, Conscious Competence* and then *Unconscious Competence*. He turned and smiled. First thing this morning you were probably here," he said, pointing to the first quarter. "You didn't know how much there was to know about designing an operation. This morning's training might now have moved you to Conscious Incompetence: you now know how much there is to know.

"I don't expect you to retain most of what we've been through this morning. Some of you will want to go on leading change. Then one day you'll be doing it intuitively – perhaps forming a hypothesis for a new area on your first walk through."

Something did resonate a little with her: she had once felt paralysed to think that the cover she had been trusted to sew would be sold for a lot of money. Now she often found herself on autopilot.

Josh had moved to the side of the room where Nigel had posted the flip-chart sheet that summarised the SPECIAL OPS mnemonic.

Specification: customer and business needs

Processes: product tree, co-location

Equipment: dedication and OEE targets

Cycle for each process: takt/balance, batches or FIFO, EPE interval

Inventory: where, how to control; approx. quantity and area required

Assimilate: on target-state MIFA diagram

Layout: fit value streams around constraints

Operators: how many, where, what cross-training?

Production control: details at each process

Standardise: how to train and sustain

"So we start with a *specification* for our operation: what the business and customers require from it. Such targets should reflect Customer requirements, Capacity, Capital, Costs and Culture. Look out, too, for specific value streams where targets might be different – like the three-week customer lead time for Aspiration. I hope you're beginning to see how we can nearly always design different systems to deliver whatever is a priority."

"Step two is to consider how our *processes* can be realigned. First, we need to understand the complexity by seeing how the number of unique product variants multiplies as we move from left to right on the flow diagram. This can be represented on a product tree. First, this will confirm whether different specifications lend themselves to separate value streams. Second, it will show us where it might be feasible to hold shop stocks of limited variants to offer shorter customer lead times. Third, we need to consider how we can co-locate processes to compress lead times."

Nigel crossed his feet at the end of his outstretched legs. He was probably still uptight after Josh had suggested that Pre-upholstery did not need to be a separate process in its own right.

"Please remember to keep an open mind. Challenge yourselves to remain objective. For example, is quality really at risk? Upholstering in the woodshed may be problematic, but would there really be any quality risk to building frames, pre-upholstering, upholstering and finishing all next to each other?"

"I still can't see the point," Nigel said.

"Then we'll continue to agree to disagree for now," Josh said.

Sue winced. She had hoped that Josh would have been good enough to patch things up instead of leaving differences unresolved.

"Step three is to determine what *equipment* is required and what can be dedicated to which potential value streams. For example, can we dedicate a cutting table to Aspiration? The core pieces of analysis here are the product-machine matrix and OEE for fully automatic machines anywhere near capacity limits. What would the OEE of a cutting table need to be to liberate enough capacity to fit all of Aspiration's orders? I hope I've at least started to convince you that the premeditated dedication of equipment might be better than running around chaotically in an effort to keep all plates spinning. If a machine can be dedicated, we can then look to relocate it within a value stream where justified.

"Step four is to design the *cycle* of work at every process. Where processes are shaped by labour, the cycle should normally be the takt time. Takt time is the available production time divided by the customer demand for that period, and it creates a customer-based rhythm for production. Every station should be balanced, with work content equal to takt and continuous flow between them. This should be relevant for the main processes from Frame Assembly to Finishing. Where equipment is significant there might be further constraints, such as changeover times, capacity or fixed machine cycle times. Then it might not be possible to process each unit First In First Out (or FIFO). Batches might be needed – for example, loads in the dye shop. If there are big differences between changeover times, even batches cannot be treated FIFO. A standard cycle should then be defined in which every variant can be produced if demanded: an Every Part Every (or EPE) interval. This will be relevant in the dye shop because if we process everything on the hoof, we can lose control by repeating the longest changeovers too frequently by urgent changes from darker to lighter colours – as well as causing delivery problems by ignoring the rarer variants.

"Step five is then to determine how much *inventory* needs to be located where and how it will be controlled. For example, does there need to be a shop stock or supermarket containing some of every variant, or do the made-to-order parts just need to be corralled before any essential re-sequencing in the next process? Remember, to minimise waste all inventory will need to be controlled in terms of quantity, location and method of replenishment. Estimate the quantities and sizes of areas required.

"Step six is to *assimilate* all of this information on a target state flow diagram. This will serve as the blueprint for the near future. We've formed an initial sketch of this for our business, but more validation and detail is required. It will help to train people and communicate how the end-to-end vision will work.

"Step seven – and only then – can we consider changing the *layout*, to fit the processes and inventory into our specific buildings, with minimal transportation. This includes co-locating as many processes as we've deemed possible, while considering practical constraints, equipment shared between value streams and any equipment where the benefits of relocation do not justify its expense."

Josh smiled. "We're nearly there!" he said. "Is everyone still with me?"

"We're *listening*," Sue said.

"That's good enough for me. Step eight is to determine how many people we need to work where, with what skills. Where takt is relevant, the number of operators should be determined by dividing the total work content per product by the takt time – assuming all constraints in equipment and training can be removed. For other areas, the number of operators required should be determined from the equipment cycles, the layout and the degree of manual intervention required. This step should also give us a target plan for cross-training that will improve team work and problem-solving.

"Step nine is to design the details of *production control* for each process. For example, how will we indicate to operators in the dye shop that a machine should be unloaded, what should be loaded next and whether everything is on track?

"Finally, step ten is to establish how the new end-to-end flow can be *standardised*. For example, a standard work sequence chart can be developed for each group of operators to outline their production control details and how they keep the whole flow working. Such standards help to sustain the change and serve as a basis for further improvements.

"That's it. Summary completed. Not much to it, eh?"

Even Nigel managed to smile.

"Now you have a flavour of what *can* be done to design an operation, it is worth comparing this with what is typically done when a new plant or business is established. The initial focus is typically for engineers to install like pieces of equipment together to fill the available space, generally in a logical overall sequence. Then it is left to the production team to work out how to run orders through the equipment and where to store Work In Process (or WIP). Material and information flows then tend to evolve over time.

"Right – let's have some lunch. Thank you all for engaging this morning – and for being honest when you have not agreed. We need to get much better at disagreeing in this organisation!"

This sounded a bit odd: *wouldn't it be better if everyone could just get on?*

"Thank *you*," she said anyway. "I'm sorry if we've been a bit unresponsive."

"Speak for yourself," Chris said.

"Don't apologise," said Josh. "Ideally this training session would have been spread over the two-week design phase."

"Do our managers already know all this?" she asked.

Josh looked at her. "Most people won't know what they don't know about designing an operation. Especially one they might have inherited."

She looked at the flip chart. *Surely their managers knew more than she did?*

15

ALONE AT THE TOP

IT was a dreary Saturday evening. In the darkness outside, surface water crashed off the undersides of vehicles carrying the carefree towards the city centre. Gregory smelt the cold putty and watched each raindrop trace the path of another. *Just like the steady trickle of failing businesses, no doubt.* Perhaps no CEO ever thought it could happen to them. He straightened his back and refocused beyond the rain: he had not come here to fritter away his time.

He afforded himself a smile. Speaking of wasting time, he looked for the anonymous fisherman in the orange hat who often did just that on the bank below. Even *he* must have found something better to do this evening! If Gregory were to ever enjoy the luxury of spare daylight hours, he would be sure to make better use of them. He turned back into the office: back to business. They were already halfway towards presenting their turnaround vision to Mountfield. Now he had mobilised everyone else, this was his first proper chance to gather his own ideas.

No one had prepared him for the isolation of shouldering the business alone. He was always giving out and never being replenished. To Mountfield, he was just another manager in his portfolio of investments. To Gregory's senior team he was their uncompromising leader who always pushed them to achieve more. To general employees he was the focus for all complaints. No one appreciated that he was just a good man doing an impossible job. No one considered the pressures he was under. Eddie had been his most loyal co-worker, but now even he had now joined the ranks of whisperers. Stephen would just be using this company as a stepping stone. Fiona might struggle the most to find new work, but she was also bohemian enough not to care. Anna was now the most dependable – but even she had spurned her opportunity to invest in the business.

Linda had always been his strongest ally. But she could offer little beyond empathy and it was not worth destabilising her for that. Friends or peers? None with a listening ear. After burning his bridges with Arthur he had toyed with engaging a professional mentor – one who could challenge and sharpen him personally. But he did not want to pay to teach someone about his industry. No, he had chosen to grasp this business as his sword of honour: he just had to man up and do so. If he could avoid falling on the sword, it would be his to wield in victory.

He doubted that Mountfield would ever replace him and his team: he simply did not have enough interest in manufacturing. The likelier option was that he would close the factory and try to sell the Eden brand. The factory closure would be chronicled in the *Worcester News*, but if Eden Furniture remained he would still be able to pass this off as an inevitable but successful transition. In practice, Gregory's main obstacle to downsizing their lifestyle was the number of people he and Linda had told about their dream home. The main person he would struggle to convince of the successful transition would be himself. Mountfield's words were buried within him like shrapnel. Shouldn't mere words just bounce off a stronger CEO? Mountfield's latest phrase still ricocheted in his head: *My only mistake was overestimating your capability.* Hatred stirred whenever he relived the scene, but he was powerless to stop the repeats.

He paced round the office. Only the other week Mountfield had introduced him to another golfer as *one of his stellar CEOs.* It was probably another victim Mountfield was trying to seduce, but he never knew which Mountfield he would encounter. It made Gregory *more* determined that he would always show consistent and straightforward leadership to his own team.

He closed his eyes. He longed to get back at Mountfield on the 23rd. The problem was that even if he could hit the ball out of the park, Mountfield would gain the most. *What had it all been for, anyway?* Mountfield's plan had always been to exit: even *success* would remove Gregory from the job he loved. It was Mountfield who had sold him the idea of the buyout. Now *Mountfield* held all the reins. Had he somehow assumed that he would be accountable only to himself? *How had he got himself into this mess?* He drove his foot against the open door and walked out.

He stood at the top of the iron stairs and looked down into what still remained *his* factory. The only approach was to fight tooth and nail to prove his ability, for himself if not for Mountfield.

It was at least ten degrees colder in the factory and eerily still. A premonition of the future? He smothered the thought. A bank of lights along the front of the factory had been left on. He descended the stairs quietly. Whenever he stopped he heard only the hissing of compressed air leaks. It was incredible that after he had hammered home the need to save costs, no one had thought to turn off the lights or the air. There was also a light beyond the roller door – in the trucking corridor to Building Two. There was a chance he had unwanted guests.

From the foot of the stairs, he inched quietly across the darkened part of Building One. If anyone *was* there, he needed to see them before they saw him. The hissing at least masked his steps. His eyes strained to make sense of dark shapes like bodies strewn over a battlefield. His eyes diffused each work-in-process as he passed.

He gave the roller door a wide berth to avoid it thundering upwards, and he slipped through the side door. Squinting in brazen light, he stepped quickly through the trucking corridor and into the darkness of Building Two. His knees clicked as he crouched beside a pre-upholstery station. There was no sound other than his breathing. He would have been in better shape for this twenty years ago. Another bank of lights was illuminated all the way to the front. Whoever it was must have found their way to the portable and valuable sewing machines. Gregory slowly worked his way towards them. Halfway up the building he was afforded a clear view across the cutting tables. Sewing was peaceful. Then a noise. It came from the toilet block, which had external windows. The door opened and a figure walked boldly out.

Gregory stood up. "Hey!" he shouted.

The figure stopped and began to turn.

What was he supposed to do now?

"Who is it?" said the figure. Mercifully, the stranger's tone was not in the least bit aggressive.

"Who are *you*?" Gregory asked.

"Gregory?" said the figure. "It's Josh."

Gregory's eyes could now confirm it, but his heart still pounded. "What are *you* doing here?" He took another step forward.

"I'm working on the improvements."

"Where?"

"In our team room."

"On a Saturday night?"

"I'm afraid so," he said. "How about you?"

"Me? Oh, I'm just catching up. As normal – there's never enough time in the week."

Joshua nodded. "If you have a few minutes I can show you how far I've got."

He did not want to oblige, but it would be due diligence to call Joshua's bluff. He followed him into what used to be the apprentices' office. The central desks were covered with pencil-drawn pages of technical drawings, sketches and text. A heater glowed on the floor.

"How much time do you have?" Joshua asked.

"Not much."

"I can take you through it properly then when you have more time. Here's the design process I've been working through," he said, pointing towards one of the flip-chart pages on the wall.

It looked like a war room. Gregory exhaled slowly and quietly.

"Is everything OK?" Joshua asked.

Mugged of perspective, he was momentarily on the brink of welling up. He dug an imaginary particle out of his eye. "Fine," he said. "Tired," he added honestly. "Busy. But everything's fine."

Joshua nodded.

He nearly felt at home when he saw that one of the flip-chart sheets spelt out a mnemonic. *SPECIALOPS* did not appear to contain anything too controversial. He turned back to the table and orientated one of the pages towards him.

"That one shows a potential layout once everything comes together. Here's an overview of a new way to control material and information through the plant, as a basis for reducing the lead times and inventory. And over there are the initial pages to check that things are possible for each process."

"So how much is everything worth then?" Gregory asked, standing up straight.

"That depends on how well we can implement," Joshua replied.

"Of course."

"On paper, there's enough potential to reduce costs by roughly a quarter and inventory by two-thirds."

Gregory smirked and raised his eyebrows.

"Plus we can halve Aspiration's lead times. Within six months and without the need for the IT solution, if you're open to this."

Gregory took a step back and folded his arms. "I'm open to anything, but as I've told you already, we've already dealt with Aspiration. *Your* job is to come up with practical ideas to reduce production costs." He smirked again. "You really think you can reduce costs by *twenty-five* per cent?"

"The potential is definitely there. But we'll only achieve it if you are prepared to make fundamental changes – as I mentioned in your office."

Gregory inhaled deeply. Despite staring at the sheet, he had barely taken any of it in. "So your ideas are based on changing the layout, then?" He drew it closer.

"They're not *based* on a new layout but they will result in one, yes."

He took a moment to familiarise himself with the new plan. "You've got the dye machines in Building Two!"

"I'm proposing we move them back there," Joshua said. "We can free up enough space again in Building Two to do so. It will improve the overall flow, as well as saving on the lease for the extra building."

"Oh, that's peanuts compared to the total costs."

Joshua looked at him. "Are you sure you can't spare thirty minutes now? It would really help to take you through the full story."

He felt far from on top of his game. "I can't, Joshua. It's nearly nine o'clock and I really need to get on. I'm sure you want to get home too." Anyway, it was unrealistic to expect a CEO to drop everything like that. Especially on a Saturday when he had come in specifically for something else. "Have you taken Stephen through it yet?"

"One or two ideas but not the whole end-to-end vision, no. This is the material that will help me to do that."

"Well, that's your first step, then. As operations director, he'll want to see it first. Once he's helped to filter and refine your ideas, I can go through it with both of you."

Joshua sucked in a yawn.

"Stephen won't want to see the dye machines moved back, though, any more than I do. He worked hard on that expansion project," Gregory added.

"What was the justification for the move?"

"The overall expansion! And the dye shop was really struggling in its old location."

"They're still struggling in their new location!" Joshua said. "Nothing's changed. Trevor is pinning all his hope on the extra buffer that the new machines will provide."

"The new machines have been cancelled. No one told me they were still struggling."

"It's chaos. And they only finished the plumbing for the new machines yesterday."

Gregory cursed under his breath. The decision had been clear: how hard would it have been for Stephen to communicate it? *And how hard could it be to run the dye shop, especially with the current low level of demand?*

"Leave it with me," Gregory said. "I'll add it to my list, which is one more reason to get back to it. I'd better say goodnight."

Joshua nodded. "Goodnight, then."

"Don't work too late." Gregory started walking back through the factory. Joshua could put on an earnest front but it was possible he was up to something. It was plausible he was trying to make them look stupid by reversing some high-profile decisions. But there would have been easier ways to go about destabilising the business. He glanced over his shoulder but Joshua was already back at his desk.

16

GUEST OF HONOUR

Peter drove a people carrier with a utilitarian interior. He did always say that he cared more about function than form. Josh made small talk while clearing some space for his feet amid the CD cases and empty drinks cans.

They had entered their second week and Peter had still not shown up for a morning meeting. Josh's repeated requests had finally yielded an invitation to Peter's home that evening to *catch up over dinner*. According to the other team leaders who had all been invited back at some stage, Joan, Peter's wife, was a live wire who had probably been badgering her husband to meet his latest recruit.

Peter turned into a cul-de-sac to the north of Worcester. Modern houses faced each other around a common green. Under a yellow street lamp a handful of children kicked a ball around. Peter turned into a driveway and a boy's ruddy face and thick black hair appeared at Peter's car window. The boy shrank back when he saw Josh: a stranger sitting in his mother's seat.

"Alright, here we are," Peter announced.

The boy ran to the house, pressed the doorbell and turned to face them.

"Nath! What did you do that for? I've got a key, haven't I?" Peter rolled his eyes.

Josh approached the discarded football. He stroked it with his right foot, flipped it onto his left and tapped it up again with each. He caught the ball and presented it to the boy, whose eyes widened.

"Hello, Nath. I'm Josh."

"Josh works for me, Nath. He's having dinner with us tonight."

"Do you play football?" the boy asked.

"Every now and then," Josh said.

"Josh plays for our factory team."

The door opened and Joan appeared. She stuffed a duster behind the radiator.

"Josh! Hello, lovely to meet you." She abruptly straightened her arm to shake his hand. "Peter's told me a lot about you."

Peter glared but her smile increased.

"Hello, dear." Joan pecked her husband on the lips.

"Mum, can Josh and I play football?"

"No, of course you can't," his dad said.

"Not today, Nathan," said his mother. "Wash your hands please, and tell your sister to do the same and come down. Let them come in, Nathan! You're letting the warm air out."

After dinner, Josh was ushered into the room at the front of the house, which seemed to be reserved for special occasions.

Peter sank into a wingback, jacquard chair with Queen Anne style legs. He invited Josh to sit on the matching sofa.

"So how did today's planning meeting go?" Josh asked.

Peter rolled his eyes. "You don't want to know." He clasped his hands and straightened his legs out. "They're creating a monster. My new resolve is to limit the damage. If I'm lucky, we might just score a bonus feature or two."

"What about a custom front end for Cutting? At the moment Shelley's visibility of orders is really limited. She also has to import everything into her own spreadsheet to sort by fabric type."

"I don't think they're offering anything that detailed."

"Couldn't they? That's an example where IT *could* really help to solve a problem."

"Josh, I keep on telling you this: sometimes you need to be thankful for what you're *not* responsible for."

"Aren't we all responsible for speaking up when we see something wrong? It can't make sense to automate broken processes. Or to waste money trying to manage complexity instead of simplifying it."

Peter pondered the comments and nodded. "That's exactly what they're doing." He jabbed his finger at Josh. "You should tell that to Gregory."

"I did."

Peter's enthusiasm evaporated. "You've been speaking to Gregory?" he said, raising his eyebrows. "When was that?"

Josh proceeded carefully. "Just the other day."

"I can't remember the last time I had a proper conversation with Gregory. He never comes out onto the shop floor."

Josh looked at his boss. "Did you know that people are saying the same about you?"

"I'm on the shop floor every day!" Peter unclasped his hands. He stared at the golden bowling ball that sat on a lacquered plinth beside him. "People can think what they like, Josh. In the good old days you *could* be on the floor all day every day. There's much more to being a *modern* production manager. Days are over-stuffed with spreadsheets, reports and meetings. It's a constant balancing act: you can never keep everyone happy all the time." Peter looked at him, stroking his moustache with finger and thumb. The mahogany clock on the mantel continued to tick. "So what *did* you talk to Gregory about?"

"The change programme."

"You didn't promise anything, did you?" Peter said with half a smile.

"Nothing unfounded."

"Well, let me be the judge of that. Go on then, come clean. Did you really tell Trevor the new machines would have been a waste of money?"

"They had already been cancelled," he said. "But yes, I told Trevor we can help him to thrive without them."

"You think you know the dye shop better than him?"

"We can help anyone to design a better way of working." He chose his words carefully because Peter and Trevor were particularly close. According to Milky, Joan rued the evening years ago when Trevor had first come for dinner: she had lost Peter to skittles every Wednesday night since. "There is opportunity to improve the dye shop, as there is everywhere. Once sewn covers have been sorted by colour, they are currently loaded into whichever machine seems most appropriate, whenever one becomes available. People are doing their best but they need help to *design* a better way of working. Capacity isn't being used wisely, order fragments are processed randomly and small loads are getting forgotten."

"OK, OK. Look, even Trevor would recognise there's always room for improvement. But don't talk about problems; give me a solution."

"If we allocate each colour to a machine, and each machine cycles through a fixed sequence, my gut feeling is that we could guarantee to dye every order within two days."

"You want to fix colours to machines?"

"Yes. We can dedicate similar colours to each machine and always rotate through them in an optimum sequence from light to dark – to limit the longer changeovers from dark to light."

"They already minimise those."

"This would do so more systematically. Always sequencing from pink to red to maroon, for example."

"What if there are no orders for red covers?"

"We'll skip that colour and go on to the maroon orders."

"What if there was only one order for red?"

"We'll put it in."

Peter looked uncomfortable. "Are you trying to put the process in a strait jacket?"

"The process has trapped itself in this mess because of the *lack* of instruction," Josh said. "These are the steps that can set it free!"

"What if we had a larger load of something else?"

"We'll stick to the sequence and do the red first."

"What if another red is just about to show up? You'll run out of capacity in no time."

"Don't you remember our long chat about capacity? We can do the analysis to show capacity won't be a problem, if you're open to the possibility that it *might* work. It's called standardising the Every Part Every (or EPE) interval. Just think about the problems we're trying to solve: if we can make *every part every two days*, we can guarantee that the longest ever process lead time will be two days. Similar guarantees all along the flow can be the basis for controlling the lead times as we've been talking about. Then we can guarantee to meet delivery dates and regain the Aspiration account, while collapsing costs and inventory."

"I'm not pulling your ideas apart for fun, Josh. Suppose I'm the dye shop team leader with cost and production targets to meet. It's getting close to the end of the month and I'm behind target. What do I do? Stick to the system and tell Stephen to *stick* his targets?"

"Don't you remember me saying that internal controls like production targets can be unhelpful, if they prevent us from doing the right thing? So this is something we need to help Stephen and Gregory to address before it happens. If we want to transform this company, we need to transform the principles we've been using to run it."

"Look, Josh. Even if you and I could convince Stephen to change his targets, do you really think we could get everyone in the dye shop to work in such a fixed way?"

"Of course. If the solution is good, implementation problems are only ever management problems, so they're in our hands. There's nothing we can't then overcome, with a capable chain of command."

"Chain of command? That's part of the problem, Josh! You can't just command people any more." Peter grinned. "Or chain them up."

"You know what I mean: a strong chain of capable managers through the organisation. Gregory, Stephen, you, Trevor and operators working towards the same vision with no weak link, sharpening and supporting each other to surface and solve problems." There were, of course, flaws throughout the chain. The culture was now so bad that managers were deliberately hiding problems to cover their personal insecurities. But there was always hope that this better culture could be transformed as part of a broader transformation, through managers learning to model it as they led one-to-one reviews and engaged the workforce.

"Don't confuse strength with style, Josh. For example, Stephen can get away with a different style with me than I could with any of you lot. It doesn't necessarily mean I'm not tough enough." Peter's moustache twitched. His eyes searched around the room before settling on Josh again.

"Strength doesn't mean toughness, Peter. It's hard to define but it manifests itself in doing the right thing, in the right way and for the right reasons. If you want my opinion about strength, I would say that it comes from our inner resources."

"You're a bright lad, Josh," Peter said. "One day you might even be in my shoes. By then you'll have realised that nothing's ever as simple as the textbooks make out."

17

THE FIRST HURDLE

"Hang on a minute…" said the hefty man in the pale mohair suit. The weight of his authority commanded everyone's attention.

Gregory was isolated at the front. Knowing better than to interrupt a Mountfield silence, he perched on the front corner of the boardroom table. It was far from comfortable but he smiled to project confidence. Otherwise he might not have much of the remaining time to prove his capability.

Mountfield continued to scrutinise their report through his ridiculous monocle, nestled beneath a wild, grey eyebrow. October 23rd had finally arrived. Gregory and Anna had worked on the document all weekend, with the last major revision completed at one o'clock that morning. Their heads had been drowning in numbers so they had resolved to get some sleep. Today had been a blur and they had not managed to check everything properly. If there was a mistake, Mountfield would find it.

Mountfield's face was changeable as he flicked back another few pages. Without errors, the material would be good enough. Gregory's normal presentation skills were good enough. The problem was that he was now running on empty. If he had not pushed himself to visit Emily on Saturday evening it may have been a different story. His mind was fuzzy, and double espressos and adrenalin were struggling to provide the scaffolding for his heavy eyelids. And Mountfield was liable to fly off the handle at any moment.

"Let me play it back to you," Mountfield said. "You're promising to reduce lead times and operating costs *everywhere*."

Gregory sucked in a yawn and blinked rapidly. *Focus*.

"Which you've promised many times before. Only now it seems you're promising to do so with *no* extra investment *and* in a way that will *further* increase capacity." He looked up at him, grinned and removed his monocle. "Have I misunderstood something?"

He tried to bury his anger: everyone was watching. He smiled and rose slowly. "No, Doug, I think you've got it just about right. Except, of course, that we *have* had a track record of reducing costs – to some degree." It needed to be said but it cost him Mountfield's eye contact. He continued to address everyone else. "We have always acknowledged the hard work needed to earn the growth from Aspiration and beyond. What we are proposing now is the fruit of this hard work – radical new approaches, particularly to the way we manage our operations – that will deliver and build capability for our future. Or rather than *new* approaches, I should say they are radical *new applications* of tried and tested principles. Everything is backed up by rigorous analysis. We needed to innovate, and that is exactly what we have done." He still had the eyes of everyone except Mountfield. "Does that answer your question for now, Doug?"

"Not really, no."

It was time to roll the dice. "So correct me if I'm wrong, but you seem to imply that proposing to deliver so many benefits at once might initially sound too good to be true." The lack of response suggested that Mountfield was listening. "I can understand that, given that we've not yet got into the details. So how about, then, we dive into the detail for one particular process now? That way we can show the specifics of how everything we've mentioned holds together."

Mountfield finally looked up. "OK," he said. "Try me."

"Great," Gregory replied. "Let me suggest we bring forward an example from the dye shop. Stephen our operations director was going to take you through it later, but Stephen, perhaps you could do so now instead? Is that OK with everyone?"

Mountfield nodded and flicked through his pack.

"It's on page – twenty-three."

He had done it – they were back on track. Now he just hoped Stephen would heed his coaching to cut the wisecracks and play it safe.

Anna brought up page twenty-three on the projector screen and Stephen sprang into action. "Good morning, everyone. OK, please do stop me if you have any questions. This page explains the current situation in the dye shop. The first thing to understand is that although we *have* had some lead time problems in the dye shop, we do *not* have a capacity problem. So, as illustrated, the situation is that we have seven machines. We offer more than one hundred colours, but as you can imagine, eighty per cent of the units are for twenty per cent of the colours. We need to dye on average eighty units a day. Now, the longer we wait to collect units of any particular colour, the more units we are able to produce in a day. However, that obviously has an adverse effect on lead time. You can see below that currently the process lead times range from just one hour to sometimes fourteen days – or even more in exceptional cases. Obviously that inflates the maximum overall lead time and therefore the lead time we can safely guarantee to our customers. On the right-hand side of the page is the proposed solution of dedicating colours to different machines and establishing rules to process all covers to a fixed cycle per machine, whatever the quantity. The analysis we've done shows it's possible to process 99.9 per cent of the units within two days. Therefore we have shown we can achieve the higher capacity despite cancelling the new machines. And without any investment we can collapse lead times, collapse inventory and collapse the associated costs."

Stephen waited for a response.

"That's it?" Mountfield said, looking up. "It doesn't sound like rocket science."

"It's not!" said Stephen. "But that's the real beauty of it. You might be shocked to hear this, but we don't have too many rocket scientists working on our shop floor." Stephen grinned. "And to be honest, we're quite happy not having to pay rocket scientist wages either!"

Gregory watched Mountfield and held his breath until he smirked.

"The rocket science lies in the way I've designed it. It's bulletproof."

"If it works as you claim," Mountfield said, "the obvious question is why it has taken you so long to come up with something so simple?"

"Well, I've actually not been here that long myself," Stephen said, "just about long enough to diagnose the problem and design this solution."

Mountfield allowed his lens to drop on its chain. "When did you join?"

"The most important thing," Gregory said, butting in, "is that we're ready to implement. Yes, the solutions are brilliantly simple, but part of the brilliance has been in making them simple, so they are accessible to everyone. It hasn't been straightforward – please don't underestimate the development time that many of us have put into them over the years."

"OK, OK. So when are you going to stop talking and get it done? Give me a date for this particular solution, in the dye shop."

Gregory glanced at Stephen. "Next Monday," Stephen said. "A week today."

Mountfield seemed satisfied.

"What about the reliability of the machines?" said Mountfield's young analyst. "In my previous life I was a production engineer. Your solution sounds a bit inflexible to me. What are you going to do when a machine breaks down?"

Stephen nodded and smiled. "We've had a lot of discussion about that. The first thing to mention is that we obviously have a Total Production Maintenance programme to ensure that our machines break down as little as possible."

"Do you measure OEE?"

"Of course."

"So what's your average OEE in the dye shop at the moment?"

Stephen glanced at the carpet. Anna filled in the silence. "I think I have that here," she said.

"Sorry, I was just trying to remember," Stephen said quickly. "It's about seventy-five per cent."

Anna stopped flicking through her document. "Yes, seventy-six, if I remember correctly," Stephen said.

Anna's smile was paper thin.

"That doesn't sound too bad, given your changeovers. But if you're going to try this, you'll need to work out what to do in advance of a breakdown."

"Yes – of course. We've done so already, actually."

The meeting had broken up after Mountfield had declared he had heard enough. Gregory was beckoned into the corridor. He wanted to believe that they had done enough.

Mountfield led him into his own office, where he sat on Gregory's desk. "Close the door," Mountfield said.

He did so.

"I'm not going to say well done," Mountfield said, "because all you've done is to develop the plan you needed a year ago. You've now got until Christmas to deliver it."

He cleared his throat. This was Mountfield's way of delivering praise. Perched on the arm of a chair, Gregory smoothed down his trousers as casually as possible. "We're going to transform ourselves into the market leader, Doug." He took care to look Mountfield in the eye, trying not to give away that inside he was jumping up and down just because they had cleared the immediate hurdle.

"Take some advice from me, Gregory. Don't be naïve. Some of your own people would rather you fail than succeed. Get rid of them and plough on regardless."

With its dirty windows and its peeling, pebble-dashed walls, The Poacher's Arms was not the most salubrious place to celebrate, but it *was* the most immediate. Inside it was a proper pub with dark polished wood, thick, patterned upholstery and the sweet smell of real ale casks.

"Cheers!" Gregory said to his extended management team, holding up his pint.

"Cheers!" replied the others, almost in unison.

"I'm sorry you couldn't all be in the boardroom. Thank you, though: it was truly a team effort. Doug was impressed with our plans and has given us full steam ahead. So here's to the transformation of Gregory Todd Ltd!"

Various strains of his phrase were echoed. The sip of beer did wonders to soothe his brain. He had cut back again on wine, but he had earned this beer. Mountfield had once again attempted to strip away the gloss of victory with his parting words. But unlike Mountfield, he had never driven anyone to plot his personal ruin.

In his peripheral vision, Joshua Eden had just walked in, with what looked like his full improvement team. It was well beyond lunchtime. Gregory might have chanced upon a wilful contractual infringement.

Joshua nodded shamelessly towards them. Stephen stood up and beckoned them over.

"Excuse me," Stephen said, nudging Gregory so that he could get out. Gregory appealed for an explanation.

"What?" Stephen said. "You told me to invite the rest of the team!"

Gregory shook his head but stood up to let Stephen out. There was a big kerfuffle as another table was brought over. It should have been obvious he had meant the *management* team. Otherwise half the company should have been in the pub.

"Go on, then; he won't bite," Stephen said. He directed the young sales analyst to take his seat.

"Hi – Chris, isn't it?" Making small talk was the last thing he wanted to do, but as CEO everyone expected him to make the effort.

"Yes."

"What part have you been working on then?"

"I was asked to bring some sales and customer insight to Production. We mapped the whole…"

He carried on smiling at Chris while tuning into the conversation on his right.

"Hi, you must be Joshua. I'm Anna. Good to meet you."

"Likewise."

"You're just the person to clear something up – are you behind the OEE numbers for the dye shop?"

"Yes. Together with Nigel and Chris."

"Are the figures in the backup pages correct? I couldn't find them on the system to double check."

"Ah – they're not on the system as they're not official KPIs. In fact, there wasn't much data available so we estimated the figures. Nigel collected data with log sheets and Chris did the calculations."

"Hold on," Gregory said to Chris. "Sorry to interrupt but I think they're talking about you over here." He now tuned in more brazenly.

"According to your backup pages," said Anna, "the average OEE was fifty per cent. Was that right? It couldn't be as high as seventy-six per cent, could it?"

"I'm not sure that's the right question, Anna," Stephen said loudly. He had pulled up a new seat on their side of the table. "Josh, just to fill you in: the good news is that our dye shop solution – and the OEE figures – generated a lot of interest from Doug Mountfield. The bad news is that because of this spotlight we really need to show him we can get OEE up to eighty per cent or more."

"Well, Anna's right: the average *is* around fifty per cent," Joshua said. "A higher average with less variability would be great, but the solution we've designed will work well at a relatively stable sixty per cent. So it doesn't need to be as high as eighty at the moment – and I wouldn't recommend sucking up unnecessary resources to achieve it, especially when there's so much else that needs to be done."

"The dye shop is *Doug Mountfield's* number one priority, Josh."

"I don't see why. The market is consistently moving away from dyed covers, isn't it?"

"Doug Mountfield wants eighty per cent! And he wants the solution implemented on Monday, a week from today," Stephen said. "So the only question is what support do you need from me to make that happen?"

"Well, from a change-management perspective it would be best if you could position the dye shop implementation within a narrow and deep programme that addresses an end-to-end flow, like I mentioned before."

"That's not what I'm asking for, Josh. Are you suggesting you *can't* implement the dye shop solution by itself, next week?"

"Or look at it this way," Gregory said to Joshua in a raised voice, gate-crashing the discussion. Joshua was far too shrewd to let Stephen corner him into submission. "As Stephen said, whether it meets our ideals or not, we now need to reprioritise your team to implement the dye shop solution. So how soon do you think you *can* implement it, by itself?"

"Look, one principle I can't compromise is that neither *I nor my team* is going to implement anything by ourselves," Joshua said. "Trevor is the line manager in the dye shop: it must be him and Peter as his line manager to lead the implementation there, if it is to stand any hope of being sustained. Of course, we will do everything we can to train Peter and Trevor and to help them engage everyone through diagnose and design initiatives. But we will definitely need your support in influencing them and ensuring they show good leadership."

"You needn't worry about any of that whatsoever," said Stephen. "They'll do whatever I tell them."

"OK," Gregory said, trying to bring things to a conclusion more helpfully. "We seem to be going round in circles. Joshua, how soon do you think you can *get Peter and Trevor* to implement?"

"If you and Stephen can help us to convince them by the end of tomorrow, Tuesday, we could prepare a workshop with the rest of the stakeholders for Thursday. If that goes well, we could finish preparations on Friday to start the implementation on Monday, as you ask."

"That does the job," Stephen said, regaining everyone's attention. "Excellent. Come on, then – I'd better get you newcomers a drink before you die of thirst."

"I'll get them," said Joshua.

"No – I insist. What would you like?"

"Well, what I'd really like is a cup of tea, please."

It was just what Gregory could have done with, if he was to get any more work done that afternoon.

"A tea?" Stephen said, smiling. "What kind of drink is that?"

Chris laughed out loud.

"It's OK," Joshua said calmly. "Sharon knows how I take it."

18

ALTER EGOS

Josh had received grief from Nigel and Sue yesterday after their focus had been redirected to the dye shop implementation by Gregory and Stephen. Chris had stayed on in the pub with Stephen, but Josh had already reckoned to wait until today to start preparing the implementation, once they were all a little fresher. Except that they were still waiting for Chris to join them.

It had been an intense end to the previous week. Having finally had his work torn apart by Stephen on the Thursday, Josh and his team had worked late on Thursday and Friday to adapt the parts that Gregory and Stephen had selected for Mountfield's document. Josh had then released his team and finished the pages himself on the Saturday. Thankfully Josh had recharged on Sunday afternoon with a wonderful, blustery walk along the Malvern Hills with his dad. This had regenerated him to deal graciously with further buffeting from management weaknesses. And to deal with Chris, who he finally saw approaching through the team room door.

He went outside to intercept him and gently closed the door. "Hi Chris," Josh said. "Is everything OK?"

"I've felt better."

"We've been waiting over two hours for you."

"So? There's no need to make a big deal of it."

"I'm not. I know how hard you've been working recently, but you gave your word you would be here at eight so we could start the training. If there are circumstances that prevent you from keeping your word, let me know. Please respect those you are working with."

Chris nodded.

"Come on, let's make a start."

Chris followed him into the office and made straight for the coffee.

"Oh dear. You look rough," Nigel said.

"Thanks."

"Did you and Stephen go on a bender, then?"

Chris shrugged his shoulders nonchalantly. "I can't remember."

"OK. We're ready to start," Josh said. "So as we heard yesterday, we have now been asked to focus our help with implementing in the dye shop. And we're aiming to make the main changes on Monday."

"I still don't understand why you gave in," Nigel said. "When are we going to finish the feasibility study?"

Sue elbowed Nigel.

"I know," Josh said. "It's difficult. You will often have to start working with people in non-ideal situations. I'm sorry to say it may well get a lot messier before it gets any better. But it will get better, I promise you that."

"So have you thrown all that end-to-end stuff out of the window, then?" Chris asked. Some of the difficulty would inevitably deflect to him personally, partly because his own team had only seen a fraction of how he had been fighting for what he believed. They had set out and were already in the messy tension between today's reality and tomorrow's more.

"Listen," Josh said, "there might not be enough belief yet for an ideal, narrow-and-deep change programme. But we're not giving up on one. In the meantime, helping in the dye shop won't *conflict* with any of our beliefs. It is unlikely the dye shop will ever be split between value streams. The main reason we would ideally want to address an end-to-end value stream is to ensure that a consistent system can be designed, so that problems aren't just shifted on to other areas. I can at least guarantee that this dye-shop design will be consistent with any eventual end-to-end solution. We'll also make sure that we implement holistically, which means we'll also work on changes to process excellence, performance management and people to support the solution which essentially concerns flow. And we will also engage people as best we can through diagnose, design, implement and refine stages, even if these won't be distinct phases of a programme. Sue, I'd like you to lead the flow changes – the new production control sequence."

She looked at her other team members. "Me?" she said.

"Yes."

"I can't." She twisted her hair tightly around her fingers.

"What are you afraid of?"

She looked around as if every reason had suddenly deserted her. "I'll never be able to do what you do."

"That's not true, Sue," Josh said. "One day you'll be doing much more than this, I promise."

She tried to smile before her eyes fell.

"Chris, I'd like you to lead process excellence: stabilisation and improvement of OEE in this case."

"OEE *again*?" he said.

"No, OEE *still*, because analysis is fruitless until it is seen through to improvement."

Chris slumped onto the table.

"Nigel, I'd like you to lead performance management: how we surface and solve problems to support the rest. And we'll all be responsible for working with people in the right way to develop skills and to ensure sustainability. OK?"

Nigel nodded cautiously.

"So, Sue. How confident are you that our solution will deliver benefits for the dye shop?"

She shook her head. "The solution doesn't bother me. I just can't do things like standing up in front of a group, if that's what you expect."

"Yes you can. Trust me; we'll do it together. Do the rest of you share Sue's confidence in the solution?"

Nigel nodded strongly. Working through the solution had turned him from fierce cynic into fervent advocate.

"Chris?"

"Ready to go," he said.

"The next question is how confident do you think people in the dye shop are with the solution?"

Sue looked up. "I don't think we know, do we?" she said. "I meant to check but we just haven't had the time."

He nodded. "That's the point. Please be careful: it's easy to become so familiar with a problem that you overlook how the most significant stake-holders think and feel. Always remember: the art of good change-management requires the right mix of urgency and empathy."

Nigel leant back, holding his chin.

"We need to consider influence before we implement. I've already mentioned the importance of influencing skills a few times: they are the foundation of good change-management. They will help you to achieve good, sustainable solutions."

They seemed to be following, although Chris was struggling to stay awake. "To bring this to life, please picture yourselves at home, relaxing on your sofa. Not quite that much, Chris." Chris smiled and pulled himself up a little. "So are you all picturing yourself in your own living room? Good. Now, imagine your next-door neighbour walks in. Without acknowledging you, he starts to rearrange your furniture. Nigel, what would you do?"

"I'd tell him to get lost."

"That's exactly how I felt when they moved my sewing machine!" Sue said.

"I get the point," said Nigel. "But surely a team leader should have the right to change things around without asking? I can't stand pussyfooting around with this political correctness."

"So if we were to ask Trevor, how willing and able do you think he would be to implement our solution?" Josh asked.

"I'm sure he'd welcome it," suggested Sue. "He's a nice guy, and he has already said he would value help."

"Well, in one sense it's commendable to take his word for it," Josh replied. "If Trevor *is* willing and able to command change, do you think his team will automatically follow?"

"Not necessarily. But they should," Nigel said.

"Consider this then, Nigel. You told me you want to give up smoking. Why haven't you stopped already?"

"Oh, that's different," Nigel said, pushing himself up in his chair.

"Why?"

"It just is."

"If someone has been doing the same job the same way every day for ten years, might that not also become a habit? You can't always expect someone to do something differently overnight. Even if he changes when the spotlight is on him, his heart may remain in the old way and revert when the spotlight moves on. The point is that, believe it or not, we all tend to be human and individual. The better you become at respecting and influencing individuals, the better you will be at effecting sustainable change – and igniting a positive culture. This is an art. There may be occasions when you neither surface nor overcome someone's resistance. But what I'll do now is introduce you to a portfolio of influencing techniques that you can learn and practise. Let's call it the ABC of influencing techniques, for reasons that might become clear."

Chris' eyelids were still repeatedly dropping like the lid on his father's old bread bin.

"Chris, can you keep a track of them for us, please?" Josh asked. Chris grimaced, dragged himself to his feet and propped himself against the flip chart.

"Now, I've not seen Nigel's living room, but let's imagine it's completely disorganised."

"Crumbs, you have seen it!" Nigel said.

"Let's imagine it's full of trip hazards and there is an urgent, important need to change. I'll introduce nine influencing skills and we will see how we might apply each one to influence Nigel to change his room. So," he continued, "the first one is very simple: *Ask*. Nigel, can you tidy your room please?"

"No!"

"Thank you. It's worth including Ask because for minor changes anything else might be overkill. But, as Nigel has demonstrated, it's rare for any one technique to succeed in isolation: we normally need to blend them to address the thoughts and feelings of any particular person or group. Chris, can you write down *Ask* please? Thanks.

"The second technique is **Bargain**: If ... then ... This can work when something you have will be of use to the other person. For example, Chris could say, 'If you're willing to do it now, I can help so that you can finish in time to watch the racing.' Be careful, though, not to stray into the realm of manipulation by offering something inappropriate.

"The next skill is one we've already mentioned. Any guesses?"

"Coercion?" Nigel suggested.

"That's not quite what I was looking for," he said, "but it does start with the right letter. Very clever."

Sue was smiling again.

"**Command**. This one is Nigel's favourite: when someone has a right to instruct somebody through the chain of command. To work effectively, it depends on a healthy, appropriate relationship between boss and direct report. Does this one apply to Nigel's living room?"

"If Sylvie told me to sort it out, I'd have no choice."

"Within the context of a healthy relationship, I'm sure," Josh said. "The next one is D is for **Demonstrate**: to model or exhibit the change we want to see." He sighed quietly. "This can be particularly powerful for cultural change: modelling how to invest in people, respect individuals, surface and solve problems, embrace disagreement and so on."

"So make sure we're not hypocrites, basically," Nigel said.

"Yes, but it's more powerful than just that," Josh said. "Some might already *agree* with the desired solution or behaviour but it might remain theoretical until they can *see* it. By demonstrating a behaviour or solution we breathe life into it. We can help people to encounter something and *show* how things can be done differently."

"That sounds like what you've been doing," Sue said. "If only the other managers could behave a bit more like you."

Josh acknowledged her kind words. He had been doing all he could to *show* people a better way of operating, but outside the woodshed there was little evidence that it had been working. "It's up to all of us to be the change that we want to see."

"That's fine for you," Sue said. "But it's ridiculous to expect *me* to be a role model."

"Of course you can be a role model," he said. "It doesn't necessarily mean being without fault – because you can use each fault as another opportunity to model a positive culture. By apologising and learning from your own mistakes."

Nigel exhaled from his cheeks and shook his head.

"There's plenty to think about," Josh said. And he had indeed been thinking long and hard about it. "But there's more to demonstrating," he continued. "As well as *modelling* softer things like behaviour, we can also *exhibit* harder things like solutions. For example, we can do this by simulating a process and a potential solution with a table-top game. This can create a powerful, shared learning experience. So that's one of the things we'll do with the dye shop. But for now, how can we *demonstrate* Nigel's need to tidy his living room?"

"Take me to Sue's," Nigel suggested. "I bet her place is spotless."

"Ooh – I don't know about that," she said.

"I wouldn't be surprised," Josh said. "It might be enough to challenge Nigel's norms – in this fictitious case, of course.

"Right – let's keep going. The next one is equally important. Any guesses? Chris?"

"Energise?" Nigel said. "That's what *he* needs." Chris smirked, but he stood up a little straighter and withdrew his arm from the top of the flip chart.

"Explain?" Sue suggested.

"Yes! *Explain*. This should be a pre-requisite in nearly every case: explain why change is needed and how any proposed solution might meet the need. It alone might not be enough to convince someone – or to influence them to change. But you should never *expect* someone to change unless you can explain sound reasoning for them to do so. Nigel, your room needs to be tidied to remove the trip hazards. There will be other benefits too: you'll never miss the start of a race searching for the remote control. And you'll avoid the stress of blitzing the room every time someone visits."

Nigel nodded. "My sister-in-law."

"So Nigel might now be able to see some rationale in tidying his room," Josh said. "But that might not necessarily be enough to make him rush home to tidy it this evening."

Nigel hung his head.

"F is for *Friendship*," Josh continued. "This is different because it is a platform for influencing rather than a technique in itself. Some people default to this when they feel influencing would be more effective if they got to know someone first. This can be a good premise – but please be careful not to stray into manipulation by *hiding* an agenda. This platform of friendship can also be applied indirectly – by approaching someone via another who already has a platform of influence with them. For example, Chris – if you had never met Nigel but you knew Sue was a longstanding friend of his, you could ask Sue to consider approaching him on your behalf.

"The next technique is *Guiding*. This means guiding someone through the process of understanding the problem and developing their own solution – chiefly by asking the right questions. This *can* be the ultimate influencing technique because if someone develops their own solution, they tend to be more inclined to implement and sustain it. How might we apply this with Nigel and his living room?"

Sue turned towards her fellow change agent. "Nigel, what can we do to improve your room?"

"Get me a bigger TV."

"And that's a good example of some of the dangers with this technique. Don't open up the question too broadly, or you may end up with ideas that you can't deal with. But if you do surface minor suggestions, fix them if you can, even if they are unrelated to the problem you're trying to solve. Often, helping someone to make a small change can make a huge difference to their day-to-day experience. Another caution with *guiding*: please don't patronise or offend by asking heavily loaded questions. For example, don't say, 'Nigel, can you think of a way of removing objects from the floor?' Think through how to ask the right questions to lead someone through the problem-solving honestly and constructively."

"That sounds like how you led us to the dye shop solution last week," Nigel said. "Maybe everyone should go through that process."

"Ideally, yes!" Josh said. "That's effectively what we're doing when we lead people through diagnose and design initiatives – and yes, we still need to do this with people in the dye shop. Starting with Peter and Trevor."

Josh stood to the side and surveyed the flip chart. "OK, Chris, you've just about got room for the last two. The penultimate one is citing a *Higher Authority*: someone in authority who has mandated something. This may come as a direction from Gregory, for example. Or a legal requirement."

"Or Sylvie," said Nigel.

"Or Sylvie," Josh repeated. "And the last technique that we'll cover today is to *Inspire*. This means appealing to someone's values and showing the benefit of the proposed change in that light. For example, it works well with people who are ambitious or who take a lot of pride in their work. How might we try and use this to get Nigel to sort out his living room?"

"If you want to be a good husband, you would keep your room tidy," Sue suggested.

"Not bad. Nigel, would that work on you?"

"Maybe. What about, 'Sort it out now or she'll come down on you like a ton of bricks?' "

"Hmmm," he said. "That sounds a bit like a threat to me. This is another negative tactic which I don't condone. Negative influencing tactics can be very powerful in the short term but their legacy is to control and destroy rather than to liberate and create, which is what we need for an innovative culture. Besides, I hope I've shown you that there's no need for negative tactics when there are so many positive ones. What do you think?"

"Definitely," Sue said quickly. She then stopped nodding. "Perhaps."

"Well, as always, the best way of learning is by doing. Have the courage to practise. Don't forget that influencing is an art rather than a science. Consider the techniques as colours – to select and blend for effective use. For example: 'Nigel, Sylvie is concerned about the trip hazards. Do you think you could do something about this, please? A tidier room should also prove more relaxing for you both.' "

"I don't think I could ever be that direct," Sue said. "What if you offend him by holding him responsible? It's like you're blaming him."

"If it's Nigel's room then he *is* responsible," said Josh. "Just avoid unnecessary offence by looking to the future instead of dwelling on the present or the past. *What* you communicate – verbally and non-verbally – will flow from your intention. If you approach someone critically, it's more likely they will feel judged. If you approach someone respectfully, desiring improvement, it's more likely they will cooperate."

"A few people here need to hear that," Nigel said. "All they do is criticise."

"Well, then, let's model the culture we want to see. Today's Tuesday. To start implementation next Monday, we'll need to arrange a workshop on Thursday for the dye shop stakeholders. That just leaves us about a day and a half to influence Peter and Trevor and to prepare for the workshop together. It's going to blend commanding, explaining, demonstrating, friendship and guiding."

"Crumbs!" Nigel exclaimed. "How long is *that* going to take?"

"About three hours," Josh replied. "Trevor should open and lead the meeting, to apply his authority. I hope he'll start by thanking people for doing their best with the current situation and then go on to explain the need to improve. Then we'll play a game to model the solution and build relationships. We can then follow this by sharing our analysis and propose how the new system will work. Finally we'll ask the operators to shape certain details of the solution. For example, by determining how a pull system can work for covers from Sewing."

"What kind of game?" Chris asked.

"I don't know yet – we need to invent one. It's always best to design a game that's tailored to the specific situation."

"When you say *we*, you mean you and Trevor, right?" Sue asked.

"No, Trevor will lead the session overall. But you and I will develop and run the game together."

19

BAPTISM OF FIRE

"I'M not comin' in 'ere to play f**kin' games!" Trish, the dye shop operator had just exploded into the room.

Sue dissolved. She was living her worst nightmare. The villain had tattoos up her neck, a ring through her nose and spite in her eyes. Barry leant back on his chair and whispered to his neighbour. Smirks crawled across their faces.

"We're up to our ears in f**kin' covers and you expect us to spend the whole morning playing f**kin' games?" Trish yelled.

Josh appealed to Peter and Trevor for either of them to apply their authority as line managers. Sue could not bear to watch any more.

"What the f**k do you lot know about dyeing anyway?"

Sue could not look up, but she still felt the full force of Trish's glare. She tried to sink lower but there was nowhere to hide. They needed a matador to tackle the raging bull.

"I'm serious!" Trish screamed. "I haven't got time to waste sitting on my backside. That may be what *you* lot do every day, but I've got the dye shop to run."

Josh stood up. *Did he have any idea what she was like?*

"Welcome, Trish," said Josh's voice. There was silence. Josh was still standing beside her. She had no idea what was happening. Finally there was a groan and a dull thump.

"Thank you," Josh said. When Sue dared to look, Trish was sitting on the floor, leaning against a filing cabinet. "The purpose of this meeting is to agree a better way of running the dye shop: to reduce stress and to meet our customer commitments. That's why we need everyone's contributions. Don't worry about production for the next three hours. Trevor and I were in early to get everything started, and you may have recognised some old friends who we've drafted in for cover."

Nigel walked to the back of the room and closed the door.

"Thank you," Josh said. "Let me now hand over to Trevor to introduce things properly."

Trevor dragged himself to his feet and leant against the wall. "Yes, I know none of this is ideal. I did try and tell them." His audience comprised several other operators in addition to Trish, a planner, Barry and one of his maintenance technicians. Peter sat at the side, with his head bent over his personal organiser. "But basically it was made clear that changes were going to happen whether we liked it or not. I insisted that we at least had a say. So here we are."

Sue was astounded: this was the man who had told her he was open to help. Nigel was seething. She put a hand on his shoulder just in case. Trevor left out most of the salient points she had spent ages explaining to him. He completely lied that *Breakthrough* had asked the dye shop to go first because they only needed minor tweaks – beyond the extra equipment and staff. Josh secured Peter's attention and urged him to intervene. Nigel and Chris took it upon themselves to correct some of the numbers, but it was pointless. By the time Trevor sat down, their fledgling transformation was dead in the water.

When Josh stood up she half expected him to call everything off. Instead, he introduced the game.

Before Josh had used a slide, everyone was on their feet. He split the audience into two teams. Trish barely whimpered but her body language was smouldering. Hopefully things would blow up way before Sue's part. The two teams were told they would compete as separate dyeing businesses, over three rounds of six minutes, each representing one quarter of the year. Before each round they would be allowed to make changes. At least people were looking more awake.

When they were ready to start the first round, sluggishness had given way to banter. This gave way to light-hearted arguments. Everyone was trying to sort and process cards that had been pre-printed with order information, placing them in and out of small boxes that represented dye machines. People even embraced her idea of using small pop-up toys next to each box to represent wash times between colours. A bead of sweat rolled down her spine: they might get as far as her part after all.

After the first round she busied herself plotting each team's results against the targets they had set for themselves: for EBITDA, inventory and OTIF. Josh then gave some hints about dedicating machines to colours. In the second round, most of the arguments had given way to encouragements. It was getting closer. She collected the scores and Josh discussed with them what had worked well. He offered them the chance to buy one or two additional, smaller dye machines with a smaller minimum batch size of two units but a longer cycle time. During the third round, everyone was so focused it was nearly silent. She escaped to the bathroom and returned as the banter resumed. She helped Nigel collect the final scores, shaking out the back of her shirt every now and then.

"YES! Come on!" Trish pumped the air. Her team, which had named themselves the *Dye-hards*, set about taunting the opposition. "L-o-o-o-sers!"

"Thanks for clarifying that for us, Trish," said Josh. "Well done, *Dye-hards*." He waited for the cheers and accusations to die down. It was nearly time: there were cramps in the pit of her stomach. "But well done to *Fabrik* too. If we look back to the first round, both teams set ambitious targets. And both teams exceeded them. So well done everyone. Thank you for entering into the spirit of the exercise. Let's now take some time to reflect on what we can learn. For that, I'll hand over to Sue."

Josh walked away and everyone looked at her. For a few dreadful seconds all she could contemplate was fleeing the spotlight, just as she had fled the stage as a schoolgirl. Josh turned to face her from the back of the room. He nodded gently. *Keep smiling*, he had said. *Just ask simple questions*.

She swallowed. "So, what did you make of it?" were the words that came out. Several people looked away. Josh appeared unconcerned. *Keep smiling*.

Don't be afraid to wait.

One of the operators started speaking. She was so relieved she forgot to listen.

"I'm so sorry," she said. "Can you repeat that please?" Mercifully he did. She took care to scribble his actual words on the flip chart. *Worked hard at start. But chaotic – like the dye shop. Never expected improvement.*

"How could you try to improve that chaos?" she asked.

"Join the *Dye-hards*!" Trish bellowed, before she was clipped round the ear. Sue wrote *Join the Dye-hards* on the flip chart. The disagreement that followed prompted her to add a question mark.

"No, he's right," Trish said. "It does seem chaotic at times, how we do things. But I can't see how we can apply any of this."

"We've always said we should get rid of covers as soon as we've dyed them," said another operator. "That's like clearing the clutter in round two."

Sue wrote down the comment. "How might this help to make better use of the machines?" she asked. *She was doing it.*

"Well, if we made more room I suppose we could try again to bring in the next load before the current one finishes," Trish said. "Again, like we did in round two. That'll help."

"Great," she said. *Trish might not be her enemy, after all!* She turned to write the comment when someone else started speaking. "Look, everyone knows the real issue," Trevor said. "We need more machines and they've been cancelled yet again. Fair enough if we had a fleet of Rolls Royces, but we've got a fleet of old wrecks!"

"Ah, but Rolls Royces aren't always best!" Sue said. "You effectively *chose* to buy bicycles for the second round."

Trevor feigned a look of amused confusion to Barry. Others laughed.

"No – you don't understand!" She could not look at Josh until Trevor knew what she had meant. Trish seemed to be listening but her arms were folded. "What I mean is that the biggest, most expensive machines aren't always the best. They can't deal with single orders of rare colours, which is what customers want. So for the dye shop, what about buying a couple of household washing machines like we used here, dedicated to rarer colours? They're the right size and a fraction of the price."

Trevor's eyes widened and he smiled at Barry. She had been forced into pulling the pin from their most explosive idea.

"Blood-y hell!" Barry said. "You want to run our dye shop with white goods?"

"No! Just two, for the rarer colours," she said. But she was already sinking. She looked at Josh.

"It's the appliance of science!" someone yelled.

"What are we supposed to do when it breaks down? Queue up at White Goods Mart?"

Peter looked up from his electronic organiser.

"Let me set some context here," Josh asserted. He walked to the front of the room and Sue got out of his way as quickly as she could. The sniggers died down. "Sue's suggested how part of the solution you applied in the exercise could be applied in practice," Josh said. "If the idea of using a household machine appears amusing, ask yourselves why. We intend to do what makes sense. Do we lack the capability to dye single covers? Yes. Does a household machine offer this capability? Yes. Would a top-end household machine be reliable? Yes. Can it deliver the quality and service we need? Let's remain objective and evaluate this. If there are valid reasons why any part of a solution won't work, we'll adjust it."

"Go on, then," Barry said loudly, from the back. "In all seriousness, you tell us what you want to do and we'll tell you why it won't work."

20

Leading Indicators

"There you go, boss." Trevor handed Peter a sheet of paper over the piles already on his desk.

"Thanks, Trev. Close the door, would you?" He wanted to keep the heat in and was beginning to sound like Joan. He had just relented on letting her keep the heating on all day at home.

"Shall I take copies for us, then?" Nigel asked. He and Josh had joined them to supposedly guide them through their first official cockpit chart review.

"It's empty!" Nigel said.

"What?" said Trevor.

"You were supposed to fill in logged problems and proposed solutions."

"There aren't any," Trevor said with a grin.

Peter wheeled his chair round to join them at the table, where he took a look at his own copy. "Let's see what this says then. Dye shop cockpit chart. Week 46. Not long till Christmas now, then."

"Don't tell me!" Trevor said. "I'm still paying off the summer holiday."

"Summer?" Peter joked. "Did we have one of those this year?"

"We certainly felt it in the dye shop," Trevor retorted. "Maybe we'll get some air conditioning units in our Christmas stocking this year."

"Not in this place, you won't," Peter said. He smiled at his visitors.

"Ready?" said Josh.

"Righty-ho."

"Would you like a copy of this?" Josh slid over a copy of the standard agenda they had discussed a while back.

"Oh. Very good," Peter said. "Let's see what we should be doing, eh, Trev? Review current performance. Five minutes. Right. Quality, cost and delivery. That reminds me – Stephen's adamant we need to get a cost graph on here."

"It's there," Nigel said.

"Is it?" Peter said.

"We agreed man hours vs. plan. That's the main cost factor within Trevor's control," Josh explained.

"Yes, I know about that. But Stephen also wants unit costs on there."

"That could encourage the wrong behaviour," Josh explained.

"Is *increasing costs* the right behaviour?"

"Unit costs are an accounting measure, Peter, as we've discussed before," Josh said. "Cash flow and EBITDA will both be damaged if people are encouraged to pull orders forward to make the unit cost numbers look better."

"We can talk about it all you want," said Peter, "but if Stephen wants unit costs, that's what's going on." He turned to his left. "Trev, make sure they're on here for next time, please."

Trevor nodded.

"Great. Let's start with quality, then. Three faults last week. What were they, Trev?"

Trevor read from a table on the right side of the sheet. "Two missing buttons, apparently. And one colour reject."

"And so?" Peter asked.

"So what?" Trevor said. "Neither is our fault – as I keep telling these guys. The faults are found at inspection. A button could have come off anywhere – if it was attached in the first place. And colour faults are normally down to raw material."

"Was it one of the standard covers from Bangladesh?" Peter asked.

"Probably," said Trevor.

"It was a streaky coral beige, sewed in house," Nigel said. "Someone tried to dye it immediately after midnight blue."

"How do you know?" Peter asked.

"Because I checked!"

"Is that right, Trev?"

"Very unlikely. But it's this lot who have messed around with the sequence. Ask *them*."

"As team leader *you're* responsible for what happens in the dye shop," Peter said. He glanced briefly at Josh before turning back to Trevor. "This lot have just been helping you to implement the changes you've agreed to, which also have the backing of your operators. So why do you still refuse to own them?"

"Because," Trevor replied, "I take responsibility seriously. As the manager of the dye shop I can only commit to changes when I see *proof* that they work."

"That kind of proof can only come *when* you make the stand, Trevor," Josh said. "You'll only see it working when you exercise your faith in it. If something stands up to analysis, then have the nerve to back it. Only then will you see it come to life."

"I *have* backed it!"

"Not until it has replaced your old way of running things," Peter said.

"How can it, when it's clear the changes aren't working? What about this colour problem, for example?"

Nigel leant against the edge of the table. "How can the new system have *caused* a colour problem?" he asked. "We've changed nothing about the value-adding parts of the process! If you've got a quality problem, you've either not followed the standard or the standard is wrong. Same as always. If it wasn't for us you wouldn't know about it. The reason we're doing any of this is to help you surface problems that you've always had so we can do something about them. But you've got to give a s**t!" Nigel diverted his eyes and finally looked like he was trying to calm himself down.

"Steady on, Nige. Let's not fall out about this," Peter said. "Trev, can you do your own investigation on that colour change?"

"Yes," said Trevor calmly. "But I'm not taking orders from a pre-upholsterer and someone who *used* to be a team leader. Even if his ideas worked over there, it doesn't mean they're going to work over here."

"So are you going to write down the action?" Peter said.

"I've said I'll do it," he said. "It's a *waste* to write something down just for the sake of it."

"OK, let's move on then. Where were we on this agenda?"

Sue was falling behind Trish as she strode across the car-park.

"So what's going on between you and Clarky, then?" Trish suddenly asked, with puffs of condensing breath.

"What do you mean?"

"Well, he goes out of his way to bump into us every time we walk through Pre-upholstery."

"Really?" She *had* seen him quite a bit. He seemed a nice guy but she had genuinely not read anything into it.

"It's not me, is it?" Trish said with a smile.

Sue's cheeks glowed and she was relieved to reach the dye shop. It would be their first proper audit of the new system and Trish was armed with her clipboard and a single sheet with twenty statements. Each referred to a change that had been implemented and could be answered either true or false on the basis of observations. They would score one point for each true answer, and the total score would indicate how well the design of the area was being followed. They had arranged to go through the first audit with Trevor to familiarise him with what he had signed off. Trish called his mobile from outside his empty office. "For f**k's sake!" she cried. "He's not answering. Let's just do it ourselves, shall we?"

Sue bit her lip. It would be a lot easier and more enjoyable, but Josh still insisted they did not short circuit Trevor as the local owner. That said, they were now wasting time searching for him, on top of all the time they had wasted in trying to influence him.

"Come on, I'm starting," Trish said.

Trish was the dye shop's unofficial leader anyway. Sue had feared the worst again when she started to come up with detailed objections to their original proposal – until she started to suggest ways around them. She had since mobilised the other operators. Thanks to Trish the dye shop looked completely different.

"All covers to be dyed clearly arranged in the correct row with the correct machine number," Trish read out loud. She marched up to one of the trolleys in the left lane. She checked the machine number painted on the trolley and the colour indicated on the order information. "Yes," she said. "Do we need to check them all?"

"Just two more," Sue advised. "It should say so."

Trish did so and ticked the sheet proudly.

"All finished covers waiting for collection are in green bins, in correctly marked rows." Trish looked up. "Yep," she announced as she made another tick.

"All empty beige bins waiting for return to Sewing in the correct lane. Yep."

"Correct number of deliveries made today." They looked at the small board on the wall by the door, where the first red disc had not yet been turned over. Sure enough, the far lanes were still full. Trish cursed and marked the first cross. They moved on to the machines. The andon lights now just rubbed salt into the wounds: they shone red on top of every machine that was not working.

"What's going on?" Sue asked.

"Machine eleven – it's probably just fluff on the drum's sensor," Trish replied. "It happens all the time."

"Is it a big job to put right?" she asked.

Trish laughed. "About as much as work as wiping the fluff from your belly button."

Ugh. "Can you do it yourself?"

"Used to, until they added this." A small padlock had been fixed to the access door. "Barry put these on after he was assigned as our lead technician. Supposedly to improve safety."

"Does it?"

Trish rolled her eyes. "When did Barry ever care about safety?"

"Can't Trevor get him to pull his finger out?"

"Trev will always stick up for Barry – he's part of his little gang."

"What about this one?" she asked.

"Machine ten – the steam injector failed about a week ago. It took two days for Barry to get underneath to check. It's their least favourite job – they have to lie on their backs in the pit. So don't expect it to be done any time soon. But what do I put on the sheet?" Trish asked Sue. "Barry claims he's still waiting for the part."

"It's a cross. Someone needs to be at the machine correcting the problem, or there must be a committed date on the board for when it will be done."

Sue set off towards the two boards beside Trevor's office, and Trish lagged behind ominously. The first board had a row for each machine and Trish had got everyone recording the total number of loads and losses, to monitor adherence to the two-day cycle.

"It's still a cross for the two-day cycle," Trish said.

"But you've got a tick for the board. It's serving its purpose, surfacing the problems."

"So what, if no one does anything about them?"

The board next to it was supposed to provide a focus for prioritising obstacles to the two-day cycle. They had made all the tweaks that Trevor had demanded but it was nearly empty.

"I wrote that," Trish said, pointing to the top line. "In our one and only daily meeting it emerged that everyone was using different pre-wash times. I was so hacked off I put Trevor's name up because he said he'd sort it."

"At least he's not rubbed it off."

"I wondered about that too!" Trish said, sniggering. "Then I realised I'd used a permanent marker – by mistake." Her smile disappeared. "We shouldn't be laughing about it."

"I know," Sue said. She brushed her hair from her face. "I don't know what to say. Except that I know Josh is still doing everything he can behind the scenes."

21

THE WALL OF FORTUNE

GREGORY placed a cup under the nozzle and pressed the *double* button. He could get away without offering one to anyone else. Stephen and Peter were deep in conversation. Chris was tapping away on his keyboard in the corner of the boardroom, which they had temporarily renamed the *Breakthrough* War Room. Judging by the empties that surrounded him, Chris had already been helping himself to enough cans from their fridge.

Only three weeks had passed since their presentation to Mountfield, but they were already a third of the way through their time to implement everything. Things were happening but Anna had not yet been able to show him any significant step changes beyond their normal cycles. He urgently needed improved transparency, insight and control. Stephen had proposed all three through a performance-management system to identify which of the *Breakthrough* improvements needed special attention. He had reprioritised Chris from the *Production Breakthrough* team to help get this implemented.

Gregory wandered over to the window and afforded himself a smile: sure enough, the fisherman sat on his bank as usual, wearing his orange beanie. They were about halfway through that morning's reviews. He and Peter flanked Stephen along one side of a single desk, facing each *Breakthrough* Champion as they walked in. Some may have felt like they were being interrogated, but it was no bad thing if it ratcheted up the pressure. His clearest instructions and full support had yet to kick some people into action.

There was a knock on the door.

"Come in, come in!" Stephen said.

Gregory turned and straightened his back. It was Joshua.

"Please, take a seat," said Stephen.

Gregory sat down too.

"Thanks for coming," Stephen began. "The purpose of this meeting is to tell you how we've restructured the *Breakthrough* programme. So let's—"

"Just to clarify," Gregory interrupted, to assert himself. "This is Stephen's meeting so I'll let him lead. I'm here to emphasise how vital it is that everyone cooperates and gives this initiative their all. OK?"

"Right," Stephen said, without giving Joshua a chance to respond. "We've only got half an hour for each Champion so let's get straight down to business. This," Stephen said, pointing to the nearside wall, "is our *Breakthrough Wall of Fortune*." It had been covered neatly with a series of A3 landscape pages.

"In the top row," continued Stephen, "you'll see a single *brick* with our *Breakthrough EBITDA Profile*. In the row below it you'll see two bricks – one for Operations with the planned cost profile and one for Sales with the planned revenue profile. We've broken these down into required performance profiles for each area of the business. In the very bottom row is a brick for each special project. In the row above is a brick for each process. On the left is the plot for cost savings in Cutting. The one next to it is for Sewing and so on. Every brick plots actual versus target. All the targets feed upwards to give us the EBITDA figure we need. So with each brick we are *building* the results we need." Stephen paused. "Are you following?" he asked.

Joshua sat up straight and breathed in deeply.

"The final step was to assign an individual Champion per brick. As you would say, each manager or team leader must be responsible for implementing in their own area. So Trevor is the Dye-shop Champion, Simon is the Project *Masterplan* Champion and so on. You're the odd one out because – as you know – your role is not exactly to implement but to facilitate improvements everywhere in Production. Your main contribution is in detailing the ideas. So people can only implement as fast as you move from one area to another. Therefore your brick looks like an implementation schedule, rather than a target profile."

Joshua shook his head.

"I've got an extra copy here that we can go through," Stephen said. "We've made a few tweaks." He placed it on the table and oriented it towards Joshua.

Joshua got up and walked towards the wall where he peered at one of the sheets. "According to this," he said, "the dye shop implementation is on track."

"Er, yes," Stephen replied. "Trevor's already been in. A £52k improvement if I remember correctly. Versus the £50k target."

Joshua tore the page from the wall and scrunched it up. Then he hurled it into the bin. "That's toxic," he said.

Gregory hoped Stephen would stand up to the test but it was Peter who spoke first. "Josh, you're getting out of order, buddy."

Joshua's face flushed red. "NO!" he shouted. He stabbed his finger towards Peter. "It's you lot that are out of order! You still pressurise people to report what you want to hear and you're so far removed from what's going on you can't see the lies."

Gregory stood up to exert his authority.

"Dad created an organisation where everyone mattered," Joshua continued. "The only things that seem to matter to you are numbers!" With one arm Joshua pointed to the boardroom door. "Get out into the factory!" With his other arm he dragged away the desk that separated them from the exit. The force of the movement rocked the table onto two legs. It crashed to the floor, taking papers and cups with it. Peter leapt to his feet. Stephen looked dumbfounded, as if this was the first insubordination he had ever encountered.

Joshua looked unashamed. "Get out and talk to people," he shouted, "if you really want to know what's going on. Help them to find better ways of working. Work together as a single team!"

If the others failed to act soon, Gregory would have to deal with the situation himself. Veins throbbed in Joshua's forehead and neck. Then he shook his head and walked out before Gregory had a chance to say anything.

Josh's heart rate was slowing down. No wonder they were in such a mess if Gregory, Stephen and Peter were so blind to what was really going on. Through his team room door he could see the large frame of someone on the other side. He squeezed through to find Trish slumped in a chair. Her face was blotchy and her eyes were glistening. Sue was crouched beside her with a box of tissues. Nigel walked towards them with two cups of coffee. When he saw Josh he rolled his eyes.

"What's happened?" Josh asked as he crouched beside Trish.

"Do you want to tell him or shall I?" Sue said.

Trish cleared her nose. "You found me like this once before," she blurted. "Remember?"

Josh smiled gently. She still remembered when he had found her abandoned by bullies behind their school gym.

"What happened this time?"

She started smouldering and her lips quivered. "They've gone and wrecked our new machine."

22

THE EMERGENCY EXIT

GREGORY stared through the pane. A series of street lights raced past, illuminating nothing in particular. He was in no rush for the sun to rise: this could be the day that it finally set on Gregory Todd Ltd.

Several weeks ago the hope had seemed genuine. After October 23rd he had dared to believe that they were on the road to recovery. Now they had hit another wall. He had shouted from the rooftops to mobilise everyone. They had pulled out all the stops with November's figures. Neither had been enough.

Mountfield had summoned him to London. Gregory's biggest fear was that he was now running out of fight. A small part of him was desperate for it to be over.

He thumbed through his defence again. He would concede that they had not turned the corner – yet. But he would show how the changes were working. He would demand more time – for Mountfield's sake as well as his own.

Gregory became aware of a commotion. It was bright. The carriage was full of passengers who were queuing to alight from the train. He quickly wiped his mouth and lapel. He picked up the sensitive document splayed at his feet and hurriedly packed away his reading glasses.

He was at Paddington Station, towards the back of the herd which sluggishly moved underground. His weary legs would be deprived of a seat for a while.

He emerged at Mansion House harassed and with almost an hour to spare. London always made him feel small – especially within the City. He walked up Cannon Street and retreated into a coffee shop, which offered a comforting view of the grand dome of St Paul's. His favourite cathedral had maintained its dignity for years despite intimidation from the surrounding towers. Armed with a large espresso, Gregory took out his notes and his glasses for a final time.

Mountfield's office was in a dark, narrow street. It was marked by a brass plaque set into a grey, granite pilaster. Its hidden innards had been extensively remodelled in steel, oak and glass.

Doug Mountfield sat behind the largest of the glass walls, with phone to ear. His heavy body periodically tilted backwards, roaring with laughter. Gregory leant forward when a phone conversation ended – and back as another began. There was no indication which Mountfield he would face. Once or twice he thought he caught Mountfield's eye, but he might have been looking straight through him.

The sofa he was sitting on was a disgrace. It represented everything he hated about the state of his industry. Someone in Mountfield's company had probably thrown away the best part of a hundred grand on sofas without even sitting on one. They were shoddy artwork, no doubt chosen from a catalogue, based on the glossy leather and polished chrome. They felt cheap and embarrassing. He was sitting on a few pounds' worth of foam and bands, without any back support, and it would have been far too deep for anyone with shorter legs. The whole market had dumbed down. *Anyone* would notice the gulf in class if he could just get them to try his better products that had been properly designed and built. Sadly, the problem of persuading domestic customers to pay for the difference would inevitably remain. If he could swallow his pride he should probably jump on the bandwagon and push poorly designed artwork with high margins to ignorant buyers in the corporate sector. It wasn't a bad idea for a business if he did ever have to start over. Except he would never put his own name to something unless it was fit for purpose.

Another conversation ended and Mountfield redialled. A phone suddenly rang beside him.

"Mr. Mountfield is ready for you, Mr Todd," said the demure, suited secretary who seemed to smile sympathetically.

"Thank you." Gregory returned the papers to his bag and stood up straight. He breathed in and filled his lapels. *He* was ready for Mountfield.

"Gregory! Welcome, welcome." Mountfield leant forward in his chair and reached out a hand.

"Please, sit down. Journey OK?"

"Fine. Thanks. How's everything with you?"

Mountfield paused. "Well, Gregory, I didn't bring you all the way down here to bulls**t you. Things aren't great, are they?"

Hairs bristled on the back of his neck. "Not amazing, Doug, but things are starting to look up." *Non-defensive and confident.* "Pre-Christmas has been a little slow, but I can show that's the case everywhere. I've got *leading indicators* that show all our improvements are working. We're well positioned for the New Year, Doug."

Mountfield stood up and walked towards his bookcase, shaking his head. "You're not listening, Gregory." He turned to face him again. "The reason I brought you here is to talk about our exit."

Mountfield's eyes disappeared under folds of skin, like those of a rhino. Gregory's arguments had dried up in his throat. When he next looked, Mountfield's eyes were possessed by an unlikely glint. "You," Mountfield began, pointing his large finger at Gregory, "are a lucky bas**rd."

His stomach curdled. His chair turned involuntarily as he watched Mountfield stroll past.

"I was still cursing myself for the cardinal sin of going into business with a chum," Mountfield continued. "Then along came an even bigger mug than me." He stopped by his bookcase and turned. "I had a call, out of the blue. He's independently wealthy, loves our products. He wants to *buy* our company, Gregory! I tested him and he's keen. The offer should be in the region of seven mill."

"Seven million?"

"Yes. Unbelievable!"

"That doesn't even cover what we put in!"

"Gregory, listen. Winning sometimes means buying before the peak. Sometimes it means selling before the bottom. Trust me – this is our lifeline to sell before the bottom. He wants the *factory* – you'll not get anywhere near that just for the brand."

"Aren't you listening to anything I am saying?"

"Of course – you have every right to be heard. But don't think for one minute that anything you say is going to change my decision. The drag-along clause will take care of the rest."

Gregory clenched his fists and pursed his lips. He was seconds from driving Mountfield against his bookcase and storming out. He might have done so had he not envisaged having to return cap in hand.

"Do you realise Linda and I would lose everything?" He could not keep up payments on their home, let alone pay it off. His car would have to go, not to mention his job. His foundation would be swept away, and he was too old and shattered to rebuild.

"Not *everything*, Gregory. Don't get all melodramatic. Think of the experience you've gained. Consider it a success! You can preserve your reputation. That's no mean feat for your first buyout. Use this as a springboard!"

Mountfield the hypocrite would do OK through his preference shares, even though this was just play money to him. Gregory had been far too focused on the upside to have thought through this scenario. His business was being ripped from him and it was hard to say how much of Gregory Todd would be left.

But no leader worth his salt would loosen his grip while hope remained. "I thought you were better than this, Doug," Gregory said. "Are you really going to pull the plug just before you reap the rewards? I thought you had more nerve than that."

"You would prefer to liquidate?"

"I intend to deliver our plan. That's what makes sense. One last chance. I know we can do it. Not for my sake – for yours."

Gregory wracked his brain to improve the argument.

Mountfield filled the silence. "The company will keep going. When it does hit bottom – which it will – you can be long gone. You'll actually look like the hero for having kept the factory going for so long."

If this was Mountfield's way of admitting that no one could have done a better job, the timing was ironic. He closed his eyes and breathed purpose-fully. The main mercy in stepping off the sinking ship was that he would finally be free of Mountfield.

"So who is the offer from?"

"I need your full focus on keeping the business going as normal, or the deal is off. There's just one section I need your help with."

"What's that?"

"Look, the offer is from a self-made man who likes to do things his own way. Hear him out: his stipulation is that we get rid of those responsible for the failings before the deal can go through. They need to be named in the agreement."

"What? That's ridiculous."

"Maybe, but he's the customer, so we have to try and see where he's com-ing from. He wants a going concern, so he probably wants to leverage our inside knowledge to strip out the dead wood before he starts. Or maybe he thinks that demanding a bit of blood will shake the business up a bit."

"Nothing's that black and white!" Gregory said. "Surely he knows that, if he's thinking of running a company?" He would never have thought it but there might be people out there who were more clueless than Mountfield about running a proper business.

"That's not necessarily a concern for us, is it?"

"So is he expecting us to get rid of everyone? No one's perfect."

"Don't be silly, Gregory. His stipulation essentially leaves it up to us. The clearest option is obviously to put your name down. No one would be able to question that. All that means is that technically I would have to fire you pretty quickly. In practice nothing will really change."

"Fire me? What for?"

"What for?!" Mountfield slapped his hand on his forehead. "Come on Gregory, do yourself a favour. Bl**dy hell, I should have fired you ages ago."

"No one fires someone, Doug, unless they know they can find better. But if I can't save this business, no one can – you've just said as much yourself!"

"It doesn't matter. Look, nothing will change. You'll still be looking for your next challenge, and no one else will see the agreement anyway. It can look like you've respectfully stepped down for the new buyer."

"Haven't you considered we were just trying to do the impossible?"

"If so, whose fault is that? It was your plan."

"*Our* plan."

"Which the chief executive officer is responsible for delivering. I can't believe we're having this conversation, Gregory. Listen to me." Mountfield placed a hand on his shoulder.

Blood rushed into Gregory's head. He sprang to his feet. "No, Doug. You listen to me, for once in your life!" He was inches away from his tormentor's face and was past caring as some of his spit landed on his shoulder. "You have no idea what it's like to put your heart and soul into running a proper business." Gregory jabbed his index finger. "If you even *try* to fire me I will fight you tooth and nail with everything I have. I promise! I don't care what it costs."

For a moment Mountfield looked rocked. Gregory's chest rose and fell. His lips remained pursed. It was true – he had finally been pushed beyond caring.

Gregory took the slightest of steps backwards and Mountfield sprouted a grin. "Well, well. Gregory, Gregory. It's good to see you still have some of that fight in you. Don't forget, though, you and I are partners." His grin grew. "We're on the same side," he said softly. He dared to replace his hand on Gregory's shoulder. "Look, if this technicality is as important to you as it seems, let's talk about it – while facing the facts. The company has been failing – no debate. If you don't want to be held responsible, make it someone else. Personally, I couldn't give a s**t who goes. And the buyer won't have a clue. Make it anyone you like with an ounce of responsibility – just make a solid case for how they've been dragging the company down."

Mountfield thought again. "Maybe this isn't such a good idea, after all." He grimaced and tossed his head from one side to the other. "If we don't name you, it shouldn't be anyone you fire personally this close to the deal or it would look too suspicious. If you find someone, feel free to make the case but get someone else to get rid of them. We can't afford a tribunal or anything that might hold up the deal. So keep everything in the open: it would need public backing from the moral majority. Ok, so two conditions. One: clear case. Two: public exit. Satisfy me on both these counts and get them out by Christmas. Otherwise your name is going down."

Gregory bit his lip. Light flickered from the end of a tunnel. It led to the same ruined landscape but now this could only be reached by crawling through filth. He was already in it up to his neck, and he was sinking. However unthinkable, it seemed his only option. If he created any further disturbance, Mountfield would have no qualms about collapsing the tunnel and burying him there and then.

Peter was at his computer when Trevor stepped into his office.

"Alright Trev, mate? Take a seat. I'll be with you in a second."

Trevor leant back on his chair and stretched. He squeezed out a yawn. "Cor, dear." He combed the hair on either side of his head with his fingers. "No Josh today?"

Peter addressed his computer screen, "No. They've moved on again, to Frame Assembly. Nigel's helping Milky put his cockpit chart together."

"They're like seagulls, that lot. They come in, crap on you and fly off!"

Peter snorted a quick laugh while glancing down at his keyboard. "Come on, why won't you do this?" he mumbled to his computer.

"Bet you're pleased then – with Milky's meeting to add to all the others," Trevor continued. "Still, it looks like we got off lightly in the dye shop. Is it true they tried to rip out half the tables in Cutting?"

"Right, that will do for now," Peter said. "I'm all yours." He picked up the sheet from his printer and joined Trevor at the round table.

"Dye shop. Week 50," Peter read out loud. "Presume you're going to the shindig this weekend?"

"Rude not to."

Gregory had stunned everyone by resurrecting the works Christmas Party. One of his first savings as CEO had been to axe the annual party in favour of the staff serving hot turkey rolls to workers on the last working day before Christmas. Apparently this low-budget event was still happening. The official reason to bring back the weekend party was to celebrate everyone's efforts and achievements with *Breakthrough*. Rumours were circulating that a different kind of announcement would be made.

"If we've turned the corner, I'll be the first to celebrate," Peter added.

"You really believe that?"

"I want to."

"If we *have* turned a corner, it's only because we're going round in circles."

"Very funny," Peter said.

"Some say the whole management team is going to step down before they're sacked."

"Don't be stupid. Why would they organise a party for that?"

"So the rest of us can celebrate?"

"Come on, let's do some work. Have the graphs been updated?"

Trevor staged a curious look at Peter's sheet before looking at his own. "Nigel's not done it."

"It's nothing to do with Nigel!" Peter exclaimed. "He showed you how to get the data weeks ago!"

"I never needed him to *show* me how to do it. I just need someone to do the donkey work. I had more than enough paperwork *before* they came on the scene – and they've just created another whole layer of bureaucracy."

"What about all the reports this has replaced! Anyway, this isn't about reporting – it's management, Trev. Like Nigel said, 'How can you steer your ship if you don't know where you are or where you need to be?' "

"I don't know why you're getting management advice from a pre-upholsterer. He's never managed anything in his life! He hasn't got a clue what it's like in the dye shop, particularly towards year end."

"So how *are* things going?"

"Nightmare!" Trevor exclaimed. "As always."

"How's the system coping?"

"What system? It started falling apart the moment we got busy. Just like the washing machine."

"It's no laughing matter, Trev. We've charged Barry with gross misconduct."

"Gross misconduct? Why?"

"Wilful damage to company property."

"The door came off in his hands! He can't help it if it's not fit for purpose."

"Barry paraded the door around the maintenance department like a trophy. It wasn't the brightest thing he's ever done."

"You've got to allow people a bit of fun."

"Maybe," Peter said. "Anyway, it's now being dealt with through the appropriate channels. We should be talking about your new system. Aren't you following it any longer?"

"Nope. If I'd have tried, I would have got nowhere near the unit cost targets."

Peter raised his eyebrows "What about the machine dedications?"

"They never worked."

Peter felt hopeless. "So what are you doing, then?"

Trevor bounced back on his chair. "Just as we did before Josh and his merry men came on the scene." A grin spread across his face and he tapped his temple with his finger. "Using this."

23

PARTY POLITICS

GREGORY ushered Linda in from the cold, to the stiff sobriety of the party's early stages. Heads turned as they joined the queue. It shuffled along the sticky carpet towards the college bar.

Jane had done a great job, given the budget and the short notice. Three lines of tables had been squeezed into the main floor area, between the bar at one end and a small stage at the other. Balloons and table directions provided finishing touches. Barry was the cheap DJ, hiding behind a set of primary-coloured lights next to the stage.

Gregory was struck by Linda's fragrance as he lifted off her fur coat. She had always been against him dropping the Christmas Party. Its reinstatement now gave a strong signal to her and others that they had turned the corner. In some ways he would still insist this was true, but the party had an extra significance. This would be his secret leaving do.

At least there was clarity, now the path had been set for him. He had no idea what life beyond the company would look like, but there would be plenty of time to worry about that. He was still trying to straighten out the final details. Mountfield's voice saying *clear case* and *public exit* repeated over and over in his mind. The necessity of choosing between bad outcomes was a fact of leadership, but he was not used to working through something completely alone like this. Others had the right to hold Gregory responsible for everything, even if he wasn't to blame. If it had been as simple as that he would have put his hand up there and then, but there was no way he was going to give Mountfield the satisfaction of firing him. Therefore, he was ironically being forced to hold at least one of his broader management team to account.

He had got used to making people redundant, but his reticence to fire people for poor performance might have been his Achilles heel. Maybe his weakness was that he had been a little too nice. If he had been a bit more like Mountfield earlier on it might not have come to this. Even Arthur had warned him not to ignore poor performance, but Arthur had also been just as sure as he had been that he could help people to improve.

"He's been like that for months," Linda commented.

"Sorry, what was that?" Gregory said. Linda was talking with Eddie's wife Helen, who had found her in the queue.

"You were doing it again," Linda said. "He gets totally consumed," she explained to Helen and they laughed at his expense. "He's always been like that when watching the rugby or reading the paper, but I've never known him zone out so much in social situations."

"Eddie can get like that too," Helen commented.

If only Eddie could have consumed himself with finding new customers.

"Don't tell me you were still thinking about work?" Linda said. "It's the Christmas party, for goodness sake!"

"It's been a busy few months," Gregory conceded.

"Yes, Eddie told me you're getting involved in much more of the detail," Helen said.

"Only *some* details he's good at!" said Linda. "It's a good job he's only got one present to buy, I can tell you."

He tried to smile. Christmas had barely registered with him but it had been a merciful distraction for Linda. Another mercy was that Eddie was off the hook, given Mountfield's insistence that he could not fire anyone personally. Eddie's case would have been hard to ignore, albeit one he and Linda would have come to blows about. He could have made an equal case for Stephen, but the rest of the senior management team were off the hook for the same reason. Instead, Stephen had become his most likely ally to help him get rid of someone. Simon was a candidate: there was a clear case that Planning had cost them the Aspiration account. The problem was that Stephen would argue that Simon was now critical in delivering the solution.

"See you later, Helen," Linda said.

"Yes, lovely to see you again, Linda." Helen's smile towards Gregory seemed pointed.

"Good to see you, Helen," Gregory said. "Enjoy the party."

As Helen turned away, another woman entered the frame. "Linda, hi." It was Peter's wife. "It's been a long time," she said.

"Hi," said Linda. "Joan, isn't it?"

"You've got a good memory!" Joan said.

"How could I forget?" said Linda. "How have you been?"

Gregory exchanged nods with Peter, who had emerged at Joan's side. Inevitably, Gregory felt obliged to make the conversation. "So, are you still tearing up the skittle alleys then, Peter?"

"Oh, I don't know about that," Peter replied.

Peter was in the frame but Gregory had no answer to *why now*? He had done nothing significantly different for years.

"Ladies and Gentlemen," came a timid, amplified interruption. "As soon as you've got your drinks please make your way to the tables to create some space. And don't forget your thirsty DJ! Thank you."

Gregory took Peter slightly to one side. "How come *he's* here?" he said quietly. "I thought we had him for gross misconduct."

"We did," Peter said. "Or rather, we do. He appealed, so we just need to be careful. It should be done and dusted by the end of the week."

"So you asked him to DJ tonight as his swansong?"

Peter wore a pained expression. "It's not that simple. Jane wanted to use our speakers to keep costs down. Barry offered the extra kit, and technically he's still employed, so we didn't feel we could prejudice anything."

"Let's hope it *doesn't*," Gregory said. Barry was down as his backup. It was the easiest option for a public exit: a team leader already on his way out for sabotage and gross misconduct. It's just that the case for him bringing down the company would look pretty flimsy if Mountfield discovered that Barry's offence was breaking the door of a single machine.

"Right then, what can I get you to drink?" Gregory asked Joan and Peter. It took an eternity to be served but it was refreshing to look along a bar filled with his employees, from all walks of life.

At the end of the bar, Joshua Eden peeled away, holding three pint glasses that he nestled together. This was the man at the top of his list. Certainly, there was no one he would rather get rid of. He had still not figured him out. There was enough value in what he said that made it hard to dismiss or even dislike him, but it was equally hard to trust him. He was an agitator who showed little deference and had directly challenged his authority on a number of occasions. He also had an obvious motive for trying to bring the whole company down. But was that enough? Gregory could not afford to look paranoid, plus what if the accusation were to provide Joshua with the spark he had been waiting for? Joshua was capable of stirring unrest that could bring the deal down in flames.

Gregory tried to shake his mind out of the rut again. It must not rob him of his big night. He looked again at the honest, hard-working people along the bar. It had always been a privilege to serve as the head of this unlikely family. He had become part of it, and it had clearly become part of him. He would savour this evening, without dwelling on how much he would miss all that it represented.

His moment had come. The atmosphere had thawed during dinner and coffee was providing essential stimulation.

"Thank you. Thank you!" Gregory dropped the microphone to his side. "Attention, please! Thank you. So, welcome to the Gregory Todd Christmas party! It is my pleasure and joy to celebrate everyone's hard work with the reinstatement of this party. It was nearly three months ago when we last got together to launch the *Breakthrough* programme. Can you believe it? Later in October our plans were approved enthusiastically by our chairman, Doug Mountfield. Since then you have all been working flat out to implement, and data confirms that we are indeed starting to see the significant *Breakthrough* we were seeking. So thank you all. I know how hard many of you have been working, so consider this evening as my way of saying thank you. But please don't give up – there's plenty to do even though we have safeguarded our future. It has always been a privilege to lead this organisation, and whatever the future looks like, I'm proud of what we have accomplished. I mean it. Please, give yourselves a round of applause." Gregory tucked the microphone under his arm so that he could clap loudly.

Gregory widened his eyes and glanced to the ceiling. "I won't keep you for much longer. I'm sure you want to get on with the dancing. And maybe a bit of karaoke, eh, for old times' sake?"

There were cries of "Bazza! Bazza!" accompanied by the banging of tables.

Gregory smiled and waited. "There's just one formality left. Just like the old days, it seems fitting to use this party to announce this year's employee of the year. The award has kept going and, as always, the senior management team has not had a say. It's your vote, designed to single out someone who embodies our values: an unsung hero, perhaps, worthy of special praise. So Jane, can you come up here please?"

Jane mounted the stage as discreetly as possible. Gregory welcomed her with a kiss on the cheek. "If I did have a vote, this lady would probably get mine. She's a complete star, isn't she? Jane, I'd like to say a special thank you for organising tonight and of course for all of your support over so many years. Can we show Jane some appreciation please?"

Her cheeks flushed at the sound of further applause. He took the large envelope from her and she left the stage.

"So, I'm pleased to announce that Gregory Todd's employee of the year is…" He pulled out a smaller envelope and held it at arm's length to read. This was a disaster. There was no way out. He looked up and stretched his mouth into a smile. "… Joshua. Joshua Eden."

Maybe this was a sign that Joshua needed to be dealt with. The commotion started at the back of the hall. Joshua was pushed to his feet by members of his change team.

"Joshua, you had better come up here then please," he said.

Joshua could have thought to take the easy route out of the back door and back into the hall again at the front, but he didn't. Instead he stayed where he was, forcing people to stand up and tuck in their chairs to let him pass. The applause grew and the ripple of people standing spread all the way to the front of the hall. People stopped clapping only to pat Joshua as he walked past. Many said something to make him smile. The journey was painfully slow.

Gregory held his smile and tried to clock where Joshua's biggest support was coming from. When Joshua reached the front, Peter and Trevor were the last to pat him and pushed him towards the stage. There was a powerful whistle from Big Dave at the side.

"Come on then, Joshua. Join me up here if you would."

He leapt onto the stage.

"Congratulations," Gregory said and handed him the envelope.

"Thank you."

"Speech!" came a cry from the back.

He would ignore it.

"Speech!"

"Come on, there's no need to embarrass him."

"Speech!"

Gregory turned to look at the man of the moment. "You really don't have to say anything, Joshua, if you don't want to."

Joshua smiled and reached for the microphone. Gregory held on to it and tipped it towards Joshua's mouth.

"Thank you, everyone," Joshua said. "Thank you for supporting our transformation. Please keep going. Keep respecting each other, and keep loving each other. That means putting collective success above the success of individual departments or careers. Wait and see what we can achieve when we finally become one team!" After a few moments, muttering spread.

"Alright!" Gregory said. "Thanks for that, Joshua. Please take a seat again. Just to the side for now."

Joshua hopped down and leant against the wall next to Big Dave at the side.

"So, love is in the air!" Gregory said. "Thank you, Joshua. That was a nice, festive message to close."

People laughed.

"Hold on – just one final thing from me. The management team is still honouring our commitment to serve Christmas rolls in the canteen this Thursday, as we did last year. I hope to join you for that. But just in case – Merry Christmas and a Happy New Year, everyone. Thank you."

Gregory stepped off the stage and walked over to return the microphone to Barry.

"Alright everyone," said Barry. "Hold on a second. Right, I've found the perfect track to get things started – dedicated to our very own Improvement King: *Love is in the Air*." He grinned and slid up the volume.

24

CHARGED UP

JOSH had sent Sue and Nigel on ahead to save him a seat. He would join them in the canteen as soon as he had responded to this urgent email about the Cutting proposals. It was Thursday, the last working day before Christmas. Two more sewing machinists had just popped in on *their* way to the canteen, to congratulate him on his employee of the year award. It was kind, but he would trade in all the praise for some progress.

He had barely returned to his email before the door opened again.

"Oh, hi Chris."

"Hi, Josh." Chris' face was ashen.

"Come on in," Josh said. "Is everything alright?"

"Fine, thanks. I've just come to say that Stephen would like to have a quick word with you urgently, if that's OK."

"Now? Shouldn't we all be in the canteen?" Josh asked.

"As soon as this is over, I think."

"What's it about?"

"He didn't say," said Chris. He hovered at the door, holding it open.

Josh quickly finished the email and picked up his file. "So what are your plans for Christmas?" he asked as they headed off together.

"Oh, not much," he replied. Chris said nothing more until they reached the spiral stairs. "After you." He gestured for Josh to go up first.

Rumours had long been circulating that Gregory was out to get him, but with Stephen nothing seemed as personal. Stephen had still not relinquished many of his views, but there was always hope that he could be convinced.

Stephen's office was empty.

"No – he's in with Gregory," Chris said.

Josh's heart dropped like a stone. Chris went ahead and knocked on Gregory's door.

"Come in."

"Please, go ahead," said Chris.

Gregory was on his feet, beside his A-1-11. He looked jumpy. Stephen sat in the opposite A-1-11 and stirred his coffee.

"Come in Joshua, please," Gregory said.

"Do you want me for anything else?" Chris enquired from the doorway.

"No, that's fine. Thanks, Chris. Thanks for your help."

The door quickly closed. This was it.

"Please, take a seat."

He took the office chair that Gregory offered, which had already been positioned beside the coffee table.

Gregory remained standing and rubbed the nape of his neck. "Joshua," he began, "you must be aware that you've been cause for some concern for a while, long before your scene in the boardroom. I gave you another chance then, because I still believed that with the right motivation, you could have offered a lot."

Gregory sat on the edge of his seat and rubbed the back of his neck. "Since last weekend, people have been coming forward to offer evidence that casts doubt on this motivation of yours." He got up and walked towards the balcony doors.

Josh looked beyond him. It was a cold, grey and damp December day. The hills were nowhere to be seen.

"We can't *prove* anything about your intentions, of course. However, it is now evident that your *so-called* bright ideas have been undermining the foundations of our previous successes. You've also been stirring up trouble and causing problems, even as you insist that we need to work closer together as one team!"

Gregory looked shattered. His eyes remained laden with the fear that had long been working itself out as control. However much Josh loathed all this abuse of power, he could not loathe the man consumed by it.

"Stephen's been gathering the evidence."

Stephen launched into action by withdrawing a sheet of paper from a plastic folder and orienting it on the coffee table. It purported to be a graph of EBITDA, covering the last eighteen months. The numbers had been disguised but the downward trend was clear. A callout had been placed above the point where Josh had formed his team.

"The tricky thing is separating your role from everyone else's. We're all working towards EBITDA, as shown on this overall graph, which is strictly confidential, by the way. It suggests there *could* be a correlation between the point at which you formed your team and the deterioration in our overall results," Stephen said. "Obviously we'd like to break this down further into the performance of your specific area. But as I was explaining in the boardroom before that little episode, this isn't really possible for your role. The next best thing has been to ask the leaders of each area for their views on the effects you and your ideas have had on their own performance – good or bad."

Stephen picked up another sheet. "Let me read some of the things people have had to say:

"He said I would be freed up to manage, but I now spend more time in meetings than ever.

"Our strength was built on flexibility and freedom. Josh tried to destroy this by tying us up with unnecessary rules and regulations.

"Before Josh came on the scene, we hardly had any problems. Now we are inundated with them.

"He actively encouraged everyone to keep coming up with further problems."

Josh closed his eyes.

"Do you want to respond to any of that?" said Gregory, who looked at him intently.

How could he be so completely misrepresented? Nothing would improve unless they sought to surface and solve problems as a team! He let the silence continue and Gregory's upper lip began to lift.

"Don't you want to defend yourself?" Stephen asked.

Gregory sat down. "He doesn't have to say anything if he doesn't want to."

Everything had already been said. He had genuinely hoped to help save the company. Now he was being crushed by the behaviours he had been powerless to change.

"Look," Stephen continued, "the theory behind some of your solutions has been outstanding. Personally, I wouldn't have questioned your attitude, either, had it not been for some of your recent remarks. Did you really tell your own team that you long *to tear this company down and rebuild it from scratch*?"

He shook his head: *This was ridiculous.* "That's true," he said and afforded himself half a smile.

"You said that?" Gregory threw up a hand. "There you are, then," he said to Stephen, shaking his head. "He's never been able to accept that his father sold me the business!"

If only Dad were here to put him straight.

Stephen looked straight at him. "Do you realise what's at stake?" he asked. "We're disbanding your team, so you face redundancy at least. If there's evidence of malpractice Gregory has the right to fire you on the spot."

Stephen's eyes were cold but there was no malice in them.

"Come on, Gregory," Stephen continued, "we need to be downstairs." He stood up. "Personally, I can't see grounds for dismissal."

"What?" Gregory said. "He's not denied anything!"

"Other people still speak positively of him. Look, fold his change team if you want, but we're already getting rid of one team leader this week," Stephen said. "Surely that's enough."

Gregory looked directly at Stephen with widened eyes. "I've already explained to you," he said slowly, "that might *not* be enough."

"Why not keep Josh by transferring him to Barry's role?" Stephen suggested.

"That might not be enough," Gregory repeated.

"Well," Stephen said, "if you want my opinion, Josh is the kind of talent we need to be developing. The difference between him and Barry is night and day."

"Just to be clear," Gregory questioned, "are you saying you're not supporting me on this issue?"

"Ask anyone who they would rather keep! Except the rest of Barry's little band of troublemakers, perhaps. In my opinion, if you need to get rid of anyone else, *they're* the ones who should be following Barry out of the door."

Gregory stood up straight. "I might just have to do that."

"What, get rid of the lot of them?"

"No – ask our people which team leader they would rather keep," Gregory said. "It's not a bad idea."

"What?"

"Well, I agree it might not make sense to lose two team leaders right now. And people have always been asking for more of a say in management decisions. And we need to be downstairs. So let's ask everyone who they would rather keep: Joshua or Barry."

"Are you crazy?"

"No, everyone's together and it's an ideal opportunity to engage people. It's a way of giving everyone a say in the type of manager they want to be managed by. Why not?"

"We're the managers!" said Stephen. "We have to manage."

"And we have to empower. Are you afraid of consulting our workforce?"

Stephen screwed up his face. "Gregory, what's got into you? I've never known you desperate to get rid of anyone."

"I'm not desperate, Stephen. I've always believed in giving people a say and I'm prepared to make a stand. We might be surprised by what we hear."

"Look, it's the last day before the holiday and we shouldn't even be talking about this, let alone in front of Josh – who has still done nothing wrong as far as I'm concerned. They're waiting for us to start serving and I've already missed four calls."

Gregory sat down again and screwed up his eyes.

"So are you coming or what?" Stephen asked.

"Go on ahead and get Big Dave to take my place in the kitchen. We'll get a message to you when we're ready for the rolls."

"Right, you're on your own, then."

The canteen was simmering. Sue had been trying not to touch the cheap paper tablecloths: they made her skin crawl. Cracker carcasses were strewn everywhere. One of them had knocked a drink over Trish's lap. She had returned the wet missile with interest on her way out to dry herself.

Sue and Nigel were now looking after two empty seats. She had no idea where Josh had got to. So far he had got lucky with the delay, but the canteen would reach boiling point if they had to wait much longer to be fed.

Cheers greeted Gregory's entrance. He held the door open and Josh followed. It seemed strange that she had now got to know someone well who also cavorted with the bigwigs.

Josh looked drained as Gregory positioned him uncomfortably to his left. Something strange was going on.

Gregory stepped forward and held his arms aloft. The crowd responded with the agility of a warship.

"Thank you!" Gregory said loudly. "Sorry for the wait. I'm sure you're all starving. There's just one last bit of business we need to cover."

The crowd groaned. Despite his animation, Gregory seemed every bit as exhausted as Josh. They were all in need of Christmas.

"Thank you. It won't take long," Gregory said. The noise gradually abated. "Most of you know that this is Barry White's last day after – how shall we say – a *minor misdemeanour* with a washing machine door. Barry, can you come up here, please?"

There was a commotion on one of the front tables and some of them started to chant. "Bazza! Bazza! Bazza!" Others started to join in. Barry dragged himself to his feet and swaggered over. The remains of a cracker bounced off his back. He swung round and missed the catch but pointed to the culprit instead.

Gregory put a hand on each of Barry's shoulders and steered him into position.

"Now, I also need to inform you there's been an important development since the weekend. Joshua, can you step forward please?"

Josh did so as a shadow of himself. This looked ominous, given the recent rumours.

"It has come to light that Joshua may not have been living up to his mantle of Employee of the Year. In fact, many of you have come forward to tell us how his supposed bright ideas have actually been undermining our previous successes."

Despite the few vocal complainants, surely most were still on their side? You couldn't trust anything that managers said any more.

"Some changes have been unworkable and some have caused no end of problems. Therefore we have had no choice but to cancel the current *Production Breakthrough* module with immediate effect."

Her mouth fell open. People turned to look at her.

"I'm sorry to announce it like this, but Nigel and Sue…" He paused until his eyes fixed on them. "There you are." Everyone was now looking at them. "You can return to your previous positions. Sadly Joshua does not have this option because his old position has been filled, so he faces redundancy. However, in discussing the accusations with Joshua just now he admitted to me that he would like to *tear this company down.* Therefore the normal course of action is that he will also leave today while charges concerning his actions are investigated."

Her head started shaking. *This couldn't be happening. Surely Gregory's personal vendetta against Josh was now plain for all to see? Were people afraid of getting in the firing line themselves?*

"In fact, the charges faced by both these young managers symbolise the degree of mismanagement that has been constraining our performance. However, many of you know that I see it as a failing of the company when we fail to bring out the best in someone. To be honest, we can also ill afford to lose two experienced team leaders at this point in time. Therefore I am prepared to drop charges against one of these team leaders today and to give him a second chance."

What was Gregory playing at? Incredibly, some people had stopped listening.

"Now, this also gives us an opportunity to innovate. I've always said this business can't be run as a democracy. But this is a chance to give you some of the greater engagement you have been seeking. I would like *you* to choose to whom you would like to extend a second chance. In a sense, this is your opportunity to choose the kind of manager you want to be managed by."

Gregory brought Josh forward so he was level with Barry on his other side. "So, who do you want to reinstate? Joshua – *the Improvement King*," he said, placing a hand on his shoulder. "Or Barry – *Mr Karaoke*?"

Sue had never witnessed anything like this. Nigel looked at her and she pushed him forward. He had to say something. She pushed him again as a chant broke from the front. "Bazza, Bazza, Bazza!"

She lurched forward. Nigel put his arm round her but that was of no use at all.

"Bazza, Bazza, Bazza!" Fists banged on tables.

Gregory held an arm aloft. "Thank you. Message received," he said calmly. "And can you give the message to the kitchen, please. Thank you."

Sue could hardly breathe. *Was that supposed to be it?*

Gregory breathed deeply. "Thank you all for engaging with that," he said loudly. "And welcome back, Barry. As promised, that's the final bit of business. Enjoy your lunch. Happy Christmas, everyone!"

Barry sauntered back to a hero's welcome at his table. Gregory walked over to Josh but everyone's attention was stolen by Stephen bursting through the kitchen doors. Peter and Big Dave followed, each carrying a platter piled high with turkey rolls. Their sleeves were rolled up and they donned Christmas aprons with flashing lights. Arms swooped in like hungry gulls.

Gregory and Josh had disappeared and the atmosphere had been engulfed by conversation. *Had anyone even seen Josh leave?* Sue covered her mouth and ran out.

25

TURNAROUND

GREGORY'S toes remained cold despite a third pair of socks. His fingers were numb and his arms ached. It was mid-morning and he had still not raked as far as the smaller cedar. The leaves were damp and a little frosty; hopefully he was not doing the lawns more harm than good. He should have got someone to do it weeks ago.

Yesterday everything was as it should have been; a perfect Christmas Day. Emily was home and happy, Linda had been in her element and everything had been capped by the best night's sleep in ages. This had been disturbed that morning by an inverse nightmare. The dawn had brought creeping consciousness of the mess he was still in. He had left Linda sleeping – there still hadn't been a good time to tell her anything. Instead of presiding over doubling Gregory Todd's fortunes, he had steered them to an urgent need to halve their lifestyle. They would have to put their house on the market immediately, and to gain even a moderate income he would have to prostitute himself to a soulless firm that churned out widgets – if they would take him.

In the cold light of day, the scene in the canteen played on his mind continuously. Stephen had forced him into the whole debacle. He had known exactly what was needed and how important it had been to him. Everything had been lined up for Stephen to finish it, in his office. Yet Stephen had acted like a loose cannon and forced him into a corner. Miraculously, some quick thinking had got him out but at what price? Mountfield had been satisfied with both the case and the exit, but Gregory had been forced into making a complete fool of himself.

It had only started to dawn on him that morning how much extra shame he had heaped on himself. He had come across as erratic and irrational – two traits he loathed in others. It made little difference whether people clocked that he had been acting out of character. He had escaped the ignominy of Mountfield firing him but so what? Might it not have been better to stomach this and maintain his integrity? He would now be stained by the act in the canteen, and yet he still had to announce that he would be selling them out. How would people react when they passed him in the street? It was for these two acts that he would now be remembered. With them he would probably undo all the good work he had ever achieved, with Eden Furniture and with Gregory Todd.

Showering had failed to cleanse him, and he had not been able to linger in front of a mirror to shave. He had rendered himself incapable of finishing the course as the leader he had set out to be.

His best hope was that shame would wear off over time. He just had to keep going, and at least there was plenty to keep him busy. A slight wobble earlier on had suggested the lawns were in danger of ballooning into an unhealthy obsession. His mind had always been busy but it had never before felt vulnerable. *It did make sense to start with the lawns, didn't it, given how much they had influenced him as a buyer?*

Linda came out twice, urging him to stop and relax. She finally left him to pop out for some milk. The crows swooped down one by one to rejoin him. At first they kept a respectful distance. They watched him for a while and then slowly closed in on him. Suddenly they scattered, because a special engine snarled along the lane. He leant on his rake to catch a glimpse. With a change-down, it morphed into a gentle burbling. The barrelled bonnet of a British Racing Green Morgan swung into their drive.

Gregory's innards shrivelled. Although the roof was up he knew instantly who was at the wheel and why he had come. The car continued up to the house, where it stopped. There was a suffocating pause before the door opened. Legs stretched out, followed by the tweed jacket. The figure straightened his back and started walking towards him, rubbing his hands.

Gregory kept his head down and carried on raking. His private space was being invaded and he was in no fit state for a showdown. He dragged his woolly hat from his head and stuffed it into his pocket. He brushed detritus off his old work jeans but that only revealed the paint stains beneath. A successful CEO would not be raking his own leaves, let alone the morning after Christmas. But he had chosen to do this. He slowed himself down. *I can justify every decision I have ever made.*

The footsteps stopped. His visitor's smile was broad and he stretched out his arms. "Come here," Arthur said. His warm words condensed in the air.

Gregory stayed his ground. His old mentor kept coming until his tweed arms gripped him.

"Good to see you, Gregory."

Gregory stepped backwards but Arthur kept a hand on each of his shoulders.

"It's good to see you," Arthur repeated. His ageing eyes supported his words – they were full of generosity, as always. *What was Arthur up to?*

"I know why you're here," Gregory said. Joshua would have told him everything. "Look, I am sorry about what happened to Joshua. You must remember that I never liked to get rid of anyone, but I'm afraid we had no choice but to fold his change team. The people were clear that his changes weren't working. As you may have heard, it was actually their choice to let him go in the end." He struggled to look at Arthur directly. He tried to assume parity but it was like addressing a gentle yet commanding headmaster. "Not that I make a habit of consulting the workforce, or indeed of letting anyone go just before a holiday but there were extenuating pressures. You must know how such situations can develop."

"I know more than you think," Arthur said with a slight tilt of his head.

Arthur knew no more than Joshua could have told him. "So how are you then, anyway?" Gregory asked. "Long time, no see."

"I'm well, thanks Gregory." He was still smiling. "Although I have to say my feet are pretty cold. I can see you're hard at work but is there any chance we could continue this chat inside? I won't stay long."

"Erm – OK. I don't see why not." He placed his rake on top of the leaves and gestured towards the house. Butterflies were trapped in his gut but were doomed to perish as much in the cold air if they could find a way out. "You'll have to excuse how I'm dressed."

"Not at all. Didn't I always encourage you to get your hands dirty? How do you like living out here?"

"It's good. We might not stay, though."

"No?"

"It's been great for a while but it's a bit isolated. And with hindsight it's much bigger than we really need, now it's just the two of us."

"Oh – what's Emily up to? How is she?"

"She's great – first year of English at Bath."

"Good. Just like her dad, then."

"Well, in some ways."

"And how's Linda?"

"Great – she's just popped out."

They had reached the portico. Arthur wiped his feet and entered the large hall that Linda had managed to fill with a giant Christmas tree. The decorations had barely stretched far enough. He bent over, flicked a switch and the tree lit up.

"There you go," he said.

Arthur smiled.

"I can't really offer you a tea, I'm afraid, as we're just out of milk. Linda has popped out to get some. Unless you want a black coffee?"

"I don't want anything, thank you. I've just come to see you."

"Right. We can go in here." He opened the door to the drawing room and winced. *It was cold.* Presents were still scattered over the floor, but nowhere else was suitable.

"Sorry for the disarray. Please take a seat. I'll start a fire."

"Ah, the Helena," Arthur said. He walked over to one of the fireside chairs. "You still can't beat a proper eight-way tie."

"Tell me about it! Sadly it's even more difficult to get people to pay for it nowadays." He crouched down to sweep out the grate. "So to what *do* I owe this pleasure, Arthur? I can safely say I wasn't expecting you."

"I have some news."

Gregory rested the ash pan on the cracked marble hearth. "Oh?"

"I'm buying a furniture company."

If Arthur was declaring war, he was too late. "What company?"

"There will only ever be one furniture company as far as I'm concerned, Gregory."

The information started to engage. He steadied himself on his knees beside the hearth. "You're the buyer?"

"Yes."

Gregory lowered his head as implications trickled into his soul. He busied himself with sweeping out the grate. Arthur would have seen everything, including all the missed targets. He will have seen his son's name in the draft agreement in black and white. "How much do you know?" he said quietly.

Arthur just looked at him.

I'm finished. He emptied the ash and hung up the brush. "I don't know what to say," he said. "I'm so sorry."

The silence underlined that it was hardly enough.

"When I took over, I genuinely thought I could make a difference," Gregory explained. "I have never claimed to be perfect but the situation became increasingly difficult. I was forced into doing things I would never have considered."

Arthur was continuing to sit still. *Why had he not come down on him?* Some of Gregory's shame might already have shifted, perhaps because there was nothing left to hide. He turned around on his knees. "So it was you who insisted that someone be named?"

"Yes."

"Why?"

"It's not in my nature to ignore poor performance, Gregory."

"So? It's not in my nature either! Nor of most other leaders – but you don't often see people insisting that blame is assigned before an acquisition goes through, do you?"

Arthur just looked at him. He didn't seem willing or able to defend himself. Just like Joshua, in his office. Gregory turned back to the fire and assembled a pyramid of kindling. He positioned some smaller logs around and a couple of firelighters within. He presented a lit match until everything went up in flames. After rubbing debris from his hands, he rocked back onto his feet.

"So that's why you're here, then?" Gregory said, retaking his chair. "To tell me it's my blood you were after?" In practice the ignominy could barely increase. "It will make Mountfield's day: he's also been itching to fire me."

"Mountfield can't touch you now, Gregory."

"What do you mean?"

"It's signed."

"What?"

"I've signed the agreement."

"As it was?" Nothing made sense. "Why would you do that?"

"Josh has already suffered."

"And you don't want to clear his name?"

"His name is clear, as far as I'm concerned. Everyone else may have had some part to play in the company's problems; Josh was doing all he could."

Gregory shook his head. "I can't see how it makes any practical difference who you name. It's hardly going to solve the company's problems."

Arthur leant back in his Helena. "No," he said. "But it's got the plan back together." He smiled. "Solving the problems may take some more time."

Gregory shook his head again, in a more pronounced manner.

"I'm under no illusions, Gregory. I know the company is infected with bad habits and afflicted with baggage. I'm still going to have to wipe the slate clean. I'm going to dismiss everyone, and I hope to re-engage them with a new contract."

"Are you sure you can do that?"

"Yes. The new contract will work out better for everyone in the long run. It'll create a new foundation, which will bring people together."

The firelighters had fizzled out. He got down again on his knees to gently blow into the remains. "It sounds risky. You do realise you may lose some of the best people?"

"Transformation won't happen by playing it safe, Gregory. I have to accept I might not keep everyone, but rest assured I'm doing everything I can. In fact, we've already started. We'll be visiting all the key players. We're asking them to commit their future to us, beyond the new contract. Which brings me to the real reason I'm here and why I'm telling you all this."

Gregory leant back to admire the flames. "Eh?"

"You're at the top of my list."

"What?"

"Gregory, I've come to ask if you would commit to us as managing director."

He fell back into his chair and studied Arthur's face. He looked away to the windows. His eyes reeled back after falling on the lawns and the leaves. Arthur's eyes remained fixed on him. "You still want me to manage the business?"

"Of course," Arthur said.

"Why?"

"Why?! I've just told you – my focus up to now has been getting the whole plan back on track. How many years did I invest in you so that you could become my managing director?"

"That was a long time ago, Arthur. A lot of water has passed under the bridge."

"I've always had a long-term perspective."

Was he serious? "It was hardly *always* your plan! Otherwise why would you have sold out to me?"

"You always did like to get to the heart of the matter," Arthur said calmly. "Of course it would never have been my choice to sell, Gregory! But if I had rejected your offer or if I had fired you, the plan would have been finished. I can guarantee you would never have come back."

"You let the company go, just to keep me in it?"

"I'm not asking you to make sense of me, Gregory. I'm just asking if you would like to start afresh. Yes or no?"

Starting afresh would be impossible. Nothing could erase his last act and there was no guarantee that he could ever repair trust. "What if I've taken the business as far as I can?"

"I still believe in you, Gregory."

His heart skipped a beat. "Why?" he asked. The fire started to crackle. "What makes you so sure I'm the right person?"

"The ground is prepared for a proper transformation. I need someone who can *lead* the organisation through it. Have you any idea how hard it is to find that expertise? It has to be learnt. You were already a good managing director. You've now been through a painful but powerful learning opportunity. If you can learn from your mistakes, Gregory, there *can* be no one better equipped for your role."

His heart stiffened but he smothered his instinct to defend himself: it would be futile to argue with Arthur that he had made no mistakes. "That doesn't make me an expert, especially if you're hoping to transform the factory."

"You don't have to be an expert. Especially when you have Josh."

"Joshua's coming back?"

"Of course."

"Well, that would never work. Has he got any idea that you're inviting me back?"

"Of course he has! He always knew that the plan was for you and him to inherit the business together."

"I can't see *he* would ever want to work with me again." *Did he just mention the two of them inheriting the business?*

"Now hold on," Arthur said in a lowered tone. He leant forward in his Helena and Gregory felt himself shrink back. "Stop for one minute and consider things from Josh's perspective. After you took the company, he went in and, despite your treatment of him, he *still* did everything he could for you. Yes, you are free to walk away if that's what you want. But don't you *ever* do so with any misapprehensions that Josh and I have ever been less than one hundred per cent *for* you."

He did not know where to look. Part of him would still rather walk than to share any business with Joshua and his dad.

"How much freedom would I have to make my own decisions?"

"You'll have more freedom than ever."

"Look, I can't get my head around it." He noticed some more soot on his hands and dusted them off on his jeans. "I suppose a thank you might be in order. I just can't help wondering, though, if it's time for me to move on."

"Move on? Of course it's time to move on!" Arthur said. His eyes sparked into life again. "Do you think this is about the past? Yes, in one sense it'll be like coming home but think how much we all love this business! This is about us doing more than you have ever imagined. There's nothing else that could fulfil you nearly so much."

Whoa! Of course there wasn't! He bit his lip. Arthur still knew him, inside out.

"I've seen a lot of leaders in my time, Gregory. Never let pride, fear or insecurity make choices for you. These are always the stumbling blocks. Make your own choice," he said. The fire in Arthur's eyes had calmed to a flicker. "And make it a good one." A small smile returned. "So, yes or no?"

His lip quivered. Surely he had tried independence, and it had been a lie. Something surged within him to sweep away the resistance. It felt like courage. *This was good.* "Yes," Gregory said. It promised all he had wanted. He would have to deal with the fallout from the entire workforce, but *this* was the once-in-a-lifetime opportunity he could not afford to miss. He extended his hand and it was gripped firmly.

"I still can't take it in," Gregory said. "Thank you. I can't believe it."

They stood up and Arthur put his arm round Gregory's shoulders.

"Welcome back, son." Arthur's eyes were lustrous. "Come on, let's shape this industry together."

The smile was infectious. He felt rejuvenated, just as he had when he had joined Eden all those years ago.

The front door opened with a key. It was Linda. "Hello?"

"Hi Linda, we're in here." He wiped the corner of his eye and hurried out to reach her just as she placed her bags on the mosaic floor. He kissed her cold lips and squeezed her tightly. "I love you," he said.

She leant back to look at him as if he had been drinking.

"We've got a guest," he explained.

She was already looking over his shoulder.

"Hello, Linda," Arthur said.

She let him kiss her on the cheek.

"It's good to see you again," Arthur said.

"Likewise." She smiled politely as she unwound her scarf. She turned back to Gregory with an undisguised quizzical look.

"You're not going to believe this," he said. "Arthur's my boss again."

"What?"

Arthur smiled and turned aside to let him explain.

"It's a long story, but he's buying back the business."

"You're *selling* it? Already?"

"Well, yes."

"Why?"

"That doesn't matter now. The point is that I'm back where I belong. Arthur and I have been reunited."

"Oh." Linda failed to mirror any of the enthusiasm that burned within him.

This is going to take some explaining.

26

AULD LANG SYNE

SUE was using untested muscles to keep her feet from skating on the frozen towpath. She had been dreading the return to work. Normally she enjoyed working between Christmas and New Year. Childcare was easy with family around, and somehow the atmosphere was always relaxed despite ramping up for the sales. This year, everything was different. Her icy fingers pulled her jacket around as tightly as possible.

Nigel looked snug inside the hood on his trusty Parka coat. She had come to appreciate his unorthodox chivalry on the way to work, but this morning's conversation had been as frosty as everything else. They had attempted the obligatory Christmas chat and Nigel had tried to quiz her about Clarky. Neither had found a way to acknowledge the spectre of the events in the canteen.

"He mustn't be allowed to get away with it, you know," Nigel said spontaneously.

"Who?"

"Who do you think?"

"Gregory?"

"Of course," Nigel said. "I've been reading up on it. Josh has got a clear case for wrongful dismissal."

"Really? My sister-in-law knows a bit about all this and she's not convinced. Whatever you can say about Gregory, he tends to do things by the book."

"But the charges were completely fabricated."

"Technically he's still only suspended. It's legal while charges are being investigated."

"You're missing the point!" Nigel said. "Gregory has been desperate to get Josh out of the door, by whatever ham-fisted approach he could find. No one should be allowed to get away with it! At the end of the day they humiliated and got rid of the one person who cared a fig about sorting everything out."

"You think I don't know? I was only telling you what I've found out because I've been trying to come to terms with it. Don't lecture me, Nigel."

"So what are we going to do about it?" Nigel asked.

"It's a bit late to ask that, isn't it? You didn't do anything when you had the chance."

"So it's my fault, is it?"

"Not just you," she admitted. "Any of us should have said something."

"What could we have done? Insisted on a vote?"

She was still angry but she had not meant to take it out on him. They struggled on for some time in silence.

"I didn't mean to shout," Nigel said. "I think I'm angry at myself for going back to how things were."

"Maybe we don't have to," Sue said. "Maybe our team leaders will let us carry on with a few of the improvements." She was trying to be hopeful, but there was nothing she felt she could do on her own.

"No, that's not what I mean," Nigel said. "*I'm* going back to how *I* used to be. Don't you realise why I reacted against any of Josh's ideas that involved moving Pre-upholstery?" He looked to the sky. "I feared I would have to return one day, and I wanted to keep the workstation I felt I had earned, by the window. How petty is that? Yet in half an hour I'm still going to fight to get it back. Then I can keep my head down and get on with the rest. Despite knowing what I know, I still can't change."

Sue had not considered *where* she would sit – or if someone else would be using her machine. She had not got beyond worrying how some of the girls would greet her return.

"He promised us everything would get better. That this place would be transformed," she said.

"I guess some things are just outside of our control."

"Yeah well, it would have been better if he had never got our hopes up. People shouldn't make promises they can't keep."

Two fishermen in thick green coats sat on the bank ahead. They had got to know the one in the orange beanie as Callum. His incurable cheer had often lifted their spirits but today she hoped they could slip past unnoticed. They both kept their heads down, hoping Callum's friend would be enough to distract him.

"Sue!"

She recognised the voice immediately. She threw her arms round Callum's friend before he could unzip his hood. "What are you doing here? I thought we might not see you again."

"Come on," said Josh. "That was hardly likely." He settled her back onto her heels and freed a hand to extend to Nigel. "Hello Nigel. I thought I might find you both here."

"You came here just to see us?" she asked.

"Of course."

"Are you OK?" Sue asked.

"I'm fine."

He looked well. Her mouth opened but her mind had jammed with a hundred questions.

"We're sorry," Nigel said.

"That's OK," Josh said. "All's well that ends well."

"You've got another job?" Sue asked.

"You could say that," said Callum.

"Where?"

"Look," Josh said. "I don't want to make you late but I want to quickly tell you what has happened before you hear any rumours. Dad is buying back the business. We'll get to do everything we hoped."

"What? You're coming back?"

"Yes."

"When?"

"Soon. Do you think you can commit to continuing as change agents?"

"Of course," Sue said, "if you're coming back."

"Nigel?" Josh asked.

"Yes. I never wanted to be chained to a window anyway!"

Josh smiled. "It will mean signing a new, improved contract."

"Have you seen it?" Nigel said.

"I'm helping to draft it."

"Then consider it signed."

"Thank you, that's great. Please don't tell anyone else just yet. Dad is developing a proper communication plan with Gregory."

Her stomach hit the floor.

"Your dad is cooperating with Gregory?" Nigel asked.

"Yes," Josh replied.

"Until the deal goes through, right?" Nigel added.

Josh stepped forward and smiled gently. He put one hand on Sue's shoulder and one on Nigel's. His green eyes were clear and shined brightly. "Everything I've been through has helped to prepare this opportunity for each of you." A warm sensation surged through her and her shoulders quivered. "And to prepare the same opportunity for everyone else."

"For *everyone*?" Nigel asked.

"For everyone."

"Except Gregory, surely?" Nigel said.

"Gregory has already accepted Dad's invitation to stay as managing director."

She covered her mouth. Nigel's mouth fell open and he shook his head. "Didn't you tell your dad what he did to you?"

"There's no time to explain now," Josh said. "But it's all good. I promise."

Callum spoke up. "Look, I know what you must be thinking. But let me suggest it should be enough for now that if Josh is willing to accept Gregory back, then we should at least try to do the same."

What right did he have to say that? He wasn't even there!

"Go," Josh said. "I'll see you soon."

Nigel looked at his watch and pulled Sue away. "Come on, we need to go! We'll see you soon, then."

"There's so much I want to know!" she called.

"Good," Josh called after them, "there'll be plenty of time for that!"

27

SEAT OF INFLUENCE

GREGORY reached the towpath and glanced downstream. The fisherman in the orange woolly hat waved exuberantly. Gregory turned but there was no one else around. He nodded towards the fisherman and set off in the opposite direction as fast as he could manage in his leather soles.

It felt absurd to be fleeing work and escaping to a place he had not risked going near for a long time. The fisherman had been the first person that morning to look pleased to see him. Jane was barely speaking but it had been bad enough at home. He could accept the grief from Linda for keeping her in the dark but not for his decision to rejoin Arthur. He had tried to explain this calmly until Linda had accused him of not putting up enough of a fight with Mountfield. Things had settled again, but only because they were avoiding each other.

A duck skidded off ice at the edge of the canal and swam away. Crooked barbed wire protected the steel-roofed shacks on the other side of the walls, which were layered with graffiti. He lifted the shoulder strap of his bag over his head as a precaution before passing through the shadows of a road bridge. If more Victorian buildings like theirs had survived, the whole area might have been gentrified by now. But then Mountfield would probably have sold out to developers, and he might never have been reunited with Arthur.

The sky was pale and heavy. The forecast had given him a good excuse to walk. He didn't relish leaving his car in Arthur's neighbourhood in any weather, but if snow fell while ice remained, the side roads would become treacherous.

All the neighbouring properties seemed to have been converted into flats or bedsits. He slowed as he approached the detached Regency house. The wrought iron gates were open. Arthur must have sunk a fortune into it. The stucco was bright white, the black paint looked fresh and there were no weeds in sight. He struggled to see anything that would need to be done even if it were to be placed on the market tomorrow. A man in a balaclava suddenly emerged from the rear of the house. Gregory held his breath and gripped his bag. He was shaken by the stranger's cheery greeting and paused to recover his heart rate before ascending one side of the sweeping stone steps to the front door. He announced his arrival with the hefty brass knocker and stood back. Reaching under his scarf, he straightened his collars. *It was good to be back.*

The door was opened briskly by a young man in an open-necked shirt and smart trousers. If he was one of Arthur's advisors he clearly felt at home. Only when he held out a hand did Gregory register his face.

"Gregory, welcome."

"Joshua!" he said. "Er – sorry, I didn't realise you'd be here."

"Well, I'm joining you for the first bit. Then I'll leave you and Dad alone to draft the communications plan. Come on in!"

He looked down at the polished tiles and stepped into the warm entrance hall. Through a door that had been left ajar he could see straight through to floor-to-ceiling sash windows and the sloping garden beyond.

"Look, Joshua. I trust your dad may have mentioned – I'm sorry for what happened. I just— I might have got the wrong measure of you. I was under a lot of pressure."

"It's OK."

"I couldn't figure you out. To be honest, I'm still struggling."

Joshua smiled. He grabbed Gregory's hand firmly and stepped forward to pat him on the back. "Welcome back."

"Thanks. You're a good man, Josh."

"So are you."

Gregory puffed out his cheeks. He could not have felt further from it.

"Let me take your coat and we'll join Dad upstairs."

The wrought-iron bannister wound upwards like an exotic shell towards a domed skylight. Josh led the way, following the hardwood handrail past the chandelier.

"Here we are," Josh said. He opened a thick, six-panelled door into an open-plan room that stretched right across the house. A boardroom table occupied the front half. A row of glass doors stretched across the back, leading onto a strip balcony. His old mentor got to his feet from behind a writing desk that overlooked the city.

"Ah, welcome," said Arthur. "You made it here before the snow, then. Did you walk?"

"Yes."

"Excellent – perhaps then we can celebrate with something special." Arthur led him to a collection of sofas by the glass doors as Josh peeled off towards a small bar in the middle of the room. "Please – make yourself at home." The sofas were Evitas, which had been reupholstered to look as new. The seats were still perfect.

"Beautiful room," Gregory said. The spirelets on the cathedral's square tower seemed poised to receive the first flakes from the colourless sky.

"Yes, we enjoy it," Arthur said.

Josh placed a tray with three glasses on the coffee table.

"I presume you'll join us?" Arthur said to Gregory.

"Thank you."

The cork popped and Josh charged the glasses.

"Here's to the new Eden Furniture," Arthur said, raising his glass. "Our new start!" A few white flakes drifted onto the balcony.

"A new start!" Gregory repeated. "Thank you. Happy New Year!"

"Yes," said Josh. "Many Happy New Years!"

Bubbles crackled lightly on Gregory's palate.

"So, then. What are your dreams for Eden Furniture?" Arthur asked.

"Growth," he said. "I'd still love to grow the business."

"Why?" Arthur asked.

Wasn't growth always good?

"Or maybe it would be better to ask *how?*" Arthur said.

"Well, we're already on the brink of meeting Aspiration's needs. That will be a great business to crack."

"Really? The *margins* didn't look that great."

He was out of practice for these little challenges. "The volumes more than make up for it," he countered.

"What if I told you Doug Mountfield was about to become chairman of Aspiration?"

Gregory's shoulders stiffened. "How do you know?"

"Let's just say that he has never been able to stop talking about his own achievements in my presence."

"*Never* been able to?"

"He didn't tell you, then? Doug became part of Eden Furniture in the start-up days, way before I recruited you. He could never accept my authority, so I had to get rid of him."

"So you knew what he was like? Why didn't you warn me?"

"I did."

Gregory puffed out his cheeks. Arthur *had* said something about Mountfield's character, in the hotel room. It had seemed a desperate, fabricated attempt to throw him off course. By then Gregory must have already allowed himself to have been taken in by Mountfield's lies about Arthur – and about what he had supposedly stood to gain.

"Doug is clever, Gregory. But he can only ever steal or destroy – he will never create or build up anything good for himself. He was always going to use weapons of charm and manipulation to try and turn you against me. But as you may have found out, he can't hide what he's like forever."

"But can we afford *not* to deal with him if he's going to be chairman of Aspiration?"

"Of course we can! We won't live hand to mouth any more, Gregory. Welcome back to the long-term view! We can afford to make our own choices, and you can be as free from Doug's manipulation and control as you want to be."

"Maybe we can set things up with a rival," Gregory offered, "and help them steal some of Aspiration's share."

"You don't need to get dragged into that kind of thinking either, Gregory."

Was fighting the competition now wrong too?

"That's what I was talking about. You don't have to worry about Doug any more, or resort to the kind of *destructive* tactic that he himself is reduced to. This business is ours to lead, and you are now free to *create* something good and new with it. So what would *you* like to do?"

"Well, I think it *would* be good to find a new, online partner." Gregory assertively replaced his empty glass on the table. "Mainly for fixed upholstery, with shorter lead times. That's where the market is heading."

"Maybe, but we've still not unearthed your creative passion. Let's try it another way. You've been in this industry now for what – thirty years? What about the industry frustrates you more than anything else?"

It was already rising within him. He tried to check Arthur and Josh for signs of whether it was really safe to unleash everything. The Arthur of old could cope with unformulated thought so he went for it: "Well, the thing I *hate* is how our industry keeps dumbing down. Why is it that *our* industry slides backwards year after year while others advance so rapidly? Sofas were better designed and built thirty years ago than they are today! People used to care about substance as well as style and value, but now all the domestic market seems to care about is looks – and cost! Cost, cost and cost! Generations of people have only ever sat on cheap bands and foam. OK, we've redrawn our battle lines for our middle market – at serpentine springs for example but never bands. It's a miracle that our customers still think they're getting comfortable sofas. But I'm convinced that's only because they don't know how much better a decent sofa would feel if only they were prepared to pay a little more! It's crazy – it's the one product people retreat to for their most precious, hard-earned moments every day, yet we still somehow can't convince them to invest in anything half decent! And until they've tried sitting on a decent sofa, which is increasingly rare, how will we ever convince them how good it can get?"

Arthur and Josh were smiling and nodding graciously.

"So that's the problem," Gregory said as objectively as possible. Mountfield would already have torn him to shreds for getting emotional about something for which he did not have a solution. "I'm sorry – I guess if there was an easy solution I'd have found it already."

Arthur nodded. "Thank you. That's exactly the kind of thing I wanted to hear. So you're passionate about helping the mass market to discover the benefits of high-end, traditional comfort – at a completely new price point?"

"Well, that would be amazing. Who wouldn't want to achieve that? But you can't deliver a £3000 sofa for £1000."

Arthur looked to Josh.

"I don't see why not," Josh said. "We would need to design the range well – by selecting the right £3000 features to incorporate. The good news is that much of the cost of incorporating many of these features – like fixed coils in the seat and serpentine springs in the back – is in our labour. We can directly influence this by designing production well, especially if we minimise the variation in work content between products so that we can keep them flowing. That might mean limiting the range we offer in the frames, but we can compensate by offering some choice in arms and an abundance of choice in fabric."

"Excellent," said Arthur. "While I think of it, I like the sound of abundant. How about that for a name? Abundant choice, value and class. We could set up a booth in a retail store which invites customers to take the Abundant test. Around the sofa we could design panels showing fabric samples. Above the sofa we could have a large LED screen showing how the sofa would look in any chosen fabric."

Gregory could imagine seeing this in SofaZone. "If the features really can be incorporated," he said, "anyone who sits on an Abundant sofa would soon discover how dull and spongy the competition feels. Maybe our sofa in the booth could be partly cut away to show people the reasons for the difference they are experiencing."

"I like it," Arthur said. "What's the best lead time you think we could offer, Josh?"

"Two weeks, delivered," Josh said.

"What?!" Gregory said

"Don't envisage anything as it is today," Josh said. "Look at how it might be. For example, I can envisage dedicating a whole building to Abundant and structuring a sub-organisation around it. With the right design of products and processes, they would fly through."

"You know how we struggle to meet twelve weeks!" Gregory said. "I admit we must still be able to do better, but don't forget that's exactly how we got burnt with Aspiration."

"Remember the details I was working on in the team room that Saturday night?" Josh said. "That work confirmed that two weeks is possible."

"Would two weeks make a difference in the marketplace?" Arthur asked.

"*Six* weeks would be more than enough to make a difference," Gregory replied. "Everyone wants a custom sofa as soon as possible, but no one is offering anywhere near two weeks unless it is finished from stock. Which seems to confirm – with respect – that it might not be as easy as you're suggesting, Josh. We don't have to risk failure by attempting anywhere near two weeks."

"So we're talking about a supreme sofa with high-end features, with abundant upholstery choices below £1000 and *possibly* delivered within two weeks," said Arthur.

It was inevitable that Arthur would side with Josh. He would have to pick it up again later to avoid ever having to say *I told you so*.

"If we're making everything from scratch," Arthur continued, "could a customer have it upholstered in their own fabric?"

"I don't see why not," Josh said, "although if it were to be pattern matched it would take a bit of expertise to prescribe how much was needed. Customers would have to send in a large enough sample so we could confirm this first."

"Would the market appreciate that?" Arthur asked Gregory.

"I'm sure some customers would see it as the route to their perfect sofa. Maybe a customer could approach an Abundant booth with their perfect fabric, scan it in and see how good their sofa would look? But hey – I get the point of brainstorming, but surely we shouldn't get carried away until we know what is possible."

Arthur smiled. "We have everything we need to make this possible. It looks like we'll need people across the business – in Sales, Operations, Design and Finance – to change the way they think and work together. So Josh, we'll need your technical expertise and your narrow-and-deep approach to navigate all the change-management issues. Although I guess it might make sense if we can to resource a broad-enough transformation to cover the whole of the Eden business? Then we can lead a similar transformation for the Abundant business. What do you think, Josh?"

"That should be possible."

Arthur turned to Gregory. "Gregory, in you we have a leader who can make things happen. You're learning the importance of doing the right things in the right way. You have what it takes to set direction, coordinate the programme and surface and solve all problems. You now know something of what it will take to *lead* a transformation, instead of trying to just *support or initiate* one. This includes changing any obstacles that prevent us from doing the right thing. This might involve employment contracts, performance measures, accounting procedures and so on. And we also need to lead by example. A changed culture will be both the means and the end for us. This organisation is going to burst into life. So, are you ready?"

"Honestly?" Gregory said. "I think I still might need a bit of help."

"Excellent," said Arthur. "Because that's my job! It won't always be plain sailing, but we'll do it together. This is the adventure we've been waiting for."

28

A Good Deal Happening

Peter ignored the doorbell. The front door opened and closed, but he remained on the sofa in the back room. Joan's heels clipped along the hall until her face appeared at the door.

"I knew you were in. Your car's on the drive."

He silently praised his wife's powers of deduction.

"So what are you doing home, then?"

He chose not to answer. Instead, he offered her the document.

Joan snapped it from his hand. "It's not an April Fool's joke, is it?" she said.

He shook his head and she began reading.

Gregory had announced at the start of the year that the business was being bought back by Arthur Eden. There had been a mixed response. Some still spoke well of Arthur, but it also seemed a step backwards. The biggest gasps and groans were heard when Gregory announced he was somehow managing to remain at the helm.

Arthur had taken charge again in March. Restructuring was announced and consultations started. Of course Gregory had promised that everything would be different – again. The main difference emerged as a hare-brained plan to shove everything into one of the buildings to make way for a secret new business in the other. It sounded like the woodshed's preoccupation with space saving but on steroids. It was obvious who was behind it. Josh had been brought back in as a special director – a role that his dad had created especially for him. Today Peter had received a draft of his own new contract. There was nothing in it to compel him to sign. Theoretically he could negotiate, but if he failed to sign the final offer he could effectively be dismissed within twelve weeks.

"So you *do* still have a job?" she asked.

He snatched the contract back. "If I want it."

"What do you mean, *if* you want it?"

"Everything's changing," Peter said. He threw the contract onto the coffee table. "Guess who's leading the consultations?"

"Who?"

"Josh."

"One of your team leaders?"

"Ex-team leader, yes. Arthur's son."

"Well, he seemed like a lovely young man."

"He's half my age!"

"So what? Stephen's a lot younger than you, too."

He picked up the silky patchwork cushion beside him. "That's different."

"How so?"

"Stephen has an MBA! Anyway, this might just be a good opportunity for me to try something else."

"Something else? I thought you loved being a production manager."

"I haven't enjoyed it for years, Joan."

"How do you know you'll be able to find another job? Other factories might want someone younger. Someone better with a computer."

"I've been using a computer for years."

"Well what about seeing if you can change jobs within Gregory Todd, then?"

"It's not Gregory Todd any more, Joan. It's Eden Furniture again." He smoothed some loose threads on the cushion between finger and thumb.

"Please don't pull those threads, Peter. You're as bad as Nathan." She took the cushion from him and replaced it in the corner of the sofa. "Isn't there something else you could do? I'm thinking of your pension, that's all."

"Didn't you read it? I've already been offered something else!" he said. "That's part of the problem. Nothing will be the same."

"There you are, then – I thought that's what you wanted. So what's your new role?"

"They want me to be the *Eden value stream manager*."

"Ooh – that sounds good."

"No, Joan, it's not. It's effectively half the job I have now. There are going to be two of us."

"But the pay looks better, doesn't it?"

"Not really. It includes an allowance to cover both shifts. They want me to take 24x7 responsibility for half of the operation."

"That's OK – we can work around that."

She had not grasped the bigger picture but it wasn't her fault. All the contracts were changing – including for all those who would be working under him. They were doing away with piecework, for a start – claiming that it was a hindrance to people working together. It was madness: they stood to lose several of their fastest upholsterers. Many of the controls he had worked so hard to maintain were being completely undermined.

"Will you still be reporting to Stephen?"

"No – he's on his way out."

"He's been fired?"

"No, he's serving his notice. He's becoming a senior something-or-other for an insurance firm in London. He's taking one of our bright young recruits with him."

"Well, I bet you'll be glad to see the back of him."

"He wasn't that bad."

"What? You've changed your tune!" she said. "So who will you be reporting to now, then? Does it say?"

"Gregory, if I take the job."

Joan sat down on the arm of the sofa. "Gregory? Wow! Then that's a promotion, isn't it?"

"It doesn't work like that. Please – do we have to talk about this any more, Joan?"

"What, about our future? I think so."

"No, I mean do we have to talk about it *now*? I'm putting the kettle on." He moved past her and drew Joan with him into the kitchen.

"You'll notice a few changes since you were here for the interview," Gregory said before climbing the stairs.

Jane's desk was now nearer the top of the stairs so that she could greet visitors. Thankfully she had been one of the first to thaw towards Gregory, given all she had seen of how Arthur and Josh had been interacting with him. They were now emerging from one of their busiest Augusts ever yet some of his workforce had still to bring him in from the cold. Ironically, the situation had helped him to practise his new discipline of trying to do the right things in the right way, irrespective of pressures and reactions from others.

"Jane, do you remember meeting Rahim, our new sales director?"

Jane stood up.

"Jane is our Executive Assistant." *Would the compliments he was about to reel off have been more similar to Arthur's praise or Mountfield's flattery?* This subtle technique of mining what he had been thinking in the moment, beneath the surface, had developed from his self-analysis that had exploded at the start of the year. The more he practised, the less heavy handed it was becoming. He had already unearthed some invaluable self-improvement nuggets, including a few that had shocked him to his core.

"Hi," Jane said. "Welcome to Eden Furniture."

"Thanks. Good to meet you properly."

"Likewise. You're joining at an interesting time."

"So it seems."

Gregory smiled at Jane and led Rahim beyond her desk, where light from the bank of tall Victorian windows fell across two rows of back-to-back desks. This was the hub for the senior management team.

"We've only recently torn down the individual offices," he explained. "We're dismantling all sorts of man-made barriers across the organisation, which have prevented us from working together. So I thought the senior management team had better practise what it preaches."

"Excellent," said Rahim. "We did something similar in my previous company and I prefer it. I found it helped us to resolve things straight away instead of waiting for the next meeting. And it should be more fun to work together, shouldn't it?"

"I hope so," Gregory said, feeling slightly relieved. "My main concern was the noise, so we left a few offices on this side. They're for general use, so feel free to use one whenever you need some space to concentrate or privacy for a call."

"I'm thinking of using one now," Anna said loudly. She looked up from her computer screen with half a smile.

"Sorry, Anna," Gregory said. "Hi, everyone, can I have a moment? I'd like to introduce – or reintroduce – Rahim, our new sales director. Rahim, this is Anna, our finance director. Paul, our purchasing and logistics director, normally sits next to her but is out with a potential supplier. He's there with Bob, our Abundant value stream manager, who sits next to him."

"Yes, I'll have quite a bit of work to do with Bob," Rahim said.

"Indeed – as with Shelley, the Eden value stream manager."

Shelley stood up. "Hi, pleased to meet you."

"Pleased to meet you too."

"As I've been saying, we've started a two-step transformation of the entire operation," Gregory explained. "The first step is to fit redesigned processes for Eden into Building Two. We've now been through diagnose and design phases and we're – what, two weeks – into our implementation phase?"

"That's right," Shelley said.

"Shelley spends most of her time at her other desk in Building Two, with the Eden team. I take it you're here for the Steering Committee?"

"Yes – just heading there to get set up."

He looked at his watch. "I think it would be a good opportunity, Rahim, if you could join us for that. It will give you a good flavour of what we're doing and how we're trying to go about it. The rest can wait."

"Sure."

"Will the meeting include another tour?" Gregory asked.

"Of course," Shelley said.

"Good. We'll also walk through Building One – where you'll see the old upholstery stations. We've completed most of the changes to the buildings, like taking down much of the warehouse. So don't be surprised to see a lot of finished goods on the floor: that will be the case until we've proven everything, so we don't fail any customers. In Building Two we've implemented most of Eden's upstream, from Cutting to Sewing. We've taken out two cutting tables that we're transferring to Abundant and we have turned the other two through ninety degrees. You'll also see the space that we've cleared for Pre-upholstery to Finishing, which we'll move in a couple of weeks."

Rahim had stopped nodding.

"Sorry, you'll hear all this in the meeting, but it will make more sense when you see it."

"It sounds like you're making a lot of changes," Rahim said to Shelley.

"Just a few."

"Have you been involved in a transformation like this before?"

"No!" said Shelley. "None of us has. I was the team leader in Cutting until a few months ago! But Josh has. He'll tell you I'm leading, but he's kind of masterminding everything."

Rahim smiled.

"Rahim already knows Josh," Gregory said.

"Oh, you're from around here then?" Shelley asked.

"Well, I am now. I came to Pershore from Persia, via London. I met Josh through a friend of my wife. She grew up in Pershore, which is why we were keen on settling there."

"I'm not sure where Josh is at the moment," Gregory said, "but you'll see him in the meeting. He has a desk on the end here, next to yours and opposite mine. This one is assigned to Fiona the design director, although she's mostly in the studio."

Rahim nodded.

"Right, we might as well go to the boardroom straight away if you're ready. See you all later."

Rahim slipped his bag from his shoulder and started to take out what he needed. Gregory thought he would be a good fit. He had sailed through the negotiation exercise, and his track record in business development was exemplary. Eddie would find it tough, but he had at least acknowledged to Arthur that he might be better suited to his new role as customer relations manager.

Gregory stopped Rahim as they passed the corner office and dropped his voice. "This office is the one we tend to use for hospitality. It's also open for general use but it's the one Arthur tends to use when he's in. Not that he's precious about it. Josh uses it too, sometimes. Just so you know, really."

"Thanks, no problem."

On dark days this office symbolised everything Gregory had lost, but on brighter days it symbolised trappings of the past, from which he had been freed. Other days found him anywhere between these extremes, but every day he was grateful that he had been given another chance. He never doubted he was in the right place.

Gregory held the door for the rest of the convoy to move out onto the raised walkway. The first part of the steering committee meeting had gone well. Once again there were no surprises with the content, since Josh had reviewed it with him in advance. Having done so it had been tempting again to think it a waste of time for each person to take five minutes presenting a point he already understood. After changes to both the format and his attitude earlier that morning, he had tried hard to get a better balance between encouraging and challenging. Josh's feedback just now was that it had been much better but he should still try to do more of *both*! He was beginning to see the meeting as a microcosm in which to model their hopes for how the organisation should work together. He set direction and the appropriate people investigated the problems and proposed solutions, which they could then probe and discuss together. He and his management team agreed the way ahead, while committing to deal with any obstacles.

The vista from the wrought-iron walkway had totally opened up. The major changes to the offices and building were completed two weeks ago, during an unprecedented two-week summer shutdown. The diagnose and design phases for the Eden transformation had been completed prior to that, mainly so that everyone could shape the site details. It wasn't ideal to split the activity over the summer but Arthur argued that if they were to wait for a perfect time, they would put things off forever. A bonus was that they had finally been able to fix the roof, just in time for the summer washout. They could hear the rain but there wasn't a bucket in sight.

Gregory had given his go-ahead for all the major changes, but that made it no less unnerving to see the factory being taken apart on his watch. It wasn't anything that could be easily reversed. He hoped that Josh knew what he was doing and that everything would fit. They would soon enter another critical period in which the new team incentives for sewing machinists, pre-upholsterers and upholsterers would be trialled. Part of him was already longing for the disruption to be over: he had already personally intervened to avert mini-crises with two existing customers.

Gregory stepped off the bottom stair. The area still looked a mess with the old upholstery stations, but he allowed himself a smile. This was where the new U-shaped Abundant line promised to transition from Pre-upholstery to Upholstery. If everything worked out, it could not have been planned any better, from the perspective of selling Abundant sofas to visiting clients.

Josh and Rahim darted out of the convoy towards a communication board in the middle of the upholstery area. They had left Gregory alone in the convoy but he was happy to collect his thoughts. He now appreciated any such moments in the midst of the maelstrom, with so much going on. He would never have tolerated so much change at once: he definitely did not feel in control. Mercifully, Josh's ability to coordinate so much detail was proving extraordinary.

It wasn't just the physical changes that were destabilising. Once out of his comfort zone, Gregory had also been forced to unlearn some things about himself. This would have been another trigger for him to have reined in the chaos, were it not for Arthur's assurance. Nothing fazed Arthur and he always brought a balanced perspective. With this help Gregory was concluding that in many ways he *had* been a good leader but primarily by locking everything down. He had allowed himself to become a bit of a cynic, leaving little room for the unexplored. There *was* also a chance that some of his supposed strengths might have been weaknesses in disguise, such as those that may have discouraged others from telling the truth. He might well have been becoming stronger by entertaining such weaknesses. At times it felt that his world was being turned inside out, yet the right way round.

"There you go," said Trish, the team leader for the dye shop. She and Sue were waiting for him at the end of the trucking corridor. "That's your copy for later. Thanks very much for doing this – it's great."

"No problem. Thank you."

He took the reading glasses from his inside pocket. It was an audit sheet for the dye shop. He had given the dye shop another chance with the simple solution that Stephen had presented to Mountfield when they were still Gregory Todd Ltd. Now they claimed the changes were finally working and he had been invited to audit it straight after the steering committee meeting.

"Just work your way down the questions," Trish explained. "It should be straightforward, but we can guide you through it. It's a simple yes or no."

It did indeed look straightforward enough. He had never been familiar with the details but he had never understood why something so conceptually simple had been so impossible to implement. This sheet now gave the details of how it was supposed to work. In fact, it told him exactly what to look out for. If he'd had this simple sheet last year he could probably have come down and made sure things were happening himself. Maybe that was the point. *This was brilliant!* He had never felt comfortable wandering around the shop floor. He had either resorted to inane general conversation or focused on a specific detail. Throughout his tenure as general manager he had often felt of little more use on the shop floor than a visiting VIP. Trish had placed a tool in his hands that now promised to pinpoint the problems he should be engaging people about.

Gregory folded the sheet in half and smiled. "It looks good, thank you."

"No problem," said Trish. "Sue helped to put it together."

They turned to welcome her into the conversation as he slipped his glasses back into his pocket. "Thank you," he said. "Well done on your presentation too, both of you."

"Really?" Trish asked. "I was so nervous."

"You came across as very knowledgeable."

"So I should be! We've been trying to do this for long enough."

"Tell me about it!" he said. "OK, so perhaps you can enlighten me. Why *did* we struggle to implement this first time around? It never did seem very complicated."

"Are you serious?" Trish asked.

"Yes." If they thought that moving the dye shop back to its old location had been significant, they could think again. "Go on. I have my views but I want to hear yours."

"Everything's different," Trish said.

"Like what?"

"Everything! No offence, but no one used to care what was going on in the dye shop before. As long as Trev was turning out the right numbers."

"Of course we cared!" he said. Trish looked away, but it was true! He couldn't let anyone get away with suggesting otherwise. "We've always cared!" Regardless of any rumours that Josh may have spread, that had been the whole point of balanced scorecards – to make sure that they were achieving the right results in the right way!

Trish was still looking at the ground.

"OK," he said to Sue, "give me a practical suggestion of one more thing I could have done to show you we cared about what was going on in the dye shop."

"You could have got rid of Trevor," Sue volunteered. "Trish is making all the difference as team leader."

"I don't know about that," said Trish.

"Look," he said. "I'm sure Trish is doing a good job but the solution isn't always to get rid of someone. So how could we have helped someone like Trevor to have implemented properly?"

"By showing him how important it was," Trish said. "And showing Peter the same."

"And Stephen too, probably," Sue added.

"We did!" Gregory said. "We told Trevor it was his number one priority! I don't know how we could have made it any clearer."

Trish sighed and looked away again.

"I think there's a difference between *telling* and *showing*," Sue said quietly.

That much was obvious! "Ok then," he said, "tell me one more thing I could have done to *show* Trevor how important it was."

"Doing one of these audits alongside Trevor would have helped. And with Peter!" Trish said. "You would either have put a rocket up them or you would have soon got the measure of them."

There was a chance that audits could surface *people* problems as well as *system* problems, but he had to be careful – people were always trying to suck him into this or that to show his support for things.

"OK," he said. "Thank you. I'll have to think about that. And how else we might s*how* people what's important, instead of just telling them." He hated the thought of overkill from too many finicky check sheets. But if people thought they were finicky, shouldn't he be able to gauge that too as some of the helpful resistance Josh spoke of, when going through the sheet with them? As long as people could be honest with him.

They joined Shelley, who was waiting beside the cutting table. The convoy had unravelled and stragglers were chatting in twos or threes all the way up the main aisle. "Excuse me," he said to Trish and Sue. "I don't suppose you could encourage the rest to join us, please?"

Shelley scurried towards an operator who was working hard, piling up bundles of cut fabric at the end of the cutting table. Shelley put one of the bundles into an empty sewing crate and placed it at the top of the new roller conveyor immediately behind them. This sparked a remonstration and he feared Shelley might have been a little too precious. Soon enough, though, there were smiles and nods. Shelley returned and the operator set about putting the backlog of bundles in crates and sending them on their way to the sewing machinists who were now whirring away in their new positions just behind. The operator glanced in Gregory's direction – without returning his smile but also without the sort of glare he had received in Building One. He had always maintained it was better to be respected than to be liked, but the truth was that he wouldn't mind both.

It was a miracle that the building was buzzing with life again, given how much had already changed. He hoped Rahim would get a sense of this, beyond the confusion of the construction site, where tape on the floor criss-crossed the old painted lines.

"Please put your hand up if you can hear me OK," Gregory said. It was a relief to be trialling the headsets given the size of the group. "You'll find the headsets work better at this stage if you put them in your ears. Please help your neighbour if he looks lost." They were clearly a novel source of amusement. "Yes, feel free to tune into something more interesting if you can find it." It was hard to believe he trusted this lot to run his business! "Right, Shelley is going to spend the next thirty minutes giving us a walk through the entire Eden value stream. Hopefully," he said, catching Shelley's eye, "she'll remind us of the vision for each stage, what's changed so far and whether we're on track. We'll then draw the steering committee meeting to a close, but there's then an optional activity in the dye shop. That's the one area of this value stream where everything's now finished. Right, Shelley?"

"Right," Shelley said somewhat sheepishly. She looked towards the back of the tour group. "Sorry, it's just that Josh has conditioned us never to suggest anything has been *finished*," she added. "I think this is just to emphasise that we've really only just started to raise and solve the problems."

Josh's passion for details was a great strength, when combined with his ability to see the bigger picture. Otherwise it could produce semantics.

"Yes, yes," Gregory said. "We understand all that, but the *implementation* has finished. The point I was making is that anyone who wants to join me for the dye shop audit afterwards would be most welcome. Right, Trish?"

"Sure."

"OK, Shelley, let me hand over to you now then, to take us through the vision here for Cutting."

"Yes, thank you. So here you can see the two Eden cutting tables in position. We'll walk the rest of the flow in a moment but to put it into context, the fabric store has stayed at the end of the building. We'll share it with Building One as we'll have many fabrics and leathers in common with Abundant. The dye shop is back in its old location in this building, where we could make use of the old trenches, plumbing and electrics. This does improve flow although it's still not ideal since it splits the fabric store in two. We just felt it was hard to justify the extra spend on another location within the same building."

Too right, but it was about cash flow as much as justifying the expense. Although Arthur had invested some more capital to see them over the hump, he and Anna had to be particularly careful about how much they spent on improvements before they delivered any savings.

"The part of the store you can see now, next to the cutting tables, contains the high-use fabrics and leathers for Eden. The higher the use, the closer the fabric is to the ground."

"I imagine this is not the first time you've tried to organise the store along these lines?" Rahim asked.

"No," said Shelley. "For those that can't hear, Rahim's just asked if we have already tried something similar. The answer is yes, particularly around stocktakes."

Rahim looked half-satisfied.

"So you're probably wondering what's different this time?"

He nodded. "The thought had crossed my mind."

"I think the main difference this time is that we were much more systematic with the design," Shelley said. "And that we involved everyone throughout the diagnose, design and implement phases. I think it's safe to say that everyone now feels some sense of ownership and knows their part in maintaining it."

Shelley was a natural tour guide. He was impressed at how she had made the step up from team leader.

"Thank you," Rahim said. "I hope you'll be proved right!"

"And are you going to audit this too?" Gregory asked.

"Yes – I'd like to see a single audit for the Eden value stream as a whole, but we're not ready yet. Even if the area looks ready, we're still waiting for the custom program that will automatically sort the orders and issue a daily plan based on due date and lay characteristic."

"And that's proving difficult?" Gregory asked.

"Not technically. Just in practice, I'm afraid."

"And why is that?"

Shelley screwed up her face and glanced at the ground. "I think IT is just under a lot of pressure at the moment."

They should not be having this conversation in public but it was too important to let go. "They agreed to the timescales, didn't they?"

"I think they're doing their best," Shelley said, "but they have got a lot on their plate at the moment, especially with the Abundant project."

"They knew all about that when they agreed to the timescales."

It infuriated him that people still promised plans that they could not deliver. He knew for a fact that Anna and the IT manager had both committed to the entire Eden and Abundant IT scope. If it had been too ambitious, they should have said so. "I'll have to ask Anna to look at our IT resources again," he said. "If we can't deliver both plans as they stand, we'll have to see what else we can do. We'll get you a revised commitment by the end of the week."

Shelley's mouth dropped open. Had she expected him to say something different?

29

POLES APART

PETER exchanged awkward smiles with his host. Trevor reached past his laptop and scraped another jam biscuit from the paper doily.

The air conditioning in their clients' training room was fierce. He was glad he had worn long sleeves: he had only done so that morning because Joan had insisted it looked more professional. The whole training room looked newly appointed, to a standard high enough for most boardrooms. The good news was that it suggested they had plenty of budget to spend on consultants. Unless, of course, they had already blown the budget on the room. They would find out soon enough: the lady they were waiting for held the purse strings.

"Did you have far to come?" asked his host.

"Worcester. Not too far," Peter said. He slowly stretched out his leg. Driving was never good for his knee, plus it was already sore from walking every inch of their plant the previous week.

"Up and round on the M40?"

"Ah, no. Cross country. Less variability, you see. Predictable lead times!"

His host smiled politely and straightened his tie. "So how long have you been involved in this game?"

"What, consulting?"

"Yes."

He was aware that theirs was the only conversation in the room. "Just over a year, now. It was June last year when I left Eden Furniture."

"And you enjoy it?"

"Yes," he said quietly. "It's very rewarding to help people. I do miss being involved operationally though, from time to time. I think I told you that prior to consulting I racked up nearly twenty years of managing plants."

For six months of the last year he had still technically been a consultant, but he had taken a contract to revamp the quality system of an equipment hire firm that Joan's cousin helped to run. It wasn't his core interest but he had hoped that the change would have been as good as a rest. Then, just as the weather turned warmer, Eden had generated a lot of press coverage with the launch of the Abundant line. That's when Peter had made the inspired move to rename his company Eden Consulting. Things had started to pick up, so much so that he had brought Trevor along on this assignment to show him the ropes.

A lady in an olive-green dress breezed in. She must have been about his age.

"Hello, Sarah," said his host. "Let me introduce Peter Nash to you. And this is Trevor Foxley. From Eden Consulting."

"Hello. Pleased to meet you. I'm Sarah Brown, operations director."

"Peter Nash."

"Hi," said Trevor, finishing his biscuit. "I'm Trevor Foxley, senior consultant."

"Hello, everyone," said Sarah. "Sorry I'm late. Let's get straight into it, shall we? I understand you were on site for a couple of days last week?"

"Yes, that's right. Long enough to find some potential."

Ron, the wiry production manager with the high-pitched voice was already shaking his head from the other side of the table. Peter had tried being reasonable but he was like a terrier. His factory wasn't bad, but Ron acted as if it was the best in the world.

"I daresay. It's funny – I heard Joshua Eden speak on Operations Design at *Manufacturing Live* a few weeks ago and I thought, *That's exactly the kind of thing we need here.* Which is why I looked you guys up. But it was literally last weekend that my husband and I decided to shop for a sofa. We went into a furniture store and saw one of Eden's Abundant booths. Has anyone else seen one of these?"

He could keep his hand down and pretend the question was for everyone else. Until he could see where the comment was leading.

"You really should," Sarah said, playing with the dark green beads around her neck. They've thought about the whole consumer experience. Half the sofa is cut away to show why it feels so good."

"So did you buy one?" Trevor asked.

"No," she said. "Not yet."

Trevor maintained his smirk and glanced around the table.

"We thought we'd take the option of choosing our own fabric. We've still got time, as they promise it only takes two weeks to build the whole thing, once they receive the fabric."

Trevor softened his smirk.

"Anyway, I don't think we'll sell too many of our own products in booths. The main message for us is how Eden has managed to incorporate so many features at their chosen price point. It's because of the way they've designed their operation, right?"

Peter nodded. "That's exactly it. Most factories focus so much on cost, customer orders have to find their own way through and waste accumulates."

"Not here, we don't," barked Ron. "We schedule everything."

"Well, the ideal for scheduling is first-in-first-out," Peter said. "We'll show you several instances we found of orders leapfrogging other orders."

"Of course they do! We have inevitable constraints in our processes: you've hardly scratched the surface."

"Sorry, I should have checked," Sarah said. "Did both of you work directly for Eden Furniture?"

"Yes, ma'am. It's where we learnt to do what we do," Peter said.

"And did you work directly with Joshua Eden?"

Peter smiled. "I was actually Josh's boss."

"Wow, OK. Very good."

"And I mentored him through his first improvements," Trevor said.

"Excellent. So you're both well placed, then, to tell us how we can become the Eden of Agricultural Machinery?"

"Absolutely! Shall I make a start?" Once he got going it would be impossible for Ron to disagree with their observations. They had photographed much of the evidence.

"Please do."

Peter flicked his mouse and waited for his laptop to wake up. "It won't be a minute."

He re-entered his password and breathed a little more easily when people started turning to face the screen.

"Well, what you need is something we call *Performance Lean.* This combines the critical aspects of *lean* manufacturing and *performance* management, which helped Eden Furniture to do what we've just been talking about."

"Haven't we already done lean manufacturing?" Sarah asked.

"Years ago," Ron said.

Here we go – she had thrown her terrier a bone. Crimson colour spread from the nape of Ron's neck. "With all due respect, I told them last week that they're bringing nothing new to the table."

"And as we said last week," Trevor said, "it doesn't matter what you know; it matters what you do. And we've found lots of opportunity in your plant that shows what you're *not* doing."

"Any monkey can find examples of the eight wastes, even in the best of plants," Ron said. "If you want to help, suggest something concrete we should do differently with our own processes."

"Come on, Ron, let's give them a chance," Sarah said. "Please make a start and I'm sure that will lead on naturally to discussing how things can apply here."

"Thank you." Peter quickly advanced the next page. "So we've classified our observations under the categories of Performance Management, Just-in-time and 5S."

"What's 5S?" Sarah asked.

"It just means keeping the plant tidy," said Ron. "It uses five Japanese words beginning with S to try and make things sound clever. They can be loosely translated into five English words that also begin with S: Sift, Sort, Sweep… and two other Ss."

"Standardise and Sustain," Trevor added. He swept his hair across his head. "We've got another page that explains this in more detail."

"Hold on," said Sarah. "I think I agree with Ron to some extent. I'm not sure there's a great deal of benefit in talking about general programmes that we may have already tried. Yes, of course we can always try and do them better. But I don't remember Joshua Eden mentioning Performance Lean."

"Ah no, he wouldn't," Peter explained. "That's our way of repackaging things to make it easier to understand."

"Well, I'm not sure I want anything repackaged. My personal hope was to hear about the *Operations Design* process Joshua had mentioned and to discover how we might be able to apply it here. To become the Eden of Agricultural Machinery."

Ron smirked at Trevor.

"We can do that, no problem," said Trevor.

"Great. Can we move on to that bit straight away then please, if you wouldn't mind?"

"Ah," Peter said. He was not about to let Trevor bluff his potential big client. He knew exactly what she needed – and he could still envisage it on the flip chart in Josh's training room. "What I think Trevor means is that it would be no problem to do so but I'm afraid there might have been a bit of a breakdown in communication. I didn't realise that this was your expectation for today."

"Oh. But you do know of an Operations Design process you could take us through?"

"Yes, of course," he said. "We developed our own design process at Eden called SPECIALOPS. It's a mnemonic for each of the steps to go through."

"Perfect. Perhaps you could take us through that now then please? With the whiteboard, if necessary."

He rubbed his moustache. "I'm afraid that might be tricky." The flip chart sheet was probably still hanging there in the team room, but he had never managed to go through it properly. The terrier was grinning – he was probably already sensing blood. *What would Stephen do?*

"The process tends to get in depth quite quickly, you see," Peter explained. "So it's difficult to give a quick introduction. And it's best to have the relevant data to work with, to suggest how it could apply to your own processes. Look, now we know what you're looking for, how about we arrange a proper workshop? That way we can give it the proper preparation and time it deserves."

"How long do you think we would need?"

"It depends on how deep you'd like to go. I'd probably suggest two to three days."

"And could you fit this in within the next couple of weeks – before the summer holidays start at the end of July? I wouldn't want anyone to miss out."

"I should think so."

"Great – let's do it. This is definitely something I would like to be involved with personally."

It was a masterstroke. He had not only bought time to prepare; he had also secured a chargeable workshop that they could stretch out for three days without getting in too deep.

30

COMING TOGETHER

PETER approached the factory with mixed feelings, especially when he saw that the gates were closed. They had never been closed throughout his reign as manager. Furthermore, everything had now been painted in gloss, and it hadn't been a rush job. If this was the budgeting priority of the so-called value stream managers, he hated to imagine what state the equipment was in.

An unfamiliar security guard sauntered over. Peter wound down his car window and nearly scorched his forearm against the dusty bodywork. It was another beautiful day: the summer had already been better than the previous year. An Eden sign had been planted in a new flower bed. Stephen would never have tolerated him frittering money away on such things, even if he had wanted to.

"Can I help you, sir?" the guard asked.

"Yes, this is all a bit formal, isn't it? Can you just let me in, please?"

"Do you have an appointment?"

"Oh, I don't need one of those. I'm Peter Nash. I used to run this plant!"

"Good morning, Mr Nash. Who are you here to see today?"

"Everyone! Old friends!"

"What are their names please, sir?"

He shook his head. "Nigel Travis." He could afford to play along if it got him what he wanted. Nigel was his most straightforward bet, anyway.

"No, I'm sorry, sir. I have no one down to see Mr Travis today."

"You let in someone just ahead of me!" The car had parked in a visitor's space and a lady was walking towards Reception. It looked like Gregory's wife.

"That lady was expected, sir."

She needed an appointment to see her husband?! "Look, she's um – Linda Todd. I know everyone here. Give Gregory himself a call if you like."

Gregory stood on the front steps, with the sleeves of his pale pink shirt rolled up. He relished the sunshine on his face and forearms.

"Hello, darling. Welcome."

"Hi," said Linda. "Well, it certainly looks different from the outside, with the landscaping and the welcome. I wish our lavender was this prolific – the smell is glorious."

There was a remonstration at the gates – a driver was causing a bit of a scene. He couldn't see who it was but it looked like everything was under control. Sycamore trees shimmered across the road.

"Thank you so much for coming."

"I might have come sooner if I had known the place now looks like a health farm."

He smiled broadly. "Well, things are pretty healthy these days." It was just over a year and a half since he had been reconciled with Arthur and they were on track for a sevenfold increase in EBITDA. That might not mean much to Linda, but it was nearly double the number in the original plan which had been enough to light up Mountfield's eyes.

"Are you ready for a tour?"

"I think so."

"Great – let's go."

"This is all different, isn't it?"

"Oh, yes." They had overhauled the reception area to give visitors a better introduction to their products. One side had been modelled as a stylish living room, featuring Eden sofas and chairs. The other side featured an Abundant sofa booth.

"This looks familiar," she said. It had not taken long to get Linda into a furniture store to see an Abundant booth. He was still nervous about showing her the factory. He really wanted her to appreciate how far they had come, but she had never seemed particularly interested in the factory. Plus she had little for comparison: it must have been years since she had been inside.

"Ready?"

"I think so."

He swiped his card and opened the door. "Here, you'll need these." She rolled the bright yellow plugs and inserted them into her ears.

"Making sofas is noisier now, is it?"

She might have remembered more than he had thought. "It might actually be a little more intense. But we always had a policy for hearing protection. Now we just make a special effort to be consistent. Please keep to the green pedestrian paths. If there's an emergency the muster point is in this front car park."

"I promise to behave."

"Good. Come on – first of all we'll walk straight through to the wood-shed. We can start the tour there and then follow the flow of material."

He ceremoniously opened the final set of painted doors, with outstretched arms. The factory was full of light and life. There was no special reaction. *Surely she had noticed the difference?*

"What do you think?" he said, leaning towards her ear.

"You're right – it is noisy."

They walked past the transition between the now-defunct terminology of Pre-upholstery and Upholstery: he would explain that later. Still, Linda was not really looking in the right places. She smiled and nodded but it might have just been to appease him.

It had taken Linda ages to accept his decision to reunite with Arthur. She said she had only done so because of the good she could see it was doing him. Why *this* had taken so long he had no idea: he had felt a new lease of life from the start. Now whenever he and Linda faced difficulties, they did so together. There was much to be thankful for.

Recently he had been re-evaluating how much of his life might have been shaped by the fear of making mistakes. It had never *stopped* him taking a risk, but he had always had one eye on potential failure. He now knew that in Arthur he had someone who would back him to profit from every honest mistake he would ever make. What were the new limits – if any – to what they could try next, if he had nothing left to fear?

Some of the operators had already acknowledged them. Now Big Dave stood in the green gangway ahead. *Please don't give Linda a bad experience.* Big Dave had caused a few problems last summer when they had been dismantling his warehouse. He had not heard much from him since, but he would never be the ideal person to give Linda a flavour of what they had achieved.

When they were just a few feet away, Big Dave suddenly turned and flung his arm towards them. Gregory flinched but Dave's arm finished with a salute.

"Steady!" Gregory said. "Linda, this is Dave. Have you met Linda, my wife?"

"Pleased to meet you," said Big Dave. "He takes you to all the best places, then?"

Linda leant in slightly towards the tattooed hulk. "Don't encourage him," Gregory heard her say. "I think he already believes that, judging by how much he talks about this place."

He wasn't *that* bad.

"Well, it's never dull," said Big Dave. "That's for sure."

"You've still got enough space for finished goods?" Gregory asked.

"Pretty much," Big Dave replied. "Do you remember my warehouse?" he asked Linda.

She shook her head.

"It was over there. It used to stretch halfway across the factory, to the loading bay. With an upper floor. I used to be team leader."

"You used to store sofas upstairs?"

"Some of them – hauled them up a roller conveyor."

"That's crazy."

Gregory grimaced to Big Dave. "It was never ideal," he explained to Linda. "But you need to understand, no one planned it that way. We just consumed the available space whenever we grew."

"Until someone suddenly realised you didn't need a warehouse, after all?" she said with a grin. She had misread the cues and had stomped on eggshells.

"No," Gregory said quickly. "It's never that simple, Linda. No one could have made a decision like that in isolation. That's why people so rarely manage to do what we've achieved – like I've been trying to explain. We've had to redesign every single process but as a system, to reduce waste and maintain the production sequence as best we can. As soon as the production lead times were much shorter and more consistent, we could release orders later so there was less need for the further waste of storing finished goods."

She nodded, with her grin safely packed away.

"We've even started sequencing within each cutting cycle based on delivery order," Big Dave added. "They're trying to cut first what needs to be delivered last," he said to Linda. "So it can be loaded into the truck first, if that makes sense."

She nodded slowly.

"That's been the real benefit," Big Dave said. "Now the walls have come down we're seen as part of the same team. We've always been the eyes of the customer but nobody listened. So we just shuffled sofas. Now we're all in the thick of sorting things out together."

Gregory smiled. He could not have put it any better.

Linda did not seem to have appreciated the full extent of what she had just witnessed.

"OK, thanks Dave. We'd better get going."

Linda shook Big Dave's hand and they moved on towards the loading bay. He stopped when they were a safe distance away.

"So that was Big Dave. He's always been one of the biggest influences on the shop floor. When he signed the new contract, a whole host of experienced workers followed. He used to symbolise the culture of 'them and us'. You've just heard it from his own mouth: he's now channelling all his effort and influence into improvement."

"Uh-huh."

"Do you know how much any leader would give for this kind of cultural turnaround? It's only come about because of all the graft we put into engaging people in diagnosing, designing and implementing the changes. It's taken us on a virtuous cycle. Attitudes have improved so much that most of the resistance we uncover is now helpful."

"Uh-huh."

"We want to be a business where people feel compelled to speak out whenever they feel something is wrong. As managers we need to be secure enough to listen – and even embrace – this feedback, to filter it and to enable things to be fixed."

"Great."

"This is fundamentally opposite to how most organisations are run!"

"Yes – I get it."

She didn't. Or at least not as much as he did. Maybe it was impossible for anyone to get it without having lived and breathed the old way. He smiled weakly. At least the physical changes would be more straightforward to observe. "Come on, we've not even started the proper tour yet."

They crossed the yard carefully. "So this is Building Three. Eden frames are now built in the left part and go on to Building Two which is behind us over there. Abundant frames are built in the right part, serving Building One behind us over there. The woodshed is still within the right part so sits within the Abundant organisation, but it makes parts for both. OK?"

"Fair enough."

He led her into the cacophony of the woodshed. "Right," he said loudly. "Wood is taken from the far end over there and cut, shaped and drilled through all these machines to replenish the components that have been taken from the shelves over here. We call this a shop stock – some call it a supermarket – for the frame builders. There's a dedicated section for a controlled quantity of each group of components. The machines used to occupy all of this space until Josh freed it up – this is where the whole transformation started. This in turn has freed up the whole area through that red roller door, which used to be a much larger store for components. It's now where the Abundant frames are being built. So what do you reckon?"

"People seem busy – but happy enough."

"Busy doing the right things," he added. "We've worked with every single person to ensure more of their time is on the things that matter."

"Don't they mind, if that effectively means being chained to a machine?"

That was an unfortunate choice of phrase: Josh spoke of deliberately *unchaining* operators from single machines, principally to free them for regular value-adding work elsewhere. But anyway – Linda hated semantics as much as he did and this would be an unnecessary complication. "What's your concern – that some might find the work too demanding?"

"Kind of – I'm not sure I'd like to do it."

"It is hard work – and it isn't for everyone. Most people who didn't want to work hard or as part of a team left instead of signing the new contract. But it's much better than before for those who did sign. There's Graham, the team leader. You can ask him if you like?"

"No, it's alright. I can take your word for it."

Hopefully she hadn't judged Graham on his appearance. "I'm afraid there was probably a time when I didn't fully appreciate how hard some of the people were working," Gregory said. "Then do you remember when Josh convinced me to try out some of the jobs, during the Eden diagnose phase?"

"How can I forget?"

"There's a real knack to a lot of it – some of them make it look so easy. Now they're starting to help each other a bit more – and we train everyone in new areas so they bring fresh eyes and ideas. Hopefully they're beginning to feel a bit more appreciated. Like those who are creating the value, after all."

"Righty ho."

"Are you ready to move on? Or would you like to see more here?"

"No, that's fine. I'm ready when you are."

They went through the red roller door to the sweet-smelling room where the Abundant frames were being knocked into shape. He stopped at the information board. "This is probably the most critical information in the whole factory. It's the fixed sequence for Frame Assembly, which has been determined by Cutting. As soon as an order is received it is assigned to a particular two-day delivery slot towards the end of its two-week customer lead time. All deliveries within a slot are arranged by customer location, as Dave explained, but orders of similar lay characteristics are brought forward to be cut with the first, to ensure we always operate within Cutting's capacity limit." He was on autopilot – he had now explained this so often. "So the fixed sequence here ensures that the frames will meet the right covers at the right point on the assembly line."

"I'll believe you."

"What do you think?"

"It sounds like you've had a lot to think about."

"There's a lot more I could say, believe me." Such as why they were now using two men to assemble one frame at a time, instead of one man assembling three at a time. He had been through it all but he would struggle to explain the full reasoning.

"There's a guy called Richard who has spearheaded a lot of the improved methods in Frame Assembly. He can explain a lot more if you're interested." Richard was in the far corner, directing a young man's glue gun to the frame's joints in a particular sequence. He remained crouching but saluted Gregory with a raised thumb. On second thoughts, Richard was so thorough they might never be able to get away. "Otherwise let's keep following the flow from here to Building One."

The completed Abundant frames were loaded onto a new track that had been built along the covered corridor, reclaimed from maintenance storage. It crossed the loading yard along the factory's perimeter that bordered the canal. He led the way along the queue of frames.

"So do you consider *this* inventory to be a waste then, too?"

She was a better student than he had credited. "Have you any idea how much inventory we've designed out?"

Her look suggested he had been a little too defensive.

"Believe it or not, this is only about two hours' worth of inventory. And at the moment we still need this time for the glue to dry before we put the frames under too much tension. So yes, it's not strictly value adding but at least this way we keep the sequence *and* allow the glue to dry while transporting the frames to the cleaner environment that Upholstery needs. Maybe one day we can find a better way. Maybe you should come and help us."

"I'm not sure you could afford me."

"We can if you've got a good vision!" They had reached Building One. "Come on, welcome to the Abundant line. All this is completely new."

The single track swept deep through the former warehouse and into the factory way further than they could see from where they stood. It returned all the way up the other side towards the loading bay. The amount of work that had gone into designing this line was unbelievable. Some had been convinced it would never work. They watched the first operator fit springs to the back of a frame.

"Look," he said, "these are like the springs on the Helena we have at home."

"Very good."

"Basically we start fitting the springs to the frame here, and it comes off the line at the far end as an upholstered Abundant sofa."

It was hard to gauge how much Linda wanted to know. Each workstation had been designed for manual work equivalent to the takt time – which for the time being was five minutes and twenty seconds. Therefore every five minutes and twenty seconds a worker would finish their allotted work on a unit and it would pass along the track to the next station.

"Around each operator we've designed the workstation to provide everything they need within close reach: components, tools, work instructions and so on. Components are delivered to either side of the line by material handlers. Except I can't give you a proper overview here. Let's go up to the raised walkway for a better view."

"OK."

From there he could also check privately why they were behind. The overhead counter showed that the line had fallen another unit behind since they had been in the woodshed. Josh's voice in his head reminded him he had been letting problems like this slip by unnoticed, day after day before they tried to standardise work to takt time. In a team-building session with other managers he had also received frank feedback that they did not find it helpful when *he rushed in to solve their problems*. He had only ever been trying to lead by example, but this led to them hiding the next problems from him. So he was now trying to allow more space for people to solve their own problems. But from the raised walkway he could at least check whether they were doing so.

He let his wife ascend the stairs first. "So from here you can get a better idea of the whole line. We've just come from over there, where the frames are loaded onto the line. You can see how the sofa progressively takes shape. Look, just below us is the best place to see all the sofa's features coming together."

"Just like in the booth."

"Exactly. Well, almost. Over there you can see the covers joining the line: there's a small buffer to ensure the line does not stop unnecessarily. Further upstream you can see the feeder line where the covers have just been sewn." It was good to see Bob on the floor, although he didn't seem to be fixing anything. To be fair, there were no red lights in sight. Given that the display counted good sofas when they came off the *end* of the line, the problem might well have been sorted a while ago.

"So, do you have any questions?" he asked Linda.

"Don't you ever wish you had tried all this before? When you were still Gregory Todd Ltd?"

She *really* didn't get how much they had achieved. "No, Linda. There was no way I could have done all this on my own."

"But you already had Joshua with you. OK, so you and he had that big episode but before that, didn't you consider asking him to help?"

Good old Linda – she had a knack of going for the jugular. "To be honest, I had no idea what he could offer."

"Didn't he tell you?"

"Maybe." He adjusted his feet and leant on the railing with straightened arms. "I've changed, Linda. Josh was young and I liked to think that I knew it all - although in some ways I knew I didn't. I just couldn't see it. Most of all, I couldn't see how Josh of all people could have been completely *for* me. Especially when he was challenging me. Hence the *episode*, as you put it.

"Now I'm starting to realise how much courage it takes to challenge someone for their own benefit, in the right way. Because we've now started trying to practise this kind of feedback in the senior management team. It's a lot easier to pass up the opportunity or to get it wrong, I can tell you. But I like to think perhaps that a bit of Josh is rubbing off on us all."

"It's good that you're getting on with each other now," Linda said. "I'm really pleased that everything seems to be working out well for you."

"Thank you, Linda. And thank you for all of your support."

"That's a pleasure. Thank you for the tour."

"Ah – we've not finished yet! But come on then, tell me: what's your highlight so far?"

"Oh, I wouldn't want to single anything out. Just to see you come alive when you talk about the whole transformation, I think. I just hope you can hold on to this sense of achievement now it's all finished."

Gregory turned to his wife and curbed his smile by keeping his lips together. "Oh, I wouldn't worry about that, Linda – nothing's finished. The transformation won't be finished until we run out of problems to surface and solve." He unleashed his smile. "In fact, everything you see here is really just the start."

www.ingramcontent.com/pod-product-compliance
Lightning Source LLC
Chambersburg PA
CBHW020832210326
41598CB00019B/1876